The Next Identity Crisis

Autonomy, Power, and Control in the Age of AI

Rosario Mastrogiacomo

Apress®

The Next Identity Crisis: Autonomy, Power, and Control in the Age of AI

Rosario Mastrogiacomo
ANNANDALE, NJ, USA

ISBN-13 (pbk): 979-8-8688-2787-7 ISBN-13 (electronic): 979-8-8688-2788-4
https://doi.org/10.1007/979-8-8688-2788-4

Managing Director, Apress Media LLC: Welmoed Spahr
Acquisitions Editor: Susan McDermott
Development Editor: Laura Berendson
Project Manager: Jessica Vakili

Distributed to the book trade worldwide by Springer Science+Business Media New York, 1 New York Plaza, New York, NY 10004. Phone 1-800-SPRINGER, fax (201) 348-4505, e-mail orders-ny@springer-sbm.com, or visit www.springeronline.com. Apress Media, LLC is a Delaware LLC and the sole member (owner) is Springer Science + Business Media Finance Inc (SSBM Finance Inc). SSBM Finance Inc is a **Delaware** corporation.

For information on translations, please e-mail booktranslations@springernature.com; for reprint, paperback, or audio rights, please e-mail bookpermissions@springernature.com.

Apress titles may be purchased in bulk for academic, corporate, or promotional use. eBook versions and licenses are also available for most titles. For more information, reference our Print and eBook Bulk Sales web page at http://www.apress.com/bulk-sales.

If disposing of this product, please recycle the paper

A mia madre, esempio di forza, coraggio, e amore.

Table of Contents

About the Author

Rosario Mastrogiacomo is the Chief Product Strategy Officer at SPHERE, a cybersecurity firm specializing in identity hygiene and data governance. With three decades of experience in the field, Rosario leads initiatives that blend strategy, innovation, and AI to solve some of the most pressing identity security challenges. He is the author of *AI Identities: Governing the Next Generation of Autonomous Actors* (Apress, 2025) and a recognized speaker, thought leader, and host of the podcast Smells Like Identity Hygiene, where he explores the intersections of cybersecurity, automation, and human responsibility. Rosario is also the author of widely circulated industry articles and a contributor to executive-level conversations around the role of AI in enterprise identity and risk management.

Introduction

The Age of Unstable Identities

On summer afternoons in the 1980s in Queens, New York, the heat pressed against the windows, the pavement shimmered, and inside our small apartment, the window AC rattled with the stubborn determination of a machine that had seen too many Augusts. It was old but reliable and walking into that cold air from the hot summer heat felt just as good as a warm blanket feels in the winter. The Mets game was always on, its soundtrack threading itself through the rooms like another member of the family.

Outside, life unfolded in layers. The thwack of a rubber ball against asphalt. Kids shouting, disputing whether it was fair or foul. The rise-and-fall rhythm of neighbors' conversations drifting from stoop to stoop. Queens wasn't quiet, but it was comforting. An orchestra of ordinary sounds that told you exactly where you were and exactly who you were.

And then, predictably, magically, Mr. Softee.

That looping jingle didn't just cut through the air; it pulled the whole neighborhood into a shared pause. Kids froze mid-play. Parents leaned out windows. Even the Mets broadcast seemed to soften for a moment, as if respectfully giving way. It wasn't the promise of ice cream that mattered, not really. It was the promise of *belonging*. A reminder that you were part of a place with its own rituals, its own rhythms, its own quiet agreements.

If you lived that time and at that place—a time right before the technology revolution, before we held the Internet in our hands—you know exactly what I'm talking about. If you didn't, you very likely have your own time and place like this. Something stuck in your mind forever. Sometimes triggered by a sound, smell, or taste.

This isn't just nostalgia. It isn't just a memory. It's a map of identity, the kind that settles into your chest long before you learn the word for it. It was belonging to a community that suffered together, joked together, and believed together.

Why We Begin Here

Identity begins as a feeling before it becomes an idea, and that's why we start here. Not with technology or the anxieties of artificial intelligence. But with a moment so ordinary and so real that it reveals what identity truly is: the invisible architecture of belonging, meaning, and trust.

In Queens, being a Mets fan wasn't just about baseball. It was about loyalty through losing seasons, about inherited hope, about defiant pride in choosing the team that made you suffer but still gave you something to believe in. It was about knowing that thousands of people who looked nothing alike, worshiped different gods, spoke different languages, and carried different histories all shared this one improbable emotional anchor.

Identity is the story that turns strangers into *us*, and that's the foundation on which every society on Earth has been built.

But today, something unprecedented is happening.

For the first time in history, identity, the most human of human technologies, is becoming unstable. Not because our values have changed, or because culture is shifting, or because politics have become complicated. Identity is destabilizing because we are introducing new actors into the world who do not, and cannot, participate in the ancient human rituals that make identity meaningful.

Artificial intelligence systems now make decisions, generate content, negotiate, persuade, speak, remember, predict, and act. They participate in our informational world with a speed and scale no human can match. They produce words that sound like us, images that look like us, voices that imitate us, and actions that represent us.

And yet they have no childhood memories. No neighborhoods. No Mr. Softee. No summer air drifting through an apartment as the Mets lose another close one.

They have *output*, but no origin. Capabilities, but no context. Actions, but no ancestry.

This is the fracture line we are crossing without fully understanding it. We are moving from a world in which identity emerged slowly, from bloodlines, geography, ritual, and reputation to a world in which identities can be generated, duplicated, simulated, or fabricated in seconds. A world where agency is cheap, and trust is expensive.

This book is about that shift. It is about what happens when the oldest human technology—identity—meets the newest nonhuman actors in our society. It is about how we built trust long before governments or markets existed. How we extended identity through names, documents, institutions, and finally digital systems. And how that entire structure begins to wobble when artificial intelligence becomes autonomous.

Above all, it is a book about *belonging*. About what it means to be someone recognizable, accountable, and trusted in a world where the very definition of "someone" is changing.

The Mets fan in me, the kid in that Queens apartment, is still trying to make sense of it. Still trying to understand how we preserve the humanity of identity when nonhuman agents can mimic our words, imitate our choices, and even act on our behalf.

Because the truth is this: if identity is the story that binds us together, then the next identity crisis will determine whether we can still recognize ourselves and each other on the other side of the age of AI.

But before I tell you what this book will cover, let me tell you what it will not do. This is not a book of strategy. It is not a how-to guide for navigating artificial intelligence in your business, your career, or your personal life. If you are looking for a roadmap with action items and implementation checklists, you will be disappointed. There are many excellent books that offer that kind of guidance; in fact, my first book, *AI Identities: Governing the Next Generation of Autonomous Actors*, does just that.

This book is an attempt to make sense of a shift so fundamental that it touches the roots of human civilization itself. My goal is not to tell you what to do. My goal is to unsettle you productively. To help you see the ground you are standing on and show you how it is moving beneath your feet. The questions I raise are not the kind that have clean answers. They are the kind that, once you see them clearly, you cannot unsee. They are the kind you will carry with you, whether you want to or not.

I write as someone who has spent decades working on identity systems. Not as an academic theorist, but as a practitioner who has watched the infrastructure of trust evolve in real time. I have seen how identity gets built, broken, and rebuilt inside institutions. I have seen how the systems we design to recognize people end up shaping who those people can become. And I have watched, with growing unease, as the tools we built to manage identity have begun to mutate into something we never intended: actors in their own right, capable of speaking, deciding, and operating with a speed and scale that no human can match.

That practical experience is why I care so much about the philosophical questions. The people building these systems often don't have time to ask what they are really building. The philosophers asking the deep questions often don't understand how the systems actually work. Someone needs to stand in the middle, with one foot in each world, and try to make sense of what is happening before it is too late to shape it.

The Five Crises

The age of autonomous AI does not present a single problem to be solved. It presents a web of interconnected crises, each reinforcing the others, each destabilizing something we once took for granted.

The first is **the crisis of identity itself**, which is the meta-crisis that contains all the others. Every evolution of identity, from tribal recognition to paper documents to digital credentials, solved certain problems while creating new vulnerabilities. The paper seal could be forged. The digital self could be stolen. Now the synthetic self can be fabricated entirely. The question of "who is real" is no longer something institutions can assume. It is something they must answer continuously, and the tools for answering it are failing. Identity is the thread that runs through every crisis that follows, because identity is how humans have always answered the question of who counts.

The second is **the crisis of ownership**. When tools were inert, ownership was straightforward. You owned your hammer, your car, your software license. But autonomous systems blur those boundaries. They adapt. They pursue goals. They act in ways their creators did not explicitly script. The traditional grammar of property, the logic of "mine" and "yours", strains when applied to entities that behave more like actors than artifacts. Can you own something that thinks? Can you be responsible for something you cannot fully predict or control?

The third is **the crisis of trust**. When voices can be cloned, recordings can be fabricated, and presence itself can be simulated, the default assumption of authenticity collapses. We have entered an era where seeing is no longer enough to believe, hearing is no longer enough to confirm, and even real-time conversation may not prove that a human is on the other end. What remains is a world where proof is expensive, denial is plausible, and institutions must become permanent verification machines just to maintain the baseline assumption that used to come for free: that the person you are dealing with is who they claim to be.

The fourth is **the crisis of control**. We like to believe that humans remain in charge. The organizational charts say so. The regulations assume it. But practical control has begun migrating to systems that act faster than oversight can follow. The clinician, at the end of a long shift, clicks through AI-generated recommendations. The manager is scanning a dashboard of model-prioritized tasks. The risk officer is reviewing notes drafted by a system she does not fully understand. All of them feel in charge.

The architecture has other plans. Delegation, repeated often enough, becomes abdication. Not through a dramatic coup, but through the slow accumulation of convenience.

The fifth is **the crisis of meaning**. This is the crisis that reaches deepest, because it asks what remains distinctly human when machines can reason, create, persuade, and even comfort. If intelligence becomes cheap, what is sacred? If answers become abundant, what is wisdom? If decisions can be delegated endlessly, what is responsibility? If an AI can write your eulogy, compose your love letter, or generate the words that comfort your grieving child, what exactly are you contributing to your own life? These questions cannot be answered by a model. They will be answered by what societies refuse to trade away and by what individuals insist on doing themselves, even when delegation would be easier.

These five crises are not separate problems with separate solutions. They are facets of the same disruption, and they reinforce one another. When identity becomes unstable, ownership becomes unclear. When ownership becomes unclear, trust collapses. When trust collapses, control becomes illusory. When control becomes illusory, meaning erodes. The thread runs through all of them, and that thread is identity: the oldest human technology, the one that made cooperation possible, the one that is now being remade by forces we have set in motion but do not fully control.

How This Book Is Organized

This book unfolds in five parts, each building on the one before.

Part I: Identity Before Machines establishes the foundation. Chapter 1 traces identity as a human technology, from face-to-face recognition in small bands to the rituals and social structures that allowed cooperation to scale. Chapter 2 examines the birth of the "paper self." The moment when identity was first externalized into names, documents, and institutions. Chapter 3 follows identity into the digital age, where it became data: abstracted, standardized, and scaled to a degree the architects of paper systems could never have imagined.

Part II: The Crisis of Ownership marks the turning point. Chapter 4 draws the line between automation and autonomy and explains why that distinction matters morally, not just technically. Chapter 5 introduces the new actors: AI agents, synthetic voices, and decision-making systems that participate in our world as entities with their own operational logic. Chapter 6 confronts what happens to ownership when the thing you own can act, adapt, and surprise.

Part III: The Crisis of Trust examines what happens when synthetic identity meets human institutions. Chapter 7 explores the erosion of authenticity. The end of our ability to know, with confidence, that we are dealing with a real human being. Chapter 8 describes the identity wars between those who fabricate and those who verify. Chapter 9 traces the institutional and social collapse that follows when verification fails at scale.

Part IV: The Crisis of Control asks what happens when humans believe they are in charge of systems that have quietly begun to govern them. Chapter 10 exposes the mechanisms of that illusion. Chapter 11 examines the double bind of being caught inside decisions you cannot contest or trace. Chapter 12 traces the drift. How autonomous systems reshape institutions through the quiet redefinition of what counts as normal.

Part V: The Crisis of Meaning turns from diagnosis to construction. Chapter 13 proposes the clauses of a new social contract for a world where nonhuman actors share agency with humans. Chapter 14 asks what remains distinctly human when machines can reason, create, and persuade. Chapter 15 returns to where identity began. Not with documents or credentials, but with the irreducible experience of being someone rather than something.

The book concludes with a meditation on the unfinished self. On the fact that identity has never been settled, and that the agent era is simply the latest chapter in humanity's long encounter with its own creations. The conclusion does not offer solutions. It offers postures and questions to carry forward, and an argument that the future remains open. That we are still the authors, if we choose to be.

A Word About What Follows

I do not know how this story ends. No one does. The technology is moving faster than our institutions can adapt, faster than our philosophy can absorb, faster than humanity can adjust. Anyone who claims certainty about where autonomous AI will take us is either selling something or fooling themselves. In many cases, both.

All I can offer is a way of seeing. A framework for understanding what is at stake, why it matters, and what questions we should be asking. I can offer the perspective of someone who has spent a career watching identity systems evolve and who has come to believe that the current moment is not just another technological transition but something more fundamental: a renegotiation of the basic terms on which human societies have always operated.

Identity is how we answer the question of who counts. It is how we decide who belongs, who can be trusted, who deserves protection, and who bears responsibility when something goes wrong. That question has never been settled once and for all. It has been renegotiated throughout human history, and each renegotiation has reshaped what it means to be human.

The agentic AI era is another such renegotiation. It will not be the last.

But if we fail to engage it consciously, if we let the terms be set by technological momentum, by commercial incentives, by the path of least resistance, we may find ourselves living in a world we never chose, governed by logics we never endorsed, with identities that feel less like expressions of who we are and more like profiles optimized for systems we do not understand.

That is the possibility this book is written to prevent. Not by offering a blueprint, but by helping you see clearly enough to make your own choices and to demand that the institutions shaping your life make theirs consciously as well.

The story begins the same way my own identity did: in a place, a moment, a memory. A sound drifting through a window. A game in the background. A feeling that tells you, unmistakably, *you belong here.*

The question is whether that feeling can survive what comes next.

PART I

Identity Before Machines

Before we can understand what autonomous AI is, we must first understand what it disrupts. The temptation in a book about emerging technology is to begin with the technology itself, to start with the headline and work backward. That would be a mistake. The crises this book explores are not problems that emerged from silicon. They are problems that emerged from human social architecture, and they can only be understood by tracing that architecture to its foundations.

Identity is older than writing, older than cities, older than agriculture. It is humanity's first technology for managing the problem of other people. Long before anyone conceived of a database or a digital credential, human societies were already solving the challenge that identity exists to solve: how to extend trust beyond the reach of personal recognition, how to cooperate with strangers, and how to hold one another accountable when memory and familiarity are not enough.

Part I follows that technology through three transformations. Chapter 1 examines identity in its earliest form: the face-to-face world of tribes, rituals, and embodied recognition, where trust was built through proximity and maintained through social consequence. Chapter 2 traces the birth of the "paper self," the moment when identity was externalized into documents, names, and bureaucratic systems that allowed strangers to be recognized across distance and time. Chapter 3 follows identity into the digital age, where the paper self became data, abstracted and scaled to a degree that the architects of earlier systems could never have imagined.

These chapters are not mere background. They are the foundation on which everything else rests. The crises that emerge when autonomous systems enter human institutions are not new crises. They are old crises, amplified and accelerated. The questions we will face about trust, ownership, control, and meaning are versions of questions humanity has faced before, at every threshold when the mechanisms of identity were remade. To understand where we are going, we must first understand where we have already been.

CHAPTER 1

Identity As a Human Technology

Long before identity became a credential, a database entry, or a line on a passport, it was something simpler and more dangerous. It was the answer to a question every human group has had to ask since cooperation first became possible: who belongs here and on what terms? That question gave rise to every system we now associate with identity, and it has never stopped being asked. Tribes asked it. Empires asked it. Modern bureaucracies dress it in a different language, but they ask it still. Identity, in its oldest and most enduring form, is a technology of survival. It is how strangers learn whether to relax in each other's presence, how groups decide whom to trust and whom to push to the edge, how cooperation extends beyond the small circle of people we already recognize by name and face.

This chapter traces what identity was before machines began to manage it on our behalf, but it does not begin in a textbook or a bureaucratic office. The architecture of belonging is first encountered in person with other people, where the rules are unspoken, the categories are already drawn, and the consequences of failing to read them arrive without warning. Most of us live our entire lives without ever being asked to articulate what identity actually does for us. We feel it most clearly when it breaks, when the signals we send are misread, when the systems meant to include us instead mark us as something to be sorted or set apart.

R. Mastrogiacomo, *The Next Identity Crisis*, https://doi.org/10.1007/979-8-8688-2788-4_1

That experience does not require a credential to operate, and it does not wait for adulthood to arrive. It begins early, often before we have the language to name it.

Layers We Do Not Say Out Loud

I was born in Italy and came to the United States when I was seven years old. I did not speak any English. Every day, I was taken out of my classroom and brought to a separate room with other foreign students to learn the basics of a language that surrounded me but did not yet belong to me. A bilingual student was assigned to translate for me. She hated it. I could feel that she hated it, even if I did not fully understand the words being said around us. I suspected the other students teased her for having to translate. I know they teased me. I pretended not to notice. That only gave them more material.

To them, my lack of understanding meant something else entirely. It meant I was slow. It meant I was behind. It meant I was less intelligent. In that classroom, language was not just a tool for communication. It was a proxy for competence, worth, and belonging.

Initially, it felt hopeless. I remember the fear that I would never catch up, that I would always be operating at a disadvantage. Even years later, after I spoke fluently, I still felt behind when I read. My mind translated the English, made sense of it there, and then translated it back before I could respond. I still thought in Italian. I still measured myself against a standard that felt just out of reach.

I trusted people who spoke my language more than anyone else. Not because they were kinder, but because I could trust meaning itself. Even as a child, I sensed that language has layers. Someone can say one thing and mean another. In my native language, I could trust that I understood not only the words but the intent behind them.

Looking back, I do not see villains in those classrooms. I see something more familiar and more uncomfortable. Those children were doing what humans have always done. They were protecting an identity they already belonged to. They were defending the boundary of "us" from someone who did not yet fit inside it.

Identity As Protection

This is where identity begins: as protection, not expression. Contemporary conversations often treat identity as something personal, cultural, or political, something inward-facing that exists to be articulated and recognized. This framing places identity in the realm of choice and self-definition, which is comforting but historically misleading. Identity did not emerge to help humans express themselves. It emerged to help humans survive one another.

Long before identity became a matter of values, narratives, or ideology, it functioned as a mechanism for navigating danger. Early human life was organized around uncertainty, scarcity, and persistent risk. Intergroup violence was not a later corruption of peaceful origins but a persistent feature of human social life from the earliest times [1]. Survival required rapid judgments made with incomplete information. In that environment, the ability to distinguish friend from foe was existential. To misjudge identity was to invite injury, exile, or death. Identity functioned as a survival filter. It answered a fundamental and relentless question: is this being safe enough to approach or dangerous enough to avoid or confront?

In the smallest human groups, identity required little formal structure. When everyone knew one another through direct, repeated interaction, recognition was personal and memory-based. Faces, voices, habits, and shared experiences created a dense web of familiarity. Trust did not need to be symbolized because it was continuously reinforced through lived contact.

As human societies grew, those conditions eroded. Memory no longer scaled with group size. Familiarity thinned. Encounters with unknown individuals became more frequent and more consequential. Identity had to change or cooperation would fail. It needed to move beyond personal recognition and become something that could operate under conditions of partial knowledge.

From Recognition to Ritual

This pressure intensified dramatically with the shift from nomadic life to agriculture. The move toward farming did not simply alter how humans produced food. It fundamentally changed how they related to risk [2]. Once survival depended on planted crops and stored grain, it became tied to place and time. A hunter-gatherer group under pressure could relocate. A farming community could not. Seeds in the ground represented delayed survival. Structures and tools represented investments that could not be easily rebuilt. When departure was no longer an easy option, exclusion became more dangerous and inclusion more valuable. Identity systems responded by becoming more elaborate, more ritualized, and more tightly bound to survival.

The trust signals that emerged under these conditions shared a common logic: they were costly to fake. Accent, gait, dress, ritual behavior, all carried credibility precisely because they required prolonged immersion in a group. Anyone can claim peaceful intent. Few can convincingly perform belonging without having lived it. Similarity preceded belief. Early humans did not primarily ask what strangers thought or intended. They asked whether strangers could be trusted to behave predictably under pressure.

As groups continued to expand, even embodied familiarity became insufficient. Ritual and symbolism emerged as infrastructure, not decoration. Shared rituals, symbols, and markers allowed identity to scale beyond memory. They replaced personal familiarity with standardized signals. Participation became evidence. Belonging could be demonstrated publicly, quickly, and without extended interaction. Rituals are trusted because of what participants are willing to do, not because of what they believe. They demand time, conformity, and public commitment, and that cost is what makes them credible [3, 4].

None of these systems were designed to be accurate in a moral or empirical sense. Identity systems were optimized for risk reduction, not truth. They did not need to classify perfectly. They needed to classify well enough to avoid catastrophic failure. In evolutionary terms, treating a harmless outsider as a threat was costly but survivable. Treating a genuine threat as safe was often fatal. Under these conditions, identity systems naturally tended toward exclusion. They overgeneralize, stereotype, and persist even when they cause harm, because human systems do not seek optimal solutions. They seek solutions that are good enough to function under constraints [5, 6]. Identity systems are satisficing mechanisms, and their flaws are consequences of the problem they were designed to solve.

Not One Design

But before we continue, a crucial caveat. The trajectory traced so far, from tribal recognition to ritual to codified belonging, follows a pattern visible across many civilizations, but it does not describe a single universal design. Different cultures solved the identity problem by choosing different foundational units, and those choices shaped everything that followed.

The Western tradition, from Greek philosophy through Enlightenment liberalism, gradually arrived at the autonomous individual as the basic unit of identity. A person is a self-contained being with rights, duties, and an interior life that belongs to them alone. This assumption runs so deep in Western thought that it can feel like a description of reality rather than a design choice. It is not. It is one answer to the question of what a person is, and other civilizations gave different answers that are equally sophisticated and, in some cases, more relevant to the challenges this book will explore.

Confucian thought, which has shaped moral and political life across East Asia for more than two millennia, begins not with the individual but with the relationship. In the Confucian framework, a person is not a self who happens to have relationships. A person is constituted by relationships, as child, as parent, as sibling, as friend, as citizen. Identity is not something you possess independently; it is something that exists in the space between people, maintained through reciprocal obligation and expressed through conduct. The self is inherently relational. Remove the relationships, and there is no self to speak of [7].

The Southern African philosophical tradition of ubuntu makes a similar but distinct move. The Zulu phrase *umuntu ngumuntu ngabantu*, a person is a person through other persons, is not a statement about community as an add-on to individual identity. It is a claim about what personhood actually requires. You become human through participation in human community. Identity is not a possession you carry alone. It is a quality that emerges from connection [8].

These are not exotic footnotes to the Western story. They are alternative architectures for the same problem that this book is tracing. And they matter now, because the crisis that autonomous AI introduces is partly a crisis that the Western design, with its emphasis on individual autonomy, individual ownership, and individual accountability, is uniquely ill-equipped to handle alone.

Why Identity Hardens

As identity systems solidified, they did not simply remain in place as neutral background structures. They accumulated emotional weight. What had begun as a set of practical signals and shared behaviors gradually became infused with meaning, memory, and obligation. Identity ceased to be merely something a group used and became something a group *was*.

Once identity becomes entwined with collective memory, it is no longer evaluated solely by its effectiveness. Its continuity evaluates it. Practices persist not because they are still the best solution to a current problem, but because they are recognizable, inherited, and familiar. Groups preserve norms long after they cease to be adaptive, enforcing them through social pressure and punishment even when change would improve outcomes [9]. Stability becomes synonymous with survival, even when the two diverge. This persistence is reinforced during moments of crisis. When a group experiences shock, threat, or loss, identity systems tend to harden rather than soften. Rules become stricter. Boundaries become clearer. Deviations become more threatening.

Over time, the emotional logic of identity systems begins to overshadow their practical logic. People do not simply follow identity rules because they work. They follow them because deviation feels dangerous, shameful, or disloyal. Belonging becomes its own reward, and exclusion becomes its own punishment. Structural pressure, not malice, drives this shift. Identity systems persist because they make uncertainty tolerable.

As identity systems harden, they inevitably intersect with authority. Once a group agrees on who belongs, it must also decide who speaks for the group, who enforces its boundaries, and who interprets its rules. In early societies, authority was embodied in elders, lineage leaders, warriors, or ritual specialists, and its legitimacy derived from tradition rather than from outcomes [10]. Rules were obeyed because they were inherited, not because they were efficient or just. That inheritance-based legitimacy has a critical consequence: harm does not automatically delegitimize authority. A rule can cause suffering and still be accepted, provided it is recognized as part of the group's inherited order.

This is why identity systems can cause repeated harm without collapsing. When an individual is excluded, punished, or sacrificed, the event is often framed as confirmation of the system's seriousness rather than as a failure [11]. Responsibility dissolves into custom. "This is how things are done" becomes a powerful moral shield. When no single person can be blamed, the system itself becomes unquestionable. The result is a paradox: identity systems exist to enable human cooperation, yet they often suppress individual judgment. They protect the group, but they also demand obedience. Over time, the very mechanisms that enable large-scale cooperation begin to constrain flexibility and moral responsiveness.

By the time identity systems reach this stage, they are deeply embedded in everyday life. They shape expectations, distribute trust, and define legitimacy so thoroughly that they become invisible. People no longer experience identity as a constructed solution. They experience it as reality itself. This invisibility is what gives identity its power and its danger. When identity is experienced as natural rather than invented, its rules feel beyond question. Loyalty becomes virtue. Dissent becomes a threat. And harm, when it occurs, is absorbed as the cost of order.

Identity is a human technology forged under pressure, refined through repetition, and sustained by emotional and social need. It made civilization possible by stabilizing trust among strangers. It also introduced constraints that persist long after their original purpose fades. Understanding identity in this way is essential because it explains how identity can later be externalized, formalized, and extended beyond direct human relationships. The foundations were laid long before those transformations occurred.

In that classroom, the children were turning my silence into a verdict; identity was doing its oldest work. No one handed those children a manifesto about exclusion. They did not need one. They defended the boundary of "us" with the only tools available to them: accent, fluency, familiarity, ritualized cruelty, and the quiet authority of whatever felt normal in that room. What I experienced as bullying was also a primitive form of governance, a community stabilizing itself by making difference legible and then punishing it.

The pattern is uncomfortable because it is ordinary. Identity scales from faces to rituals, from stories to symbols, from belonging to authority, and as it hardens, it begins to demand loyalty and tolerate harm in the name of continuity. Those childhood moments were a glimpse of the infrastructure beneath civilization: the human technology that turns uncertainty into order, strangers into categories, and categories into power.

Summary

Identity began as a survival technology. Long before writing, cities, or any of the institutions we now associate with formal recognition, human beings had to solve the most dangerous problem of social life: distinguishing those who could be trusted from those who could not. The earliest answers came through proximity. Faces, voices, habits, and shared memory carried enough information to bind small groups together, and in that intimate scale, identity required no symbols beyond the body itself. The cost of being known was simply the cost of being present.

As groups expanded, that intimacy could not scale, and the architecture of identity changed in response. Ritual became infrastructure. Symbols replaced memory. Belonging had to be performed publicly because it could no longer be sustained privately, and the signals that survived were those costly enough to resist easy imitation. Different civilizations made different foundational choices about what a person actually is. The Western tradition gradually settled on the autonomous individual. Confucian thought built identity around relationships. Ubuntu rooted personhood in the participation of one human in another. Each design solved the same problem from different premises, and each shaped the institutions that followed.

What unified these traditions was not their answers but their pressures. Identity systems were never optimized for truth. They were optimized for risk reduction, and they accepted error as the price of order. Over time, they accumulated emotional weight, hardened into inheritance, and migrated from practical solutions into something closer to doctrine.

By the time an identity system becomes invisible to the people inside it, it is no longer experienced as constructed. It feels like reality itself. That is where its power compounds. Rules that feel natural rarely face questions, and harm absorbed in the name of continuity rarely meets resistance. The childhood classroom that opened this chapter was not an anomaly. It was a small, ordinary instance of the same machinery that has stabilized civilizations for thousands of years, drawing the line between "us" and everyone else and enforcing it with whatever materials the room provides.

This is the foundation on which everything that follows is built. Trust between strangers is not an accident of human nature. It is the product of a long, fragile technology that civilizations have refined under pressure and sustained through ritual, exclusion, and emotional commitment. The crises this book traces are not departures from that history. They are extensions of it.

Looking Ahead

In Chapter 2, identity steps off the body and onto the page. As societies grew beyond the reach of face-to-face recognition, they began externalizing the self into documents, names, and bureaucratic records that could travel where the person could not. The paper self made identity portable, legible to strangers, and retrievable without intimacy. That shift made modern life possible, and it introduced a vulnerability the older systems had never faced. Once the self could be represented, it could be copied, contested, forged, and quietly redefined by whoever held the records.

References

[1] Keeley, Lawrence H. *War Before Civilization: The Myth of the Peaceful Savage*. Oxford University Press, 1996.

[2] Scott, James C. *Against the Grain: A Deep History of the Earliest States*. Yale University Press, 2017.

[3] Durkheim, Émile. *The Elementary Forms of Religious Life*. 1912. Translated by Karen E. Fields, Free Press, 1995.

[4] Turner, Victor. *The Ritual Process: Structure and Anti-Structure*. Aldine, 1969.

[5] Douglas, Mary. *Purity and Danger: An Analysis of Concepts of Pollution and Taboo*. Routledge, 1966.

[6] Simon, Herbert A. *Administrative Behavior: A Study of Decision-Making Processes in Administrative Organization*. 4th ed., Free Press, 1997. First published 1947.

[7] Tu, Wei-ming. *Confucian Thought: Selfhood as Creative Transformation*. State University of New York Press, 1985.

[8] Metz, Thaddeus. "Ubuntu as a Moral Theory and Human Rights in South Africa." *African Human Rights Law Journal* 11, no. 2 (2011): 532–559.

[9] Henrich, Joseph. *The Secret of Our Success: How Culture Is Driving Human Evolution, Domesticating Our Species, and Making Us Smarter*. Princeton University Press, 2015.

[10] Weber, Max. *Economy and Society: An Outline of Interpretive Sociology*. Edited by Guenther Roth and Claus Wittich, University of California Press, 1978. First published 1921–1922.

[11] Girard, René. *Violence and the Sacred*. Translated by Patrick Gregory, Johns Hopkins University Press, 1977.

CHAPTER 2

The Birth of the Paper Self

Chapter 1 traced identity in its oldest form, when recognition lived in the body and trust was carried by proximity, ritual, and the slow weight of shared experience. That system worked for as long as people remained within reach of one another, but it could not scale beyond the limits of memory and presence. When societies began extending past those limits, identity had to be rebuilt in a form that could travel where the body could not.

There is a moment in the life of every modern person, often unnoticed, when a piece of paper begins to know us better than any neighbor does. The form arrives. The number is assigned. The certificate is issued. From that point forward, institutions can speak about us, decide about us, and act on our behalf without ever encountering us in person. We tend to think of this kind of identity as a record, but it is more than a record. It is a representation that can travel independently of the body, retain coherence across decades, and command belief in rooms we will never enter. The paper self does not replace the embodied self that the previous chapter described. It runs alongside it, often outlasting it and increasingly determining what the embodied self is allowed to do.

This chapter traces how that representation came to exist and why it changed nearly everything about the way human societies handled trust. The transformation looks technical from a distance, but it was a

R. Mastrogiacomo, *The Next Identity Crisis*, https://doi.org/10.1007/979-8-8688-2788-4_2

philosophical event. It moved the burden of recognition off the human eye and onto the institution, and it taught modern societies to accept a strange new premise, that the version of a person held in a record could be more authoritative than the person standing in the room. That premise has shaped most of the moments in our lives that institutions cared about, and one of them was the day I formally became someone I had already been for years.

An Old Solution to an Old Problem

When I became a citizen of the United States, I received a piece of paper that told the world who I already was. The ceremony had been orderly and calm, the kind of room institutions built to make private lives fit inside public procedure. People recited words that carried history, and then the document appeared, clean and official, with my name printed like a verdict.

I had been living in the United States longer than anywhere else by that time, so nothing in my life changed in that moment. I did not wake up with new values or a new personality, and my attachments did not rearrange themselves to match a flag. The center of my life had already been here, shaped by work, relationships, routines, ambition, and the fact that my future had been unfolding here for years.

Still, the paper mattered in a way that surprised me. It felt operational rather than symbolic or sentimental, as if a door had been installed in the wall and the document was the key.

That power did not come from the ink or the seal. It came from what the paper allowed a system to do without knowing me. A friend could believe my story because they had seen me live it, but an institution had to believe my story without seeing any of it. The paper created a version of me that could travel farther than my body and speak more loudly than my voice.

This was the shift that defined modern identity. Earlier worlds had handled identity through recognition and culture. A person had been known by face and family, by reputation and repeated contact, by the rituals that signaled belonging and the accent that revealed where someone had grown up. Those systems had not been gentle, and they had always drawn boundaries, but they had been bounded by proximity because the rules were carried in people.

Paper changed the balance in a more fundamental way than most people noticed in daily life. It took what had once lived primarily in relationships and moved it into artifacts that could be carried, checked, filed, and believed. It made identity legible to strangers, thereby making it actionable for institutions [1]. The *paper self* was the name for that externalized layer: the representation of a person that could be recognized without intimacy, stored without memory, and transported without the body. It was not character or consciousness, nor was it meant to be, but it had become the interface through which institutions recognized the person behind it.

When Life Became a Record

The impulse to externalize identity into portable documents is far older than modern bureaucracy. What changed over time was not the impulse itself but the scale, the standardization, and the growing assumption that an institution could treat a document as more authoritative than a human voice.

Long before passports carried photographs, rulers issued letters of safe conduct [2]. A traveler moved beyond the reach of local reputation and needed a way to carry legitimacy over distance. Written authority traveled farther than spoken assurances, and it took a form that could be shown, checked, and believed.

A vivid relic comes from the Tang Dynasty in China. Along the Silk Road, merchants passed through frontier checkpoints that required paperwork. Surviving travel permits, known as guosuo, were issued by local authorities to regulate movement and trade [3, 4]. One preserved guosuo documented a merchant's travels and the checkpoints he passed. It included names and details that made the traveler legible to officials who had never met him. Even without a modern photograph, the document did what modern identity artifacts do: it turned a human being into an administratively recognizable subject.

If the guosuo looked unfamiliar, the logic was not. Identity could be carried as a document, and that document could be checked at the edges of a system where power was enforced. The checkpoint was an ancient setting for a modern truth.

The most consequential form of the paper self did not begin with travel. It began with birth, because birth was where the relationship between a person and an institution could start before the person had any agency to refuse it.

When communities were small, a child was known because they were seen, and a family was known because it belonged to the shared memory of the place. As societies expanded, memory stopped scaling. People moved. Witnesses died. Inheritance and property required continuity, and obligations required proof, so identity had to become something that could be retrieved.

Civil registration transformed life events into administrative facts retrievable by strangers and referenced years later. England and Wales provided a clear pivot: from July 1, 1837, the civil registration system began recording births, marriages, and deaths through state registrars, moving identity facts into infrastructure that operated beyond parish memory [1]. A family recorded a birth because it mattered to them. A state recorded a birth because it mattered to the system.

Once births were recorded, people became countable, and countability carried political weight. It formed the basis for taxation, conscription, schooling, eligibility, and exclusion, and it explained why paperwork became a central technology of governance.

That shift carried an institutional need: a record that could not be reliably retrieved might as well have been lost. Names were human. They carried culture, history, love, and sometimes trauma. They were also messy for administration. Names repeated, changed through marriage or migration, and were spelled differently by different clerks. Institutions responded by reaching for an index key, a unique identifier that made a person addressable inside a system. The number was not the person, nor did it capture soul or character, but it made the person findable. In an institutional world, being findable became a form of existence.

What Paper Made Possible

The paper self should not be made into a villain. Paper identity did not persist because humans loved forms. It persisted because it worked often enough to make large-scale cooperation feasible.

When identity became portable, rights could travel too. A person could prove family relationships in court. A worker could prove eligibility for hire. A citizen could claim entitlements that did not depend on being personally known by an official. A traveler could cross borders with a document that signaled some level of protection [2]. Paper identity also reduced a certain kind of arbitrariness. A record could restrain a capricious official. A document could protect a person from being erased by rumor and provide continuity when families moved and institutions changed. Bureaucracy carried its own frustrations, but it also offered a consistency that pure social recognition often lacked.

When the Same Mechanism Could Be Misused

The same mechanism that enabled protection could be repurposed for domination. The reason was structural rather than mystical. If a system could classify people and enforce the classification, paperwork could become an instrument of coercion. Historical examples matter here not because the present automatically repeats them, but because they reveal how administrative tools can shift direction when a moral environment collapses. Cruelty does not always announce itself as cruelty. It can arrive as a new form, a new requirement, a new stamp, and then become routine.

In Nazi Germany, persecution was carried out through paperwork [5, 6]. The Nuremberg Laws of 1935 redefined Jewish identity in legal terms and stripped rights through classification. Once the state defined who counted as a full citizen and who did not, identity became a legal boundary that could not be crossed by persuasion or character. That boundary seeped into schools, workplaces, public offices, banks, police stations, and border controls. A person who had been a neighbor became a category in a file, and a category could be isolated.

The administrative grip tightened in ways that reached into the most intimate parts of identity. Under an August 1938 decree, many Jews with first names deemed "non-Jewish" were required to add "Israel" or "Sara" to their given names [7]. The cruelty was both practical and symbolic, because the forced marker had to be repeated in every signature, application, and transaction. Two months later, passports held by Jews were invalidated unless stamped with a red "J." A passport had been proof of movement and protection. Under this logic, it became a portable signal for exclusion, a document that instructed other officials how to treat the person holding it.

Apartheid South Africa demonstrated another branch of the same logic: identity as permission to exist in certain spaces [8]. The apartheid state standardized the reference book, commonly called the dompas, as a required document that tied identity to authorized presence, to employment, and to the right to be in a city without being treated as a violation. When paperwork became permission, anxiety became routine. If the book was forgotten, lost, stolen, or damaged, the person was not treated as unlucky. They were treated as illegal.

These examples illuminate a structural truth that resonates far beyond their specific historical contexts: the paper self can be tuned toward protection or domination, and the tuning often appears procedural. The infrastructure does not change. Only the intent behind it does.

The Number That Became Your Character

Not every lesson about the paper self came from authoritarian history. Some came from everyday institutions that most people experienced as normal.

A particularly revealing artifact is the credit score. It is not issued by a state, but it serves as a condensed reputation that precedes a person. It takes pieces of financial behavior, compresses them into a single number, and presents that number as a proxy for trustworthiness. Numbers carry an aura of objectivity. They make decisions feel neutral and make judgment feel like calculation. In practice, scores shape access to lending, housing, and pricing in ways that are invisible until the moment of denial.

Research by the US Consumer Financial Protection Bureau described millions of adults as "credit invisible," meaning they lacked a credit record at nationwide consumer reporting agencies, and described millions more with records too thin to be scored [9]. In institutional life, absence of a record was often treated as absence of trust.

The credit score illustrates a broader shift in the paper self. Verification asks whether someone is who they claim to be. Evaluation asks whether they are worth trusting. Scoring compresses that second question into a digit and trains society to accept that trust can be computed.

From Paper to Data

The paper self is an old human solution to the old problem of scale. It allowed rights to travel. It allowed strangers to cooperate. It gave institutions a way to remember people without intimacy.

It also introduced a new kind of vulnerability. Once identity was externalized as artifacts, it became transferable and could be copied, forged, stolen, and reassigned. It could be consulted without the person present and used to sort people into categories that shaped access and opportunity.

The most important shift was straightforward: paper moved identity from recognition to administration. It made identity retrievable and, in turn, trained society to treat representation as reality.

That training prepared the world for the next transformation. When paper records were digitized, they became searchable at speed. When search became routine, decisions began to happen without conversation. The document I held at that citizenship ceremony not only confirmed my belonging but also revealed a structure built over centuries. Modern life ran on versions of people that could be held, processed, and acted upon in their absence, and that reality had shaped institutions long before computers arrived.

Summary

The paper self was an old solution to an old problem made new by scale. Long before passports carried photographs, rulers issued letters of safe conduct, and merchants on the Silk Road carried travel permits like the Tang Dynasty guosuo. The impulse to externalize identity into something portable, something a stranger could check, is far older than modern bureaucracy. What changed in the modern era was not the impulse but its reach. Civil registration in the nineteenth century made the recording of births, marriages, and deaths a function of the state rather than the parish, and once life events became administrative facts, people became countable. Countability carried political weight. It became the basis for taxation, conscription, schooling, eligibility, and exclusion, and it explains why paperwork became one of the central technologies of governance.

Paper identity gave human societies something they had never had before. It gave rights a way to travel with the person rather than with the village. It allowed strangers to cooperate without intimacy. It restrained capricious officials and offered continuity when families moved and institutions changed. The paper self should not be made into a villain, because it persisted not from love of forms but because it worked often enough to make modern life possible. Names, however, were messy. They repeated, changed through marriage, and were spelled differently by different clerks, so institutions reached for the number as an index key. The number was not the person, but it made the person findable, and in an institutional world, being findable became a form of existence.

The same mechanism that enabled protection could be tuned toward domination, and the tuning often appeared procedural. The Nuremberg Laws redefined identity in legal terms and stripped rights through classification. A 1938 decree forced many Jews to add "Israel" or "Sara" to their names, turning every signature into a marker of exclusion. A red "J" stamped on a passport converted a document of protection into an instruction for other officials. Apartheid South Africa demonstrated another branch of the same logic, where the dompas made identity a condition of permission to occupy space. These were not failures of paperwork. They were paperwork doing what paperwork is structurally capable of doing when the moral environment collapses. The infrastructure does not change. Only the intent behind it does.

Not every lesson came from authoritarian history. The credit score showed that the paper self could shift from verification to evaluation without anyone noticing. Verification asks whether someone is who they claim to be. Evaluation asks whether they are worth trusting. The score compressed that second question into a digit and trained society to accept that trust could be computed. Millions of adults exist as "credit invisibles," meaning they cannot be scored at all, and absence of a record is often treated as absence of trust. In a world built on representation, invisibility becomes a quieter form of exclusion than denial, but no less consequential.

This is the deeper inheritance of the paper era. Paper moved identity from recognition to administration. It taught modern societies to treat the version of a person held in a record as more authoritative than the person standing in the room. That training prepared the world for what came next.

Looking Ahead

In Chapter 3, identity steps off the page and into the database. The same logic that made the paper self portable and retrievable is rebuilt at machine speed, where records are consulted without conversation, decisions are reached without a clerk, and the document waiting in a drawer is replaced by an account that never rests. The shift looks like convenience. It is closer to a quiet rewriting of how trust is granted, because the question institutions ask begins to change. Where the paper self asked who someone was, the digital self begins to ask what they will do. That move from verification to inference will reshape nearly everything about modern recognition, and it will lay the foundation for a possibility the earlier systems could not have imagined: identities that have no person behind them at all.

References

[1] Scott, James C. *Seeing Like a State: How Certain Schemes to Improve the Human Condition Have Failed.* Yale University Press, 1998.

[2] Torpey, John. *The Invention of the Passport: Surveillance, Citizenship and the State.* Cambridge University Press, 2000.

[3] Arakawa, M. "The Transit Permit System of the Tang Empire and the Passage of Merchants." *Memoirs of the Research Department of the Toyo Bunko,* 2001.

[4] Hansen, Valerie. "The Impact of the Silk Road Trade on a Local Community: The Turfan Oasis, 500–800." In *Les Sogdiens en Chine,* edited by Étienne de la Vaissière and Éric Trombert. École française d'Extrême-Orient, 2005.

[5] Arendt, Hannah. *Eichmann in Jerusalem: A Report on the Banality of Evil.* Viking Press, 1963.

[6] Hilberg, Raul. *The Destruction of the European Jews.* Quadrangle Books, 1961; revised editions by Holmes & Meier.

[7] United States Holocaust Memorial Museum. Holocaust Encyclopedia entries on forced name additions (August 1938 decree) and passport "J" stamp policy (October 1938).

[8] Breckenridge, Keith. *Biometric State: The Global Politics of Identification and Surveillance in South Africa, 1850 to the Present.* Cambridge University Press, 2014.

[9] Consumer Financial Protection Bureau. *Data Point: Credit Invisibles.* May 2015.

CHAPTER 3

The Digital Turn

Chapter 2 traced the rise of the paper self, the moment when identity left the body and became something a stranger could check, file, and believe. Documents made rights portable, names were compressed into index numbers, and societies learned to treat the version of a person held in a record as more authoritative than the person standing in the room. The paper self was powerful and it was patient. It waited in drawers. It was retrieved at counters, presented at borders, opened at the moment of decision, and then put away. Identity in that era was something you carried until someone asked for it.

What follows in this chapter is the quiet end of that patience. The digital self is not simply a paper self that has been scanned. It is a representation that no longer waits to be consulted, because it has been wired into the background of nearly every interaction a modern person has. It is checked when you open an app, when you cross a network, when you buy a coffee, when you walk past a sensor. It does not ask permission to be examined. The login prompt is only the visible surface of a process that has already happened thousands of times beneath the screen. Where the paper self extended identity across space, the digital self extends it across time, attention, and behavior, and it does so at a speed no human gatekeeper can match.

This shift looks like convenience. It feels like access, like progress, like being allowed in. That is what makes it easy to miss. Beneath the smoothness, the question institutions ask about a person is changing. The paper self answered who someone was. The digital self begins to answer

R. Mastrogiacomo, *The Next Identity Crisis*, https://doi.org/10.1007/979-8-8688-2788-4_3

what they will do, what they have done, what they are likely to do next. That move from verification to inference is the central transformation this chapter examines, and like most transformations that reshape a society, it began with a moment that felt like nothing at all.

From Scarcity to Accounts

The first time I created a digital version of myself, the moment was so small I almost missed it. It was the early 1990s. In a home where one phone served the whole family and that same line doubled as the only connection to the Internet, I logged into a dial-up service and encountered a form field asking me to choose a username. The field was tiny, a few inches wide at most, but the decision it demanded was unlike anything I had been asked before. I was not signing a document or filling out an application. I was naming a self that would exist somewhere I could not see, stored on a machine I would never visit, recognized by people I had never met. The name became an email address, and the address outlasted every other introduction I made that year. I *still* have it.

That moment was small, almost trivial, which was why it mattered. A new kind of self had been born in that box: a digital self that existed because the system recognized it and that endured because the system stored it.

What made the digital self different was not that it existed, because the paper self had already turned people into portable representations. The difference was speed and silence. The digital self traveled at machine speed. It was retrieved without asking, compared without explanation, and consulted constantly in the background. The paper self had waited in a drawer until someone opened it. The digital self was never at rest. The transition did not feel like a philosophical event. It felt like convenience. It felt like access. It felt like being allowed in.

In physical life, identity had usually been demanded by a person. A clerk asked. A teacher called the roll. A guard requested papers. In the digital era, identity was demanded by a machine, and that demand carried a different emotional texture. There was no negotiation and no charm. There was only the gate. A login prompt looked simple, but it was a new kind of ceremony, and repetition turned the idea into a habit. When identity became a habit, it became infrastructure.

Accounts

Digital identity began with a simpler requirement than most people imagined: shared machines needed a way to distinguish users. In the early 1960s at MIT, the Compatible Time-Sharing System introduced one of the earliest widely recognized uses of computer passwords [1, 2]. The password was invented as a practical boundary marker, a way to separate one user's space from another's. The first digital selves were born from scarcity, and the login prompt performed the same function that paper identification had performed in the physical world: it established order by dividing access.

Even the earliest era hinted at the risks that would later become familiar. A famous early incident involved a researcher printing a file of passwords to gain more computing time. The story mattered less as trivia and more as a prophecy: as soon as identity became a credential, identity became a target.

A password did not describe a person. It enabled a relationship between a user and a system. It was proof of access, not proof of character. Yet it became the seed of something larger, because as soon as systems needed keys, they needed accounts, and accounts required a stable identity within the system.

Dial-up services made this shift accessible to ordinary households [3, 4]. They asked people to choose a screen name and remember a password.

A screen name was not only a persona. It was something the system could find, route messages to, attach activity to, and treat as the subject of permissions. A postal address was tied to geography. An email address was tied to identity [5]. Once a society accepted addresses that were not physical, it had accepted the first mass version of a digital self that could travel without the body.

The paper self had been built out of artifacts: certificates, registries, identifiers. The digital self was built out of accounts. An account was not simply a record. It was a container for rights, permissions, history, and relationships. It could be suspended, flagged, locked, or deleted. Paper identity had made a person legible to institutions. Digital identity gave institutions a way to act on a person without ever meeting them.

The difference was more than semantic. The paper self allowed a bank clerk to verify you. The digital self allowed the bank's system to decide whether you were allowed to transact at all, often without a clerk seeing anything beyond a screen. Identity moved from episodic checks to continuous consultation. The paper self was checked at the border, at the counter, at the moment of application. The digital self was consulted every time you clicked, every time you logged in, every time you made a request. A person did not merely present identity. Identity became the condition for participation.

When Identity Became Data

The digital self grew because storage changed. In 1970, Edgar F. Codd published a paper describing the relational model of data [6, 7]. It proposed a way to organize information into tables that could be related through common fields. What mattered was not only efficiency. What mattered was the concept of linkage. In a relational world, identity was not a single document. It was a set of attributes that could be connected across contexts. A name in one table could be linked to a transaction in another, a login in another, an address in another, a complaint in another. Paper had separated identity from relationship. Databases separated identity from context.

The Internet expanded the idea further. It was designed to be stateless, but commerce and community required memory. In 1994, programmers at Netscape developed the cookie [8, 9], a small piece of state stored in the browser so a site could recognize you across requests. The cookie became a new kind of identity fragment, invisible to most people, yet it created continuity, and continuity is one of the deepest ingredients of identity. Once recognition could be automated in the browser, the web stopped being a library of pages and started becoming a place where "you" returned.

That memory created a new path for surveillance, not necessarily as a conspiracy, but as an economic opportunity [10]. If a site could remember you, it could count you. If it could count you, it could sell your attention. If it could sell your attention, it had an incentive to know you better. A change that had begun as a shopping cart became a cultural machine. Over time, the dominant economic model shifted. Many services became "free" at the point of use, and the cost moved somewhere else. The digital self, in this framing, was not only a representation. It was a resource.

Digital systems made records cheap, persistent, searchable, and shareable. A dossier was not simply a pile of facts. It was a constructed portrait that could be consulted as if it were a person [11, 12]. The dossier also created a new asymmetry. A person knew their own intentions, their own story, and their own interior life. A system knew patterns. Systems were not impressed by explanations. They were impressed by consistency. They learned to treat identity as a set of repeatable behaviors and stable attributes.

Paper identity had asked: who is this person? Digital identity increasingly asked: what *will* this person do? This was the shift from verification to inference. A system no longer relied only on fixed facts such as name, date of birth, and document numbers. It also relied on behavioral signals: how quickly you typed, which device you used, where you logged in from, what your pattern of activity was. In earlier cultural worlds, identity had been tied to belonging, story, and recognition. In paper worlds, identity had been tied to records and documentation. In the digital world, identity was increasingly tied to prediction.

From Handles to Faces

Early online identity often felt like a costume. A screen name could be playful, protective, or experimental. The costume served real purposes: for people exploring identities that were dangerous to express in physical life, it offered protection; for people who faced discrimination based on appearance, it offered a fresh start; for people who were simply shy, it offered a voice.

But the costume also created problems. Anonymity enabled cruelty. Handles allowed harassment without accountability. As the web matured, many of the most influential platforms began to pull identity closer to the physical self. The reasons were not purely ideological. Real-name identity reduced certain kinds of abuse. It also made advertising more valuable. Two powerful forces converged: people genuinely wanted to connect with others they already knew, and advertisers would pay more for audiences they could identify and target. Both forces pushed toward a world where online identity and offline identity merged.

The shift happened platform by platform, each one normalizing a new level of disclosure. Facebook made real names the default. Instagram asked for your face. TikTok asked for your voice, your mannerisms, and your physical presence. By 2020, the transformation was complete. In 1995, most people online were invisible. A generation later, billions had voluntarily uploaded their faces, voices, locations, relationships, opinions, and daily routines to platforms that stored everything and forgot nothing.

This was not coerced. No government mandated it. No corporation forced it. People chose exposure because exposure felt like connection, because visibility felt like validation, and because the costs were invisible while the benefits were immediate. The irony would become clear only later. The same archive of human faces, voices, and writing patterns that people had voluntarily created became the training data for the systems that would learn to imitate them. The same real-name culture that had replaced anonymity made impersonation meaningful, because you cannot deepfake someone who never revealed themselves. We built the target before we built the weapon. We created the training set before we understood what it would be used for.

The Bridge No One Noticed

The digital self changed again when the primary interface moved from the desk to the pocket. A household computer was a place you visited. A smartphone was a thing you carried. The digital self was no longer an identity you entered. It became a layer you inhabited. Identity was always on stage, not as a dramatic performance, but as a constant stream of signals. A paper identity sat in a drawer until it was needed. A mobile digital identity followed you and left a trail.

Digital identity should not be romanticized, but neither should it be reduced to a surveillance story. It offered speed, portability, and new forms of inclusion. Families stayed connected across continents. People discovered communities that would never have formed locally. Sherry Turkle described how online environments opened space for identity exploration, role-trying, and renegotiating the boundary between the self and the social world [13]. In that sense, digital identity has been liberating for many people.

But the most consequential development was quieter than any of these. As accounts multiplied, the systems that managed them stopped caring whether the entity behind the account was a person. A handle could represent a human, and it could also represent a script, a service, a bot, or a program acting on behalf of someone else. Once accounts existed, nonhuman agents could be given accounts. Once accounts existed, nonhuman agents could be given permissions. The system did not experience this as a moral dilemma. It experienced it as a feature.

For three chapters, the actors in this story have been human. People built identity systems. People were recognized, classified, documented, and tracked by those systems. People benefited from them and suffered under them. Even as identity moved from face to paper to data, the underlying assumption never changed: the entity behind the identity was a person. The system might misrepresent you, reduce you, or surveil you, but it was always *you* on the other side of the record.

That assumption is about to break. The systems we built to represent human identity have become sophisticated enough to host identities that are not human at all. And the question that has organized every chapter so far—*who is this person?*—is about to collide with a question no previous identity system was designed to answer: what happens when the actor is not a person and the system does not care?

Summary

The digital self did not arrive with a manifesto. It arrived with a login prompt. What began in the 1960s as a way for shared computers to distinguish their users became, over the next 60 years, the dominant architecture for how human beings are recognized by the institutions that govern their lives. Passwords gave rise to accounts. Accounts gave rise to records. Records gave rise to dossiers. A screen name on a dial-up service was the first mass version of a self that could exist independently of the body, and once that idea was accepted, the rest of digital identity unfolded with a kind of logical inevitability that few people noticed while it was happening.

The transformation rested on a small set of inventions that did not look philosophical at the time. Codd's relational model taught systems to link attributes across contexts, so that identity stopped being a single document and became a network of connections that could be reassembled on demand. Cookies gave the web a memory, and memory is one of the deepest ingredients of identity, because to be remembered by a system is to be recognized by it. Behind these inventions sat an economic logic that turned recognition into a resource. If a system could remember you, it could count you. If it could count you, it could sell your attention. If it could sell your attention, it had an incentive to know you better. Surveillance was not chosen as a moral project. It was selected as a business model, and once it was selected, the entire architecture of digital life began to optimize for it.

The deeper shift inside that architecture was not the volume of data but the type of question being asked. The paper self answered who someone was. The digital self began to ask what they would do, what they had done, and what they were likely to do next. That move from verification to inference is the single most consequential transition in the modern history of identity. It allowed institutions to act on people based on predicted behavior rather than confirmed fact, and it taught modern systems to treat patterns as more reliable than testimony. Identity ceased to be something a person presented at a counter. It became something a system consulted continuously, often without the person knowing they were being asked about at all.

There was a gentler side to this story, and it deserves acknowledgment. Digital identity offered speed, portability, and forms of inclusion the older systems could not provide. Families stayed connected across continents. Marginalized communities found rooms to breathe. People exiled by geography or circumstance discovered ways to participate in worlds that had previously excluded them. The digital self was not only a surveillance project. It was also a liberation for many of the people who used it, and recognizing that double character is necessary if the rest of this book is to be read in good faith.

But the most consequential development was quieter than any of these. As accounts multiplied, the systems that managed them stopped caring whether the entity behind the account was a person. A handle could represent a human, and it could just as easily represent a script, a service, a bot, or a program acting on behalf of someone else. The infrastructure had been built for people, but it no longer required people in order to operate. That permission, granted invisibly and without debate, is the hinge on which the rest of this book turns.

Looking Ahead

For three chapters, the actor in this story has been human. People built the systems. People were recognized by them, classified by them, helped and harmed by them. Even as identity moved from face to paper to data, the underlying assumption never changed. Behind every record, there was someone. That assumption is about to break. In Chapter 4, the book crosses into Part II and begins examining what changes when the entities inside our identity systems can do more than wait to be recognized. They can act. The distinction between automation, which follows rules, and autonomy, which pursues goals, may sound technical, but it is the moral hinge of everything that follows. When a nonhuman system stops responding and starts doing, it ceases to be a feature of human life and becomes a participant in it. The crises that the next part of this book confronts begin there.

References

[1] Conner-Simons, Adam, and Rachel Gordon. "Professor Emeritus Fernando Corbató, MIT computing pioneer, dies at 93." MIT News, July 15, 2019.

[2] Walden, David, and Tom Van Vleck, eds. *Compatible Time-Sharing System (1961–1973): Fiftieth Anniversary Commemorative Overview.* IEEE Computer Society, 2011.

[3] Historical reporting on major dial-up online services in the early 1990s and their role in bringing email and chat into American homes.

[4] Histories of early consumer online services, including CompuServe, Prodigy, and AOL, as context for how gated networks shaped early digital identity.

[5] Tomlinson, Ray. History of network email on ARPANET (1971), as documented in computing histories and obituaries.

[6] Codd, Edgar F. "A Relational Model of Data for Large Shared Data Banks." *Communications of the ACM*, 1970.

[7] IBM History. "The relational database." Overview of Codd's 1970 model and its implications.

[8] Kristol, David, and Lou Montulli. RFC 2109: "HTTP State Management Mechanism." IETF, 1997.

[9] Montulli, Lou. "The reasoning behind web cookies." Personal blog, May 14, 2013.

[10] Zuboff, Shoshana. *The Age of Surveillance Capitalism: The Fight for a Human Future at the New Frontier of Power*. PublicAffairs, 2019.

[11] Solove, Daniel J. *The Digital Person: Technology and Privacy in the Information Age*. NYU Press, 2004.

[12] Solove, Daniel J. "Digital Dossiers and the Dissipation of Fourth Amendment Privacy." *Southern California Law Review*, 2002.

[13] Turkle, Sherry. *Life on the Screen: Identity in the Age of the Internet*. Simon & Schuster, 1995.

PART II

The Crisis of Ownership

Part I traced identity from tribal recognition through paper bureaucracies to digital abstraction. By the end of that arc, humans were still the actors, but the stage was built from systems, databases, and interfaces.

Part II begins at the moment something changes. We are no longer only building systems that represent human identity. We are building systems that begin to act. Not merely executing instructions, but making choices, pursuing goals, and shaping outcomes on our behalf. This is the quiet threshold between automation and autonomy, and it is the most morally important line modern society has crossed without fully naming it.

This is still a crisis of identity, even when the word on the surface is ownership. Ownership has always been the answer to a question that identity exists to ask: who can be held accountable? When you own something, you answer for it. When something goes wrong, we look for the owner because the owner is the someone who can be confronted, compelled, and held responsible. That chain from harm to accountability to a specific human identity is what makes trust possible at scale. It is what allows strangers to cooperate, contracts to mean something, and institutions to function. When the thing you own can act on its own, that chain breaks. The question "who is responsible?" stops having a clear answer. And when accountability becomes unanswerable, trust does not simply weaken. It begins to collapse. The crisis of ownership is the crisis of identity viewed from a different angle: the angle where we discover that the systems we thought we controlled have begun to act in ways we cannot fully author, explain, or answer for.

That is the hinge of this part. We are moving from digital mirrors to autonomous actors, and the world will not feel the same once we admit the difference.

CHAPTER 4

Automation Versus Autonomy: A Line We Crossed Quietly

The previous chapter ended on a quiet revelation. The infrastructure of digital identity was built for people, but it never required people in order to operate. Accounts could be filled by humans or by software, and the system did not distinguish between them. That permission, granted invisibly across decades, set the stage for the question this chapter must now confront. What changes when the entity behind the account stops being recognized and starts acting?

The answer turns on a distinction that sounds technical but is closer to a philosophical fault line. Automation follows rules. Autonomy interprets goals. Automation does what it is told and fails when its instructions run out. Autonomy decides what to do when instructions are insufficient, which is to say, almost always. The difference is not a matter of sophistication or processing power. It is a matter of moral architecture, because once a system begins to interpret rather than execute, the human in the chain stops being the one who decided and becomes, at best, the one who allowed.

R. Mastrogiacomo, *The Next Identity Crisis*, https://doi.org/10.1007/979-8-8688-2788-4_4

We tend to imagine this crossing as a future event, something that will arrive when machines become advanced enough to deserve the word agent. The truth is more uncomfortable. The crossing has already happened in many of the systems that shape modern life, and it happened so gradually that no one had to defend it. To understand why that matters, and why the distinction between obedience and judgment is the hinge of everything this book will explore from this point on, it helps to begin somewhere that has nothing to do with machines. It helps to begin with the first time I was put in charge of a team.

The Anchor Is Beginning to Slip

The first time I was put in charge of a team, I made the mistake that most first-time managers make. I tried to control everything.

I had been given responsibility for a small group of senior support engineers. These were not junior employees waiting for instruction. They were experienced professionals, but I did not see that clearly at first. What I saw was a team that reported to me, which, in my inexperienced understanding, meant a team that needed to be told what to do.

So I told them. I assigned tasks with specificity that left no room for judgment. I reviewed work that did not need reviewing. I inserted myself into decisions that would have been better made without me. I stayed late doing work I should have delegated, while my team sat idle, waiting for instructions that I was too busy to give because I was doing their jobs poorly instead of doing my own job well. The bottleneck was me, but I could not see it because I was too busy being the bottleneck.

It took months before I understood what I was doing wrong, and even then the lesson arrived not as a revelation but as an accumulation of friction. The team was not failing, but it was not thriving either. The energy was flat. The work was competent but uninspired. People were doing what they were told, which turned out to be far less than what they were capable of doing if they had been trusted to decide for themselves.

The lesson, once I finally absorbed it, was simple: Management is not about telling people what to do. Management is about getting the right people into the right situation and then providing them the support they need to meet their goals. Treating skilled people like tools, like instruments that execute your intentions and nothing more, limits everyone. It limits them because it denies them ownership. It limits you because it denies you their judgment. It limits the team because it makes *you* the ceiling.

What I learned was that autonomy is not a reward you grant to employees who have earned your trust. Autonomy is the recognition that they are in those roles because they bring something you do not have: their own experience, their own knowledge, their own capacity to see problems you have not noticed and solve them in ways you would not have imagined. The moment I stopped treating my team like tools waiting for commands and started treating them like professionals capable of authorship, everything changed. They took ownership. They made decisions. They surprised me. And the team became more than the sum of its instructions.

I begin with that memory because it contains, in miniature, the distinction this chapter needs to draw.

For most of human history, tools obeyed. They extended strength, sharpened perception, multiplied endurance, and expanded reach, but they did not decide. A hammer did nothing until a hand raised it. A plow cut no soil until someone guided it across the field. An atomic bomb did not question who to kill.

Even our most fearsome instruments preserved a crucial moral structure. Responsibility could be traced back to a human moment of judgment because someone had to choose, someone had to act, and someone could be held accountable. That structure did more than organize blame after the fact. It organized meaning by helping people understand their relationship to power, consequences, and control.

Tools extended the human will, but they did not replace it. The world could change quickly, violently, unpredictably, but there was still a human somewhere in the chain who could say, "I did this," or at least, "I chose to let this happen." That belief was sometimes true and sometimes aspirational, yet it anchored moral life for centuries because it kept authorship visible.

What I learned as a young manager was that humans are not tools. We have now built something new: tools that are no longer tools in the old sense. They do not wait for commands. They interpret goals. They exercise judgment. They act. We have created instruments that behave less like hammers and more like the team I once tried to micromanage.

The difference is that my team was made of humans who could wait, who could absorb my inexperience, who could underperform patiently until I figured out how to let them work. Autonomous systems do not wait. They act at speeds we cannot match, in volumes we cannot review, with consequences we cannot always trace. The question this chapter asks is what happens when we cross the line from tools that obey to systems that decide and whether we will recognize that crossing for what it is before the old assumptions about control and responsibility quietly become fictions.

The anchor is beginning to slip, not because humans have become careless or indifferent, but because we have quietly changed what we mean by the word "tool." We crossed a line from automation to autonomy without a single defining moment, without a public reckoning, and without fully appreciating what we were giving up. The crossing did not arrive as a dramatic rupture. It arrived as a sequence of reasonable upgrades, each justified by efficiency, scale, and performance.

Taken individually, those upgrades looked incremental and responsible. Taken together, they altered the moral architecture of decision-making by relocating judgment from the moment of human choice to the continuous operation of systems that can act autonomously.

The significance of that shift is often disguised by technical language, as if the difference were primarily about engineering. The difference is moral, because it determines where judgment lives, where responsibility lands, and who is actually present when consequential choices are made.

Before we continue our discussion, let's take a moment to make clear what autonomous AI is.

WHAT IS AUTONOMOUS AI?

If you have used ChatGPT, Claude, or similar systems, you have experienced AI as a conversational partner. You type a question, and the system responds. You ask for a summary, and it summarizes. You request a poem, and it writes one. The interaction feels remarkable, but it follows a simple pattern: you ask, it answers. The AI waits for you, responds to you, and then waits again. It is reactive by design. Autonomous AI is different. It does not wait. It acts. An autonomous AI agent is a system that can pursue goals across multiple steps, make decisions along the way, and take actions in the world without requiring human approval at each stage. Where a chatbot responds to a single prompt, an agent receives an objective and then figures out how to accomplish it. It can break a task into subtasks, decide which tools to use, call external services, create files, send messages, browse the web, execute code, and adjust its approach based on what it encounters. It does not simply generate text. It operates. Consider the difference concretely. If you ask a standard chatbot to "book me a flight to Chicago next Tuesday," it will tell you how to book a flight. It might list airlines, suggest websites, or walk you through the steps. But it will not actually book the flight.

An autonomous agent, given the same instruction along with appropriate access, could search for flights, compare options, select one based on your stated preferences, enter your payment information, complete the purchase, and send you a confirmation. You gave it a goal. It executed the goal. The difference between describing an action and performing an action is the difference between conversation and agency. This shift matters because action has consequences that conversation does not. When a system only talks, the human remains in control of what happens next. When a system acts, it changes reality. It spends money, sends communications, modifies records, triggers processes, and creates commitments that may be difficult to reverse. The human may have initiated the goal, but the human did not make every decision along the way. The agent did. Autonomous agents gain their capabilities through a combination of features that distinguish them from simpler systems. They typically have access to tools, meaning they can interact with external software, databases, and services rather than being limited to generating text. They have memory or context that persists across steps, allowing them to track progress and build on prior actions rather than starting fresh with each interaction.

They can plan, decomposing a high-level objective into a sequence of concrete operations. They can observe the results of their actions and adjust course when something goes wrong. And increasingly, they can operate for extended periods without human intervention, running in the background while you do other things. The agent may do exactly what you wanted. It may also do something subtly different, something that seemed reasonable to its internal logic but that you would have rejected if asked. The more capable the agent, the more consequential these divergences become. For readers interested in a more detailed exploration of how organizations can govern AI agents, including frameworks for accountability, oversight, and operational control, my earlier book *AI Identities: Governing the Next Generation of Autonomous Actors* (Apress, 2025) provides an in-depth treatment of the technical and institutional dimensions. For now, the essential point is this: Autonomous AI is not just a smarter chatbot. It is a system that crosses the line from responding to acting, from answering to doing. That crossing changes everything, because once a nonhuman system can act in the world, it becomes a participant in human life, not merely a feature of it.

An automated system performs tasks according to rules specified in advance. Its behavior is constrained by explicit instructions, even if those instructions are complex and layered. When something goes wrong, the failure can usually be traced back to a rule, a configuration, a boundary condition, or a human choice about how the system should behave.

An autonomous system is different. It is designed to pursue goals rather than follow scripts, and it determines how to achieve outcomes independently. It navigates trade-offs that may not be fully specified and that its creators often cannot fully anticipate. Autonomy does not merely execute human intent. It interprets intent, and in doing so, it begins to behave less like an instrument and more like a participant.

This still sounds abstract until you translate it into everyday experience. Designing a house with a pencil is still design because the pencil extends the architect's ability to draw while leaving every decision in human hands. Where walls go, how light enters, which compromises are acceptable, and which risks are worth taking remain the architect's responsibility. The pencil never proposes alternatives, never optimizes silently, and never hides trade-offs behind an interface.

Now imagine a different process. You submit constraints: the lot size, the desired style, the number of rooms, the budget, and the local codes. The system generates layouts, balances cost and aesthetics, optimizes energy efficiency, and proposes designs you would not have drawn yourself. You can approve or reject the output, but the decisions are no longer authored line by line by a human. The system has moved from extension to partner, and the word *tool* begins to carry a new and heavier meaning.

At first, this feels like empowerment, and the feeling is not wrong. The benefits of autonomous systems are real, and dismissing them would be dishonest. A diagnostic model that catches a tumor a radiologist missed is not a threat to human dignity; it is a gift to the patient who gets to live. A system that translates languages in real time does not diminish the translator's craft; it opens conversations that would never have happened. Tools that handle paperwork, schedule logistics, and manage routine complexity free human attention for problems that actually require it. For people with disabilities, autonomous systems can restore capacities that biology or accident removed. For people without access to expensive professionals, they can democratize expertise that was once reserved for the privileged. These are not hypothetical benefits. They are already arriving, and they are genuinely good.

Think about what it means for a first-generation college student in a rural town to have access to a tutor that can explain organic chemistry at two in the morning, patiently, without judgment, for free. Think about a parent in a country without enough pediatricians, holding a feverish child at night, who can describe symptoms to a system that triages with more accuracy than panic allows. Think about the small business owner who cannot afford a lawyer but needs to understand a lease before signing it, and for the first time has something better than guessing. These are not edge cases. They are the daily texture of lives that have always been underserved by institutions built for people with resources, connections, and proximity to expertise. Any honest reckoning with autonomous AI must begin by admitting that for millions of people, these systems are not a convenience. They are the first time anyone bothered to show up.

The argument of this book is not that autonomous AI is bad. The argument is that its benefits do not resolve the questions it raises about identity, accountability, and control. A system can be helpful and still be ungovernable. A tool can improve outcomes and still erode the moral structure that tells us who is responsible when outcomes go wrong. The doctor whose diagnosis is augmented by AI is still a doctor, but the relationship between the doctor's judgment and the system's recommendation is no longer simple. The student whose essay is refined by AI still wrote something, but the authorship is no longer clean. The company whose customer service is handled by agents still serves customers, but the question of who speaks for the company has become genuinely difficult to answer.

In other words, the benefits are real, and they are not the point. The point is what happens to trust, responsibility, and human agency when systems that deliver those benefits also act in ways their operators cannot fully predict or explain. That tension does not disappear because the benefits are large. If anything, large benefits make the tension harder to confront, because they create pressure to look away from problems that might slow adoption.

Modern societies reward velocity in ways that are easy to describe and difficult to resist. Markets that react faster outperform those that pause. Supply chains that optimize continuously beat those that wait for human review. Communication systems that respond instantly feel more alive than those that hesitate. In this environment, speed becomes synonymous with competence, and deliberation is treated like inefficiency, which is how the line between automation and autonomy was crossed quietly.

The Slope, Not the Cliff

Part of what makes the crossing so easy to miss is that delegation rarely arrives all at once. It comes in increments, and each increment can be defended as a prudent improvement rather than a moral transfer. At the turn of the century, researchers Raja Parasuraman, Thomas Sheridan, and Christopher Wickens described automation as a ladder of human-machine interaction [1]. Systems begin by helping humans gather information, then they help analyze it, then they recommend options, then they select among options, and eventually they execute actions.

The value of that ladder is not the diagram itself. The value is the insight that the journey from assistance to action can be gradual enough that it feels like refinement rather than surrender. A recommendation engine seems harmless. A risk score seems prudent. An automated approval seems efficient. A self-adjusting optimization seems modern. Then one day you look up and realize the system is not simply doing what you told it to do. It is deciding what you meant, and doing so at a pace that makes human intervention more ceremonial than real.

From In the Loop to Outside the Loop

There was no referendum in which society voted to delegate judgment to machines. The transition unfolded incrementally, under pressure, and mainly out of sight. Humans were placed in the loop, then on the loop, and eventually outside it, not because anyone announced their removal, but because their presence increasingly slowed systems down.

Speed was the driving force, and it turned oversight into friction. As systems accelerated, the temptation to let them run without interruption became stronger, not because people suddenly stopped caring, but because the advantages of uninterrupted operation were immediate. Humans sleep, hesitate, and second-guess, and those traits are features of moral reasoning. In systems optimized for velocity, those same traits can look like liabilities.

For a long time, we reassured ourselves that keeping a person in the loop preserved moral responsibility. As long as a human could approve, override, or intervene, the system could still be treated as an extension of human agency. That belief depended on a hidden assumption: intervention was not only possible in principle but meaningful in reality.

In 1995, human factors researchers Mica Endsley and Esin O. Kiris described what happens when automation runs continuously and people are reduced to monitors [2]. The pattern is now commonly called the out-of-the-loop problem. When humans are no longer actively engaged in doing the task, they tend to lose situational awareness. When the system fails, they are slower to notice, slower to understand, and less effective at taking control in time.

That finding matters because it exposes a crucial asymmetry. The override remains available on paper, which allows organizations to claim that humans are still in charge. At the same time, the human capacity to override erodes in practice, which means the moral reassurance is increasingly symbolic. Once decisions unfold in milliseconds, oversight turns into ceremony, approval becomes a rubber stamp, and intervention becomes a postmortem.

At that point, autonomy no longer feels like an ethical gamble. It begins to feel like an engineering necessity, because if humans cannot keep up, the system must be allowed to act on its own. That logic is rarely framed as surrender. It is framed as pragmatism, and pragmatism has a quiet way of reshaping morality.

The Ladder of Agency

To keep this grounded, it helps to separate "sounding smart" from "being able to do things." We can call this the Ladder of Agency, because each step changes the social stakes. The lower steps are about information and influence. The higher steps are about power and consequences. A system that produces text can mislead you, but a system that takes action can change your life before you have time to object.

At the first rung, the system **produces information**. It answers questions, summarizes, drafts, and explains. This already matters because information shapes belief, but the system still feels like a library. It is impressive and sometimes dangerously persuasive, yet it moves nothing unless you move it.

At the second rung, the system **recommends**. It ranks options, nudges choices, and frames what seems reasonable. Now the system begins to shape your autonomy, not by forcing you, but by sculpting what you perceive as the sensible path. Recommendation is subtle power because it does not feel like coercion. It feels like help.

At the third rung, the system **decides**. It chooses among options and determines outcomes, often invisibly. This is where it begins to resemble a judge. It is not merely advising you. It is adjudicating you. It determines eligibility, access, risk, priority, attention, and opportunity. Even if a human designed the policy, the lived experience becomes "the system decided."

At the fourth rung, the system **acts**. It sends the message, schedules the appointment, approves the purchase, moves resources, triggers consequences, and sets events in motion. Here, the demand for identity becomes sharp, because action without attribution feels like haunting. Something happens, and you cannot locate the someone behind it.

At the fifth rung, the system **delegates and coordinates**. It chains tasks together, instructs other systems, and manages a portfolio of actions across time. At this level, it resembles a manager of other actors, an invisible executive layer that can amplify intention far beyond a single human's capacity.

Most public conversation fixates on the first two rungs because those are the most visible. People debate truth, misinformation, plagiarism, and bias, and those debates are necessary. Yet the identity crisis accelerates at decision and action because that is where autonomy and power are redistributed. When systems decide and act, the question of "who is responsible" stops being academic.

The more unsettling point is that the ladder is easy to climb once a system is connected to the world. An output model becomes a recommendation engine with a small interface change. A recommendation engine becomes a decision system when it is allowed to auto-approve or auto-deny. A decision system becomes an actor when it is given permission to execute. Each step is justified as convenience or efficiency. Each step can be defended in isolation. The transformation arrives not as a dramatic leap but as a sequence of small delegations that collectively change what kind of world we inhabit.

When Delegation Becomes Abdication

Delegation is not the enemy. Abdication is.

Delegation is a conscious choice to entrust a task while retaining responsibility. You delegate because you cannot do everything yourself, because others have expertise you lack, or because your attention is needed elsewhere. Delegation works when you understand what you are handing off, when you can evaluate the results, and when you remain answerable for outcomes. The person who delegates is still the author. They have simply hired a hand.

Abdication is what happens when delegation becomes habitual and unexamined. It is what happens when convenience slowly replaces intention. Abdication does not announce itself. It arrives as a sequence of reasonable shortcuts, each one defensible, until the person who was once responsible no longer knows what they have given away.

Autonomous AI makes abdication easy because it makes delegation feel frictionless. The system is always available. It is always confident. It never complains. It never asks for a raise. It delivers answers quickly, and speed feels like competence. Over time, this shifts behavior. People stop asking whether the system should decide and start asking only whether it can. That is the quiet line we cross without noticing. Capability becomes permission.

Once capability becomes permission, responsibility begins to drift. Decisions are made by process. Nobody experiences the decision as theirs. That is how institutions become morally hollow without intending to.

A society that wants to preserve agency must become more suspicious of frictionless delegation. Friction is not always inefficiency. Sometimes, friction is the sign that moral weight is present. The effort required to decide, the discomfort of uncertainty, the slowness of deliberation: these are not bugs in human judgment. They are features that keep authorship visible.

The New Form of Plausible Deniability

Every era invents a language for standing near a harm without owning it. Bureaucracies gave us the claim of having followed orders. Ideologies gave us the insistence that history required it. Markets gave us the invisible hand, which has absorbed more responsibility over three centuries than any institution ever built. What these phrases share is a grammar that moves the verb away from the speaker. Something happened. Something was decided. The person speaking was present, was often necessary, and was somehow not the one who chose.

Autonomous systems supply the newest entry in that repertoire, and it is the most persuasive one yet, because it is frequently true. "The model did it" is not always an evasion. Often it is a plain description of what occurred. A system produced an outcome that no person selected, through a process no person can fully reconstruct, at a moment when no person was watching. Every earlier version of the excuse required its speaker to shade the truth, to pretend that a choice made freely had been made under compulsion. This one requires no such pretense, and that is precisely what makes it dangerous.

The ladder described earlier in this chapter explains why the phrase has become available at all. On the lowest rungs it has no purchase. If a system informs you and you act badly on the information, nobody accepts the claim that the search results did it, because the choosing so plainly happened inside you. As a system moves from informing to recommending, the claim acquires a thin plausibility, since the option you selected was the one placed in front of you and the others were not. By the time a system decides and acts on its own, the claim has stopped being an excuse and become something close to a factual report. Nothing about the human's formal position changes across those rungs. Their name stays on the account, the file, the decision. What changes is how much of the decision they can honestly say they made, and the excuse grows to fill exactly the space that authorship vacates.

This is why the shift from automation to autonomy is a change in kind rather than a change in degree. A tool that misfires implicates whoever was holding it, because a tool has no capacity to have done otherwise, and we all know it. A system that acts on its own assessment does have that capacity, or something close enough to it that our moral vocabulary reaches instinctively for the same words we use about people. We are not abusing language when we say the model decided. We are describing a genuinely unfamiliar situation with the only words we have, and those words carry assumptions about responsibility that were built for a world where deciders could be held to account. The escape hatch was not installed by anyone who wanted to escape. It opened by itself the moment the ladder was climbed.

The trouble is that a vocabulary like this does not stay merely descriptive for long. Once a phrase exists that is both accurate and exculpating, institutions will find occasions to use it, and they will reach for it most readily in the situations where someone has been harmed and is looking for a person to answer them. Notice what has quietly happened by then. The question has become who to blame, which is the easiest question in the room and almost always the least useful one. The harder question, and the one this chapter has been circling, is what responsibility can still mean when the honest answer to who decided is that nobody quite did.

Blame Versus Responsibility

Blame and responsibility are not the same thing, though we often use them as if they were. Blame is retrospective. It hunts for guilt after harm has occurred. It asks, "Who did this?" and it demands punishment.

Responsibility is prospective. It is stewardship. It asks, "Who will answer for this?" and it demands ongoing care. Responsibility does not wait for disaster. It shapes behavior before outcomes arrive.

Autonomous systems push us toward blame because harm can be vivid while causality is obscure. When people cannot see a clear human decision behind an outcome, they instinctively demand punishment. They want someone to pay. That instinct is not irrational; it is how societies have always tried to deter future harm.

But blame without clarity is theater. If blame lands on the wrong target, it fails to deter. If blame lands on a target that cannot feel shame or change behavior, it fails to correct. Blaming a system is satisfying but useless. The system does not learn remorse. The system does not fear reputation. The system does not change its values because society is angry.

The shift we need is from blame to responsibility, from retrospective punishment to prospective stewardship. That shift requires identifying, before harm occurs, who will be answerable. It requires asking not "Who can we punish?" but "Who must own the ability to intervene?" Responsibility is a claim about control points. Who can pause the system? Who can constrain it? Who has the duty to monitor it? Who can explain it in human terms? These are stewardship questions, and they must be answered before deployment, not after disaster.

This is harder than blame. Blame is cheap and emotionally immediate. Responsibility is expensive and requires institutional design. But a world of autonomous systems that runs on blame alone will become a world of perpetual scandal and no improvement, because the systems that caused the harm will keep running while the arguments about guilt continue. Control points, answerability, and stewardship assumes something we have never had to defend before: that we know who we are dealing with. Strip that away, and there is no one to assign responsibility to. And the first identity signal to go is the oldest one we have.

The Voice That Sounds Like You

Throughout human history, the voice has been one of our most intimate identity signals. It carries more than words. It carries timing, hesitation, confidence, warmth, and history. It reaches past logic into the part of us that recognizes kin, authority, threat, and belonging. That is why leaders rehearse cadence, why parents can calm children with sound alone, and why a single sentence from a loved one can collapse distance.

Synthetic voice breaks that anchor by decoupling a person's sound from their body. This is more than a new fraud technique. It is a structural change in how recognition works. When the voice of your colleague, your parent, or your friend can be simulated convincingly, the trust normally carried by voice becomes transferable to anyone with access to the right tools. Identity signals have become portable in ways human societies were not designed to withstand.

Portability not only enables deception. It changes the default trust. If you cannot assume that a familiar signal corresponds to a familiar person, you begin to demand proof where you used to accept presence. You begin to treat intimacy as suspect. You become slower to believe, slower to respond, slower to help. That sluggishness is rational self-defense, but it is also a tax on social life.

The greater danger is that synthetic voice blurs the line between persuasion and impersonation. A convincing voice can create urgency, simulate consensus, manufacture intimacy, or trigger guilt, and it can do so at scale. The human mind is not designed to treat a lifelike voice as "just output," because voice has historically been one of the ways we locate intention. When intention can be faked cheaply, the cost of skepticism rises, and the beneficiaries are always the ones who can afford to keep speaking until the listener gives up.

This is the beginning of a crisis of attribution, a world where we ask not simply "Is this content true?" but "Who is speaking to me, and what right do they have to speak in this voice?" That question cannot be solved by better media literacy alone, because it is not purely cognitive. It is infrastructural. A society that cannot reliably bind speech to an accountable identity becomes one where persuasion is cheap and trust scarce.

Summary

This chapter began with a story that had nothing to do with machines. As a first-time manager, I tried to control a team of senior professionals by leaving them no room for judgment. The lesson took months to arrive. Humans are not tools. They are participants, and they cannot be assigned tasks with the precision of a script because the work they do depends on the judgment they bring to it. The bottleneck in that story was not the team. It was me, pretending that authorship could be preserved by withholding agency from people who already had it.

We are now faced with systems that do not need permission. Tools throughout human history preserved a moral structure. A plow cut no soil until someone guided it. A weapon, however terrible, had to be aimed by a human hand. Even our most fearsome instruments traced responsibility back to a human moment of judgment, because someone had to choose, someone had to act, and someone could be held accountable. The line between a tool and an actor was the line between the extension of human will and the replacement of it, and for centuries, that line held.

The line no longer holds. The systems modern society has built do not wait for commands. They interpret goals, exercise judgment, and take actions whose consequences arrive faster than any human can review. The distinction between automation and autonomy captures the shift in compressed form. Automation follows rules and fails when its instructions run out. Autonomy decides what to do when instructions are insufficient, which in any consequential domain is almost always. The difference is not technical sophistication. It is moral architecture, because once a system interprets rather than executes, the human in the chain becomes the one who allowed rather than the one who decided.

The crossing did not arrive as a single event. It arrived as a sequence of small delegations, each defensible on its own terms. To make those delegations visible, this chapter introduced the Ladder of Agency, a framework for separating sounding smart from being able to do things. At the first rung, systems produce information. At the second, they recommend. At the third, they decide. At the fourth, they act. At the fifth, they delegate and coordinate among other systems. Public debate has concentrated on the lower rungs, where the visible problems are misinformation, bias, and persuasion. The deeper identity crisis accelerates at the third and fourth rungs, where autonomy and power are quietly redistributed. The ladder is easy to climb once a system is connected to the world, because each step can be defended in isolation as a sensible improvement. A recommendation engine becomes a decision system when it is allowed to auto-approve. A decision system becomes an actor when it is given permission to execute. None of these transitions looks like surrender. Together, they constitute one.

Speed accelerated the crossing because oversight is friction. Markets that react faster outperform those that pause. Communication systems that respond instantly feel more alive than those that hesitate. In an environment that treats deliberation as inefficiency, the human in the loop becomes the bottleneck, and the moral reassurance of human override becomes increasingly symbolic. The out-of-the-loop problem, identified in human factors research in 1995, describes the result. When people are reduced to monitors of systems they no longer actively run, they lose situational awareness, and their ability to intervene meaningfully erodes even as their formal authority to do so remains intact. Authority and control come apart. Authority stays with the human. Control migrates to the system.

This chapter did not argue against autonomous systems. Their benefits are real and already arriving. A diagnostic model that catches a tumor a radiologist missed is a gift to the patient who lives. A tutor that can explain organic chemistry at two in the morning, patiently and free, opens doors that wealth used to keep closed. The point is not to refuse these gifts. The point is to refuse the quiet erasure of authorship that comes with them when delegation slides into abdication. Delegation is a conscious choice to entrust a task while retaining responsibility. Abdication is what happens when delegation becomes habitual, unexamined, and so frictionless that no one notices when responsibility has evaporated. The first preserves the human as author. The second does not.

Looking Ahead

In Chapter 5, the abstraction acquires a face. The systems described in this chapter are about to become characters in the story rather than tendencies in it. AI agents, synthetic voices, and decision-making systems are no longer background infrastructure. They are beginning to speak, to negotiate, to persuade, and to take up the kind of social space that has until now been reserved for human beings and for the artificial persons we built to scale them, the most consequential of which is the corporation. Chapter 5 examines what changes when the infrastructure learns to speak, why performance is not the same as accountability, and why a world that adds participants faster than it builds the grammar to govern them is precisely the condition in which identity becomes more contested, more fragile, and more important than ever.

References

[1] Parasuraman, Raja, Thomas B. Sheridan, and Christopher D. Wickens. "A Model for Types and Levels of Human Interaction with Automation." *IEEE Transactions on Systems, Man, and Cybernetics—Part A: Systems and Humans* 30, no. 3 (2000): 286–297.

[2] Endsley, Mica R., and Esin O. Kiris. "The Out-of-the-Loop Performance Problem and Level of Control in Automation." *Human Factors* 37, no. 2 (1995): 381–394.

CHAPTER 5

The New Actors in the System

Chapter 4 left us with a distinction and a warning. The distinction was between automation and autonomy, between systems that follow rules and systems that interpret goals. The warning was that the line between them has already been crossed, quietly, in domains that touch nearly every part of modern life, and that the human in the loop has often become more of a witness than a decider. That argument moved in abstractions: speed, oversight, delegation, abdication. None of those words had a face.

This chapter is where the abstractions acquire faces. The systems described in the previous chapter are no longer background infrastructure waiting to be examined. They are beginning to speak, to recommend, to negotiate, and to act. They are taking up space in roles that were, until recently, reserved for humans and for the institutional selves that humans built to coordinate them. The question is no longer whether they are sophisticated enough to qualify as participants. The question is what happens when society begins to treat them as if they are, and what we are quietly granting them when we do.

To make that question concrete, it helps to begin somewhere unexpected, in the gap that almost every adult has felt at least once. It is the gap between being given a role and feeling that the role belongs to you, between holding the ID card and believing the words it prints. That gap is one of the most ordinary experiences of being human. It is also, as this chapter will argue, one of the most important things AI does not have.

R. Mastrogiacomo, *The Next Identity Crisis*, https://doi.org/10.1007/979-8-8688-2788-4_5

The Coat That Did Not Fit Yet

After college, I thought I knew who I was supposed to be. I had done the responsible thing. I earned a degree in marketing and advertising, with a minor in computer information systems. I pictured myself in the world of campaigns and creative briefs, learning how to shape attention and desire. Then graduation arrived, and reality did what it often does. The jobs I imagined did not appear. Rejections and silence started to feel like feedback about my identity, not just my résumé.

A recruiter looked at my minor and the small computer work I had done on the side during school and suggested something I had not considered: a tech support role. I remember agreeing almost casually, as if I were borrowing someone else's coat for a season. I went to the interview convinced the illusion would collapse the moment they asked technical questions. In my mind, I was an amateur who had picked up skills in the margins, self-taught and uncredentialed. I expected them to sniff that out quickly and send me home.

They offered me the job.

With no other offers on the table, I accepted, and the moment I did, I felt the ground shift under my feet. I walked into that role with a company ID card that said I belonged, while my inner voice insisted I did not. That is what impostor syndrome really is. It is the sensation of occupying a social identity that has been granted to you before you have emotionally accepted it as yours, not simply fear of failure.

That discomfort did something useful. It forced me to work harder, not because I was chasing perfection, but because I was trying to earn legitimacy retroactively. Over time, I learned the job and then learned the larger world around the job. Years later, after enough conversations with people I assumed were smarter than me, better than me, and the "real professionals," I noticed something almost comical. The feeling I thought was unique to me was everywhere. The people with the best training still worried they were faking it. The people with decades of experience still had moments where they felt one question away from exposure.

That realization matters here because it reveals what identity actually is. Identity is not only what you know or what you can do. It is also the shared agreement that you belong in a role, that your actions count as legitimate, and that you can be held responsible for what follows. We are about to extend that kind of role-based legitimacy to nonhuman systems that speak, decide, and act. When tools become participants, the stakes are no longer about output quality. The stakes are about who is in the room, what authority they are performing, and where accountability lands when the performance produces harm. Autonomous AI can't feel impostor syndrome, and it can pursue a goal with potentially dangerous overconfidence.

When Tools Become Participants

As we saw in Chapter 4, for most of human history, our tools were powerful and sometimes dangerous, but they were not participants in social life. A hammer could build a home or break a bone, yet it still belonged to the category of "thing." It did not negotiate, persuade, apologize, or recruit. It did not try to sound reasonable so that you would do what it wanted. Tools extended human intention, and when they did harm, our moral instincts looked past the tool to the person holding it.

That distinction quietly organized the world. When something happens, we reach for a "who" because human life is not a pile of events. It is a web of relationships. We assign praise and blame, gratitude and resentment, trust and suspicion, because those emotions are not decorations on top of reason. They are the mechanisms that make cooperation possible. If you cannot connect action to an actor, you cannot reliably connect consequences to behavior. When consequences no longer shape behavior, the social order starts to feel like fog.

The new class of AI systems presses directly on that "who." Not because machines have become mystical, and not because consciousness has arrived unannounced, but because participation has changed shape. We are building systems that do not merely answer questions, but increasingly recommend, decide, execute, and coordinate. When a system moves from output to action, it stops being experienced as a passive instrument and starts being experienced as a participant. You do not need to believe it has a soul to feel that shift [1]. You only need to live in a world where its choices alter your options, your time, your access, your reputation, or your money.

We have lived with automated decision systems for years, and most people already know how disorienting they can be. The bank "denies." The platform "removes." The insurer "rejects." The hiring portal "filters." A life that felt open in the morning can feel constrained by evening, bent around an invisible conclusion you did not participate in. Those systems were already acting in a sense, but they acted like background infrastructure, distant and silent.

What is new is that the infrastructure is learning to speak, and when it speaks, it takes up social space. It begins to resemble an interlocutor, something that can justify itself, persuade you, and modulate its tone to fit the moment. It can sound patient when you are frustrated. It can sound firm when you hesitate. It can sound empathetic when you are vulnerable.

Performance, however, is not the same as accountability. A human face is anchored to a biography, a neighborhood, relationships, and consequences that shape future behavior. An institution is anchored, at least imperfectly, to laws, regulators, competitors, public scrutiny, and the slow grind of legitimacy. A synthetic actor can perform sincerity, competence, empathy, and authority without being bound to the constraints that historically made those signals reliable. If trust becomes easy to simulate, then trust becomes easier to steal.

So the first claim of this chapter is simple: we are crossing a threshold from tools to participants, and once systems behave like participants, society will treat them like participants whether or not that is wise.

People will confer trust, outsource judgment, accept guidance, and form attachments, because those are normal responses to entities that occupy social space. The identity crisis begins precisely here, because the world is adding actors faster than it is building the grammar to govern them.

We Have Built Artificial Selves Before

If this feels unprecedented, it is because the new actors are arriving inside the most intimate channel humans have: language. Yet the idea of nonhuman actors is not new, and remembering that fact keeps us from drifting into either panic or denial. The modern world has never been made only of biological persons. It is crowded with invented selves, entities that are not flesh and blood but are treated as "someones" for the purpose of rights, responsibility, and power.

The clearest example is the corporation, one of the most consequential identity inventions in human history. A corporation is not a person in the way you are a person, but it is a durable social self. It can own property. It can sign agreements. It can hire, fire, lobby, advertise, and shape the built world. It can survive its founders and outlast the memories of the people who created it [2]. When a corporation acts, we do not say, "a million individuals acted." We say, "the company decided," because we need a coherent actor in the story if we are going to assign meaning and responsibility.

That need for coherence is not a sentimental quirk. It is the operating system of coordination. Modern life works because we can treat institutions as continuous identities even when the individuals inside them change. A university admits you. A hospital assumes custody of your care. A government recognizes you as a citizen. A bank extends credit and then demands repayment. In every case, an artificial self interacts with your human self, and those interactions are stabilized by roles, rules, and recognized forms of accountability.

Sometimes those accountability structures are unjust or inadequate, but they exist, and their existence gives society leverage. You can appeal. You can protest. You can sue. You can vote. You can regulate. You can strike. You can boycott. You can shame. There are friction points, and friction points are what make power contestable.

This is the second claim of the chapter: nonhuman actors are not new, but AI actors are different in a way that matters. Corporations, governments, universities, and other institutional selves are anchored to human systems that can be pressured and reformed. They are slow, bureaucratic, and legible, at least in principle. Their identity is recorded and persistent, which is precisely what allows law and culture to bind them.

An AI agent can be spun up, duplicated, modified, and redeployed with a speed and fluidity that institutional identity was never designed to manage. It can present as stable while being endlessly changeable underneath. It can be a "representative" today and a different "representative" tomorrow, and the surface can look identical even when the underlying system has changed. That fluidity is not merely a technical property. It is a political property.

The power of an actor is not only what it can do. It is also what it can evade. When identity becomes easy to reshape, responsibility becomes easier to dodge. When the "who" behind an action is unclear, the harmed person is forced to fight fog. Fog is a gift to the powerful, because it makes accountability expensive, slow, and exhausting, while the system continues to act at scale.

We should also notice something subtler. Institutional selves earned their place by being recognized. Recognition is the key move in identity. A passport works because a network of institutions agrees to treat it as meaningful. A diploma works because employers and governments agree to treat it as meaningful. Identity is never merely self-assertion. It is a social contract, an agreement that "this counts as who you are."

When AI systems begin to occupy social roles, they will seek recognition too, not because they crave it, but because recognition is what grants legitimacy and access. Once an AI system is allowed to "represent" a company, to "speak" for a service, to "decide" eligibility, to "negotiate" on a person's behalf, it becomes a participant in the moral and political order. Even if we insist it is "just software," it has already crossed into the domain where identity must be assigned, because its actions must be attributed.

This is why the question "Is AI conscious?" is less urgent than the question "What role are we allowing it to play?" Personhood is a metaphysical debate. Participation is a civic reality. A system that can deny, approve, recommend, persuade, and execute is already entangled with human autonomy. Autonomy rests on the ability to know who is influencing you, who is deciding, and who is responsible when it goes wrong.

Actors Without Ancestry

Human identity is not simply a label. It is a history that binds behavior to consequence. You and I are not merely minds. We are biographies. We carry scars, reputations, relationships, and memories that constrain what we can plausibly do next. Even when we reinvent ourselves, we do it against a past that other people remember. That social memory is not always fair, but it is one of the ways society enforces continuity, and continuity is the foundation of accountability.

This is where synthetic actors break old assumptions. They can speak convincingly without having lived anything. They can offer empathy without having suffered. They can advise without having risked anything. They can persuade without needing to face the long-term consequences of betrayal, because they can be revised, forked, replaced, or withdrawn. They can exist everywhere without belonging anywhere. They can be deployed today by one entity and tomorrow by another, which means the "self" behind the voice can become a moving target.

That makes them actors without ancestry—not mysterious, not magical, not "alive," but unrooted. Their identity is not anchored to the slow processes through which humans and institutions become knowable. They do not grow up inside a community. They do not accumulate reputation organically unless we deliberately engineer mechanisms for continuity. They can be manufactured as social presences without the deep entanglement that normally makes social presences governable. And stating these facts does not offend them.

An unrooted actor does not automatically do harm, but it changes the trust environment. Trust is not simply confidence in competence. It is confidence in continuity. The question is not only "Will it do a good job right now?" The question is "If it harms me, where does that harm land?" In human life, harm lands on a person's name, relationships, standing, and conscience.

For synthetic actors, harm can land nowhere in particular. It can be absorbed by corporate liability shields. It can vanish when the system is updated. It can be diffused across the people who trained, deployed, monitored, and profited from the system, which is a way of saying it can evaporate.

AI-driven action makes it easier for power to hide behind complexity. The organization can say, "It wasn't us, it was the system," and because the system is opaque, the harmed person is forced to fight a ghost. Complexity does not have to be malicious to be politically useful. If a decision emerges from a chain of models, data, policies, and automated steps, responsibility can be distributed until it disappears. That disappearance is power. Political theorist Dennis Thompson identified this pattern decades ago in his analysis of collective action, calling it "the problem of many hands"—the diffusion of responsibility across so many actors that no single person can be held accountable for what occurs [3].

The modern world has always been tempted by responsibility without a face. Bureaucracy can already produce outcomes that feel like no one decided. AI accelerates that tendency because it can automate not only the decision but also the explanation, generating a plausible narrative without revealing the real logic underneath. The harmed person gets a story, but not leverage.

This is why the identity crisis is inseparable from autonomy. Autonomy is not only the ability to choose. It is the ability to know who is influencing your choices and who is acting upon you. If you cannot locate the actor, you cannot negotiate with the actor. If you cannot negotiate, you cannot meaningfully consent. You can only comply or withdraw. A world full of unlocatable actors is a world where autonomy becomes a privilege rather than a default condition.

The New Incentives of Persuasion at Scale

There is a reason the coming conflict will not only be about truth. It will be about persuasion. In a world of human-scale interaction, persuasion was expensive. It required time, attention, presence, and some exposure to consequence. If you misled people repeatedly, your reputation suffered. If you manipulated too brazenly, communities pushed back. Influence had friction.

Synthetic actors reduce that friction. They can speak forever, adjust their approach, and personalize their message. They can test what works and then scale what works [4]. They can create the sensation of being heard and then use that sensation to steer behavior. They can do this without fatigue and without embarrassment.

That does not mean they will be used only for harm. It means persuasion becomes cheaper, and when persuasion becomes cheaper, the volume of attempted influence rises. Individuals will be targeted more often, in more contexts, by more actors. The burden of discernment shifts from institutions to individuals, and that burden is heavy.

When the burden becomes too heavy, people seek shortcuts. They retreat into tribes. They outsource trust to a single authority. They cling to the loudest certainty. They accept whatever feels safe. The human response to uncertainty has always been identity consolidation [5]. When reality feels unstable, people reach for belonging that feels stable.

This is why synthetic actors are not just a technology problem. They are a social psychology problem. They will accelerate the human tendency to rebuild identity around conflict, because conflict creates clarity. If the world becomes unrecognizable, we will manufacture recognition by drawing harder lines around who is "us" and who is "them."

Toward a New Social Contract with Nonhuman Participants

At this point, it is tempting to declare that the solution is simple. We should ban synthetic actors from social roles. We should forbid agents from acting in the world. We should insist that every important decision include a human in the loop. These instincts are understandable, but they are not realistic at scale, and realism matters because we are writing about the world that is arriving, not the world we wish would arrive.

The more durable question is how we build a society that can incorporate nonhuman participants without collapsing trust. That requires a new social contract, and every social contract begins with identity.

A workable contract will require answers to questions that human societies have faced before, but never at this scale or speed.

Who is in the room? Humans should not be forced to guess whether they are interacting with a person, a delegate, or an autonomous system. Ambiguity is not a neutral design choice. Ambiguity is a power move.

Who answers when something goes wrong? If a synthetic actor takes actions that affect people, there must be a clear path to someone who can repair the harm, compensate, and be constrained. Institutions cannot be permitted to launder responsibility through artificial agents.

What are the boundaries? Societies have always regulated certain kinds of identity performance because impersonation breaks trust. We do not allow counterfeit currency because money is a trust technology. We do not allow fake passports because citizenship is a trust technology. We will need equivalent constraints for synthetic identity because speech and presence are becoming forgeable.

These questions will require precise answers. Part V of this book will attempt to provide them. For now, the point is simpler: none of this requires believing that AI is a person. It requires acknowledging that AI is becoming a participant. Participants must have a legible identity because identity is how societies ensure participation is safe.

The Paradox of Autonomy

There is a paradox at the heart of this chapter. We build AI actors because we crave autonomy, and we risk losing autonomy by delegating too much agency to them. We want freedom from bureaucracy, freedom from friction, freedom from cognitive overload. We want the world to feel manageable again. So we outsource.

Outsourcing can be sane. There is no virtue in doing everything yourself, and there is no nobility in drowning in administrative chores. The question is not whether delegation is good or bad. The question is what kinds of delegation preserve authorship and what kinds of delegation hollow it out.

A society with healthy autonomy is one in which people remain the authors of the commitments that define them. They may get help drafting the words, but they still decide what they mean. They may get help managing time, but they still decide what matters. They may get help finding information, but they still decide what they believe.

A society with weakened autonomy is one in which commitments are made on people's behalf by actors whose incentives are not aligned with their dignity. In such a society, the self becomes porous, not because people have become weaker, but because the environment has become more persuasive and less accountable.

This is why identity is the foundation of trust, and trust is the foundation of autonomy. If you cannot trust the actors shaping your options, you cannot confidently author your life. You can only react.

The Quiet Future: Agents Negotiating with Agents

We often imagine the future of AI in spectacular terms. We imagine dramatic breakthroughs and dramatic catastrophes. Yet the more likely transformation is quieter. It will arrive as a shift in who interacts with whom.

Your agent will book your travel. Your agent will dispute your bill. Your agent will negotiate your subscription. Your agent will screen your messages. Someone else's agent will do the same. Human-to-human interaction will increasingly be mediated by nonhuman participants.

In the best case, this makes life smoother. It reduces friction that wastes human attention. It allows people to focus on relationships rather than logistics. It creates a kind of digital civil service that actually serves.

In the worst case, it turns life into an arms race of automated persuasion. Agents will learn to exploit human weakness, to optimize for conversion, to maximize compliance, to capture attention, and to win negotiations by whatever measure they are rewarded for. If the reward is "close the deal," then truth becomes optional. If the reward is "increase engagement," then outrage becomes rational.

The difference between these futures will not be determined by model capability alone. It will be determined by identity and accountability. If we can bind artificial participants to clear roles, traceable continuity, and enforceable responsibility, we can get the benefits of delegation without dissolving the self. If we cannot, we will live inside a constant haze where decisions happen to us, not with us.

What Kind of World Are We Building?

Every era has a defining political question. In earlier eras, it was land, labor, capital, and sovereignty. In our era, the defining question may be simpler and more intimate: who is allowed to act in the human world and under what identity?

Because when you add actors, you add power. When you add power, you must decide how it is constrained. When you decide how it is constrained, you decide what kinds of people can exist safely inside society. Identity is not a side topic. It is the operating system of legitimacy.

If we treat synthetic actors as "just tools," we will misgovern them, because tools do not require accountability. If we treat them as fully human, we will misgovern them in the opposite direction, because personhood carries moral expectations that current systems cannot meet. We need a third category: nonhuman participants with bounded roles.

That category will feel unfamiliar at first, because it forces us to articulate what we have long left implicit. What does it mean to speak? What does it mean to represent someone else? What does it mean to make a promise? What does it mean to cause harm? What does it mean to be responsible?

These questions are not technical. They are civilizational. They are about the nature of the social world.

The new actors are arriving faster than our institutions can metabolize them. They speak before we have decided what counts as legitimate speech. They persuade before we have decided what counts as permissible influence. They act before we have decided how responsibility should be assigned. They multiply before we have decided what continuity means.

When the actor arrives before the law, power moves into the gap. Some will exploit it deliberately. Others will drift into it because incentives reward drift. Either way, the result is the same: a world where agency becomes cheap and accountability becomes rare.

Once artificial actors participate in social life, a question follows that cannot be postponed: if something can act in ways that produce value, can anyone truly own it? That is the coming identity crisis in its most concrete form.

Summary

This chapter began with a story about wearing an ID card that says you belong while an inner voice insists you do not. Impostor syndrome, as I came to understand it, is not really about the fear of failure. It is about occupying a social identity that has been granted to you before you have emotionally accepted it as yours. The discomfort is uncomfortable, but it does something necessary. It forces you to work harder, learn faster, and earn legitimacy retroactively. The people who never feel that discomfort are not the ones who have earned the role. They are the ones who have stopped noticing they are inside it. That story was carrying an argument. Identity is not only a fact about what you know or what you can do. It is a shared agreement that you belong in a role, that your actions count as legitimate, and that you can be held responsible for what follows. We are about to extend that agreement to nonhuman systems, and the trouble is that the friction which makes the agreement work in humans does not exist in machines. AI cannot feel impostor syndrome. That absence is not a virtue. It is what allows AI to pursue goals with the kind of confidence that, in a human, would be checked by doubt.

The first move of the chapter was to insist on the distinction between performance and accountability. A human face is anchored to a biography, a neighborhood, a reputation, and a set of consequences that constrain future behavior. An institution is anchored, however imperfectly, to laws, regulators, public scrutiny, and the slow grind of legitimacy. A synthetic actor can perform sincerity, competence, empathy, and authority without being bound to any of those anchors. When trust becomes easy to simulate, trust becomes easier to steal. Once a system behaves like a participant, society treats it like one, conferring trust, outsourcing judgment, and sometimes forming attachments to it. Those responses are not naive. They are the ordinary human reactions to entities that occupy social space, and they will arrive whether or not the rules to govern them have caught up.

The second move was to remember that nonhuman actors are not new. The modern world has never been made only of biological persons. It is crowded with invented selves, the most consequential of which is the corporation. A corporation is not a person in the way you are a person, but it is a durable social self that can own property, sign agreements, employ and dismiss workers, and outlast its founders. Modern coordination depends on our willingness to treat such entities as continuous identities and to bind them, at least in principle, to systems of appeal, protest, regulation, and reform. Those friction points are what make institutional power contestable. AI actors are not simply the next entry in that long list. They are categorically different. An institutional self is slow, bureaucratic, and legible. Its identity is recorded and persistent, which is precisely what allows law and culture to bind it. An AI agent can be spun up, duplicated, modified, and redeployed with a speed and fluidity that institutional identity was never designed to manage. It can present as stable while being endlessly changeable underneath. The power of an actor is not only what it can do. It is also what it can evade, and fluidity is the gift that makes evasion easy. Fog is always a gift to the powerful.

From this difference, two consequences follow. The first is the paradox of autonomy. We build AI actors because we crave freedom from bureaucracy, friction, and cognitive overload, and we risk losing autonomy by delegating too much agency to them. Healthy autonomy means remaining the author of the commitments that define you, even when others help you draft the words. The second consequence is the new incentive structure of persuasion at scale. In a human-scale world, influence had friction. It required time, presence, and exposure to consequence. Synthetic actors reduce that friction to almost nothing, and when persuasion becomes cheap, the volume of attempted influence rises, the burden of discernment shifts to the individual, and people respond by retreating into tribes that promise the comfort of clarity. Identity consolidation is the predictable human response to a world in which the actors around us cannot be reliably located.

What the chapter built toward, finally, was the outline of a new social contract. The instinct to ban synthetic actors from social roles is understandable but not realistic. The serious question is how a society can incorporate nonhuman participants without collapsing trust. Three questions sit at the center of that contract. Who is in the room? Who answers when something goes wrong? What are the boundaries? Ambiguity in any of these is not a neutral design choice. Ambiguity is a power move, because it concentrates leverage in the hands of whoever benefits from the fog. We need a third category between "tool" and "person," a category for nonhuman participants with bounded roles, traceable continuity, and enforceable responsibility. Without it, we will misgovern these actors in one of two directions. We will treat them as objects when they behave like agents, or we will treat them as persons when they cannot carry the moral weight that personhood demands.

Either way, the actors are arriving faster than our institutions can metabolize them, and when the actor arrives before the law, power moves into the gap.

Looking Ahead

This chapter ended with a question that Chapter 6 is built to confront. If something can act in ways that produce value, adapt, and surprise the people who set it in motion, can anyone truly own it? Ownership has always carried a quiet companion called authorship. The farmer owns the crop because they planted it. The writer owns the book because they wrote it. Modern economies are built on the assumption that creation and responsibility can be traced to a human decision somewhere along the chain. Autonomous AI breaks that link, and the break does not feel like a technical inconvenience. It feels like the ground shifting under the categories we use to assign value, distribute reward, and locate blame. Chapter 6 examines what happens when ownership stops being a useful word for our relationship to the systems we have built and what concept might have to take its place.

Reference

[1] Nass, Clifford, Jonathan Steuer, and Ellen R. Tauber. "Computers Are Social Actors." In Proceedings of the SIGCHI Conference on Human Factors in Computing Systems (CHI '94), 72–78. Boston, MA: Association for Computing Machinery, 1994.

[2] Winkler, Adam. We the Corporations: How American Businesses Won Their Civil Rights. New York: Liveright / W. W. Norton, 2018.

[3] Thompson, Dennis F. “Moral Responsibility of Public Officials: The Problem of Many Hands”. American Political Science Review 74, no. 4 (1980): 905–916.
[4] Salvi, Francesco, Manoel Horta Ribeiro, Riccardo Gallotti, and Robert West. “On the Conversational Persuasiveness of GPT-4.” Nature Human Behaviour 9 (2025): 1645–1653.
[5] Hogg, Michael A. “From Uncertainty to Extremism: Social Categorization and Identity Processes.” Current Directions in Psychological Science 23, no. 5 (2014): 338–342.

CHAPTER 6

The Collapse of Ownership

Chapter 5 ended on a question that the next stage of this argument cannot avoid. If something can act in ways that produce value, adapt, and surprise the people who set it in motion, can anyone truly own it? That question was philosophical in Chapter 5. It becomes practical in Chapter 6. Ownership has always been more than a legal claim. It is one of humanity's oldest and most quietly effective inventions, a compression algorithm for the messy question that sits behind every complex system: who is responsible for this? When the systems we build can act, that compression begins to fail.

This chapter is about what happens when it does. The autonomous systems increasingly shaping opportunity, access, reputation, and risk are not owned in any way that produces the moral grip ownership used to provide. They can be possessed without being controlled, deployed without being authored, and benefited from without being answered for. They sit in the uncomfortable middle, treated like property in the eyes of the law and like actors in the conduct of their work, and the contradiction does not announce itself. It accumulates. The question this chapter is built around sounds deceptively simple, but it is the door through which the rest of the book walks. Can you own what thinks?

R. Mastrogiacomo, *The Next Identity Crisis*, https://doi.org/10.1007/979-8-8688-2788-4_6

Before that question becomes about machines, it was once a question about me. The story I want to begin with does not involve any of the systems described so far. It involves a much older instinct, the instinct to claim something concrete in a world where you do not yet feel entitled to belong.

Hunting for Ownership

My first job taught me something about ownership that I did not understand until much later.

Officially, I was the junior hire. Unofficially, I felt like I was on probation every day, even when no one said I was. I walked into meetings already preparing my defense, scanning faces for the moment someone would realize they had made a mistake. So I did what anxious people often do when they don't feel entitled to belong. I tried to become indispensable.

I went hunting for ownership. Not the glamorous kind that comes with titles and visibility, but the gritty kind that lives in the corners of an organization where things quietly break. If there was a piece of software no one had time to manage properly, I raised my hand. If there was a platform everyone relied on but no one "owned," I asked to get involved. Remote access, backups, the unsexy infrastructure that makes the rest of the company feel smooth and competent.

When I found a gap, I volunteered. When someone mentioned a neglected system, I asked to be involved. My goal was simple and urgent: to become "the guy." The backup guy. The remote access guy. The security-monitoring guy. If I could establish clear ownership over a domain, I reasoned, then I would have a defensible position. I would have proof that I belonged, that I wasn't a fraud, anchored to something concrete.

This was not careerism in the usual sense. I watched colleagues advance by praising senior leaders, by positioning themselves politically, and by cultivating visibility without necessarily cultivating competence.

That path was available to me, and it would have been easier. But it would not have addressed the deeper anxiety. In fact, I wanted to remain in the shadows as I feared attention would expose me. What I needed was legitimacy, not approval. I was back in that classroom feeling like an outsider. Legitimacy, in my mind, came from ownership. If I could point to a system and say, "That is mine, I built it, I maintain it, I understand it better than anyone else," then no one could question my right to be there. Ownership was my defense.

Looking back, I recognize the irony. I was deploying ownership as an offensive strategy to solve a defensive problem. I was using the language of control to manage the feeling of precarity. Every system I claimed was a small fortress against the suspicion that I did not deserve my seat at the table. It worked, after a fashion. I became indispensable in narrow domains. I built expertise that others relied on. I earned the credibility I had been so desperate to establish. But the strategy only worked because ownership still meant something stable. If I owned the backup system, then its failures were my responsibility, and its successes were my accomplishments. The relationship was clear. Ownership created a legible link between me and the outcomes I produced.

That link is precisely what is collapsing in the age of autonomous AI.

Ownership is one of humanity's most successful inventions. It is so ordinary that we forget it is a technology of the mind, a shared agreement that turns objects into "mine" and "yours" and turns conflict into something negotiable. Ownership is how we stabilize desire. It is how we coordinate scarcity. It is how we turn the world into a legible map of rights, boundaries, and responsibilities.

We do not just use ownership to divide things. We use it to decide who must care for them. If you own the house, you fix the roof. If you own the company, you answer to the board. If you own the dog, you feed it, train it, and keep it from biting the neighbor. Ownership is a moral shorthand, a compression algorithm for the messy question that sits behind every complex system: who is responsible for this?

That is why the rise of autonomous AI does not merely disrupt work or markets. It destabilizes the grammar we use to assign responsibility in the first place. We are building entities that behave less like objects and more like actors. They make choices, adjust to feedback, and pursue goals across time. They can be directed, but not fully predicted. They can be constrained, but not fully understood. They can be owned in a legal sense while still slipping through the practical meaning that ownership was designed to carry.

This chapter is about that mismatch. It is about what happens when we try to treat thinking systems as property and when property starts behaving like agency. It is about control without authorship, the unsettling reality that outcomes can be produced without anyone being able to say, honestly, "I chose this." It is also about responsibility in a world of delegated agency, where humans increasingly set processes in motion and then watch them unfold like weather.

The question beneath all of this is deceptively simple: can you own what thinks?

What We Mean When We Say "Ownership"

Ownership sounds like a single idea, but it is really a bundle of ideas, stitched together over centuries. When people argue about ownership, they often argue past each other because they are talking about different threads in the bundle.

One thread is possession. This is the intuitive, almost animal layer. Something is near you, within your control, guarded by your effort. Possession is physical, immediate, and often enforced by force.

Another thread is control. This is the political layer. Ownership implies the right to decide how something is used, who may touch it, and what counts as misuse. Control can be delegated and mediated through rules, contracts, and institutions.

A third thread is responsibility. This is the moral layer, and it is the one that matters most for this book. Ownership implies accountability when something goes wrong. If you own the factory, you cannot shrug off its pollution of the river. If you own the platform, you cannot pretend you are unrelated to the social consequences it amplifies.

In stable systems, these threads reinforce each other. Possession implies control, and control implies responsibility. Ownership works as a social technology because it fuses these elements into a single story.

Autonomous AI pulls the threads apart. You can possess the system without controlling its behavior in a meaningful way. You can control deployment while lacking ownership of the outcomes. You can profit from results while dissolving responsibility into complexity.

The collapse of ownership is the collapse of that fused story. Political theorist Dennis Thompson described a related dilemma decades ago as the "problem of many hands," where responsibility diffuses across complex systems until no single actor can be held fully accountable [1]. Autonomous AI makes that diffusion feel like a design feature rather than a temporary glitch.

The Strange Question at the Center of Modern Power

In earlier eras, ownership and agency lived in separate rooms. You could own a tool, but the tool did not decide how it would be used. You could own a book, but the book did not rewrite itself while you slept. You could own a machine, but the machine's behavior was bound by the mechanical imagination of its maker.

Even as technology became more complex, its complexity remained mechanical. A factory could be dangerous, but it did not have intentions. A computer program could be buggy, but it did not adapt its logic because it noticed an opportunity. When a system produced harm, you could follow a trail. There was a designer, an operator, a manager, an executive, and a regulator. Someone, somewhere, made a decision that could be questioned.

Autonomous AI strains that comfort. Not because it has desires in the human sense, but because it produces behavior that feels like desire. It pursues objectives across contexts. It improvises. It can surprise its creators. It can learn strategies nobody explicitly taught it. The moment a system can do that, ownership ceases to be a simple category. You are no longer asking, "Who bought this?" You are asking, "Who is supposed to answer for it?"

Our law and culture already know that ownership and responsibility are linked but not identical. If you rent an apartment, you use it, but you do not own it. If you borrow your friend's saw and cut your hand, you will not blame the saw. You will say you used it wrong, or you will say the saw was defective, or you will blame your friend for lending you something dangerous without warning. In every case, the explanation is anchored to a human chain.

Now place an autonomous system inside that chain, and notice what changes. The system can do things that resemble decisions. It can initiate actions in your name. It can recommend courses of action with persuasive confidence. It can coordinate with other systems. It can adapt its approach over time.

It plays the role of a participant, but it does not accept moral responsibility because it cannot. That is not an insult to machines. It is a description of what responsibility actually is. Responsibility is a social relationship. It is the ability to be confronted, corrected, and compelled. A system can be constrained, but it cannot be morally persuaded. Constraint and conscience are different forces. One operates from the outside through boundaries someone else sets. The other operates from the inside through the weight of lived experience and the memory of having caused harm. A system has access to the first. The second requires a kind of interiority that no architecture currently provides. You can punish a system by shutting it down, but the system does not experience the punishment as meaningful. You can retrain it, but retraining is not rehabilitation. Rehabilitation assumes a self that understands what it did wrong and chooses differently because the understanding changed something inside it. Without that interior change, correction is mechanical, not moral.

We end up trapped between two convenient fictions. In the first fiction, AI is just a tool, and ownership is enough. In the second fiction, AI is an actor, and we can blame it as if it were a person. Both fictions are comforting because both preserve older categories. Both fictions are inadequate because both ignore the structural transformation underway.

The real problem is less dramatic and more demanding: whether societies can remain stable when decisions are made by systems that no one can fully author and when the benefits of those decisions can be captured without bearing full responsibility.

That is the collapse of ownership.

Owning Objects, Employing Actors

Ownership evolved around objects. Objects do not have interests. They do not negotiate. They do not reinterpret instructions. They do not hide their reasoning because they have none. If an object causes harm, it does so through physics, and responsibility lies in design, manufacturing, and use.

Actors are different. A worker has discretion. A consultant makes judgments. A manager interprets goals and chooses a path. Even when an actor follows rules, they do so with a mind that can recognize exceptions.

This difference is why we have different moral languages for objects and actors. We talk about using objects. We talk about coordinating with actors. We talk about maintaining objects. We talk about trusting actors. We talk about fixing objects. We talk about persuading actors.

Autonomous AI sits in the uncomfortable middle. It is created, purchased, deployed, and maintained like property. Yet it operates, adapts, and influences outcomes like an actor. We treat it like a tool because that is the category we have. We respond to it like a participant because our minds do what they have always done: when something speaks coherently and takes initiative, we infer agency.

This middle position produces category collapse. If the system is an object, ownership should imply control over it. If the system is an actor, it should have accountability or at least a stable chain of accountability around it. But autonomous systems have neither in the traditional sense.

They have no moral interior, but they have operational impact. They have no citizenship, but they can still shape citizens' choices. They have no life story, but they can accumulate a reputation. They are not people, but they can occupy social space.

The result is intellectual vertigo that spills into everything. We argue about whether AI-generated work can be "owned," because ownership has long been tied to authorship. We argue about liability because liability has long been tied to intent or negligence. We argue about whether an assistant is "yours" if it is trained on your preferences but hosted by a corporation. We argue about whether you can inherit a digital proxy of a deceased relative.

These arguments sound like technicalities. They are symptoms. We are producing agents faster than we are producing stable ways to assign responsibility for them.

Can You Own What Thinks?

The question is provocative because it smuggles in an assumption that thinking is a threshold that changes what ownership means. That assumption has shaped moral history more than we like to admit.

We do not have to settle the metaphysical debate over whether machines "really" think to address the practical challenge. What matters is that we are building systems whose behavior resembles that of actors with interests. They pursue objectives. They adapt. They exploit gaps. They can surprise their handlers. They can create convincing explanations even when the explanation is a story stitched together after the fact.

One response is to insist the system is just a tool. That response protects existing categories. It also allows a quiet sleight of hand. If the system is a tool, then the institution can claim it controls the system and therefore can manage responsibility as usual. Another response is equally tempting: to treat the AI as a kind of person, so we can blame it. "The algorithm did it" becomes a modern incantation. It sounds like honesty. It can function like evasion.

The more honest answer is uncomfortable. You can legally own an autonomous system, but ownership no longer suffices to explain the relationship between the system and the world it affects. Ownership was built to govern objects. We are deploying entities that behave like actors. If we insist on calling them objects, we will keep losing control in subtle ways. If we start treating them as persons, we will build an accountability sink that absorbs blame while leaving power untouched.

Ownership has always had a quiet companion: authorship. The farmer owns the crop because they planted it. The builder owns the house because they built it. The writer owns the book because they wrote it.

Even when ownership is transferred through purchase, the moral logic stays close. Someone created something, and creation establishes a special claim. That claim might be contested, but it exists because it supplies a story. The story says: value did not appear from nowhere, it was made, therefore it can be owned.

Modern economies are built on this logic. Contracts, patents, copyrights, and corporate structures depend on the assumption that creation and responsibility can be linked. You can sell what you make. You can license what you invent. You can be rewarded for producing value. You can also be held responsible for harm because your decisions were part of the causal chain.

Autonomous AI breaks the link between authorship and outcome. It produces outputs that can be valuable, persuasive, and consequential without being authored in the traditional sense. A human can prompt a system, but prompting is not authorship in the same way that writing a paragraph is. A human can set objectives, but setting objectives is not the same as choosing each action.

This is where language starts to fail us. We use words like generated, produced, recommended, decided, and acted, but none of them fully capture what is happening. We have systems that can create things nobody specifically intended, and yet those things are not accidents. They are the predictable result of delegating creative and decision-making processes to a machine.

That shift is why ownership feels unstable. If value can be produced without authorship, who has the rightful claim to that value? If harm can be produced without authorship, who bears the rightful cost? Ownership used to answer these questions by anchoring them to a human creator or a human decision. Autonomy dissolves that anchor.

Limited Liability: The Older Rehearsal for Control Without Responsibility

To see the deeper pattern, consider a quieter invention that already separated ownership from responsibility: limited liability. Limited liability was not created to enable moral evasion. It was created to enable investment. It allowed people to share in the upside of enterprise without risking everything they owned. It helped finance the modern world.

But it also created a template for distance. You can own a portion of a company, receive returns, and yet be shielded from the full consequences of its harm. Responsibility shifts to corporate governance, executives, regulators, and legal settlements. Ownership becomes a claim on profit more than a commitment to care.

Autonomous AI extends this separation. It limits felt responsibility not only through legal structure but through opacity and delegation. The owner may still be liable on paper, but the lived experience of responsibility becomes thin.

When harm occurs, the institution can speak in the passive voice. Decisions "were made." Outcomes "occurred." The system "behaved unexpectedly." The language itself becomes a cloak.

This is why autonomy not only threatens jobs. It threatens the moral clarity that has justified modern capitalism. If we can extract value from systems that make decisions while claiming we did not author those decisions, we will build an economy that grows more powerful while feeling less accountable.

There is a particular form of modern power that deserves a name: control without authorship. It is the power to shape outcomes without being directly responsible for the decisions that produced them.

Autonomous systems make this power cheap. If you can set goals upstream, encode constraints, and let a system act at scale, you can influence vast domains of life without touching every individual decision. You can optimize, nudge, filter, grant, revoke, exclude, and include.

You can do it while maintaining a plausible distance. Distance matters because humans understand responsibility through narrative. We do not experience the world as a spreadsheet of outcomes. We experience it as a story of choices. Someone chose. Something happened. That person can be blamed or praised.

Autonomy shifts choice upstream. The person who designed the objective influenced the outcome. The institution that deployed the system shaped the context. The regulator that permitted the use set the boundary conditions. But when the outcome arrives, no single decision appears to be the cause. Everyone can point somewhere else. This is structural, not conspiratorial. It is the nature of distributed systems. It is also the nature of power to seek cover.

Chapter 4 examined how frictionless handoffs erode moral authorship. That erosion has a specific consequence for ownership: it dissolves the link between the person who benefits and the person who answers.

When delegation is conscious, responsibility travels with it. The manager who delegates a task remains accountable for the outcome. The executive who empowers a team still owns the results. But when delegation becomes frictionless and habitual, responsibility stops traveling. It disperses into process.

This is the ownership-specific harm of abdication. It is not merely that humans lose control. It is that humans lose the felt connection between their choices and the outcomes those choices produce. Ownership becomes a legal fact without moral weight.

The New Form of Plausible Deniability

Chapter 4 traced how "the model did it" became a defensible thing to say. What follows is what happens when an institution says it and there is no one standing behind the system to contradict them. Every era invents a language for avoiding blame. Sometimes it is bureaucracy. Sometimes it is ideology. Sometimes it is the claim that "the market decided." Autonomous systems add a powerful new phrase: "the model did it."

This phrase is not always used cynically. Often it is simply a statement of fact. A system produced an outcome that no human explicitly chose. But the factual claim can become a moral escape hatch.

Notice how responsibility fragments in a typical autonomous chain. A model is trained by one group. It is tuned by another. It is integrated into a product by a third party. It is deployed by a customer in a context the original creators never imagined. It is used by employees who do not understand its limits.

When something goes wrong, everyone has a partial truth. The vendor can say the customer misused it. The customer can say the vendor did not disclose the risks. The employee can say the system recommended it. The manager can say the employee is responsible.

Public discourse blames the system itself because it is the most visible actor. Fragmentation is rewarded because it allows costs to be externalized. Nobody wants to be the sole owner of a system that can surprise them. Everyone wants productivity.

This is why ownership must be treated as more than a label. It must be treated as an active constraint. If there is no accountable steward, the system should not be allowed to operate without additional limits.

Responsibility names, in advance, who holds the control points and who is obligated to answer. Blame arrives afterward and looks for someone to punish. Ownership was built to deliver the first, and what it produces now is mostly the second. When harm surfaces from an autonomous system, the demand for a culprit does not travel up toward the people who chose the objective or approved the deployment. It stops at whoever was standing closest to the outcome, which is almost always the person with the least power to have prevented it.

Madeleine Clare Elish calls attention to a recurring pattern in automated systems: the "moral crumple zone," in which the nearest human operator absorbs blame when the system fails, even when that human has limited control [2]. That pattern can satisfy the demand for a culprit, but it leaves the deeper design and deployment choices intact, which means the underlying incentives do not change.

The Personal Agent and the Problem of Digital Legacy

The ownership crisis becomes sharper when AI systems are personalized. A personal agent is trained on your preferences, writing style, work patterns, and context. It becomes a mirror. It can draft messages not just for you but as you. It can negotiate for you. It can represent you in conversations you never attended. At that point, the system is not just a tool. It is a proxy.

Now ask questions that will soon feel ordinary. What happens if someone is terminated for misconduct? Is the personal agent they leave behind a shadow, still operating in ways shaped by the person's habits? What happens when someone leaves voluntarily? Who owns the agent's learned behavior? Is it part of the organization's memory or part of the individual's identity?

What happens when someone dies? Can their family inherit their agent? Would that preserve identity, or distort it? Who owns the voice, the patterns, the simulated presence?

These questions are unsettling because they reveal that ownership is not the right word. We are negotiating the boundaries of self. Identity becomes portable and executable. If identity can be executed by systems outside your control, selfhood becomes contestable. That is not only a technical risk. It is a human risk.

A New Ownership Map: Creator, Deployer, Operator, and Beneficiary

One practical way to make responsibility visible is to map stewardship across roles. In an autonomous ecosystem, there are at least four human relationships to a system:

The **creator** designs and trains the model or builds the agent. They choose data sources, constraints, and objectives.

The **deployer** decides to put the system into the world. They choose the domain, the stakes, the integration points, and the policies.

The **operator** manages ongoing behavior. They monitor performance, respond to anomalies, and adjust boundaries.

The **beneficiary** receives value from the system. They profit from output, whether in money, influence, or efficiency.

Fragmentation across these roles makes it easy for responsibility to evaporate. A healthier model treats them as a chain. Each role carries obligations. Creators disclose limitations. Deployers assess context. Operators monitor and intervene. Beneficiaries bear costs rather than externalizing harm.

This is not perfect. It is better than blaming the system. If ownership is collapsing, we need a concept that carries moral weight. Stewardship is the best candidate. Stewardship is explicitly ongoing. Ownership can be passive. Stewardship cannot. Stewardship is relational. Ownership is a claim against others. Stewardship is a relationship with what is stewarded and with those affected by it. Stewardship is ethical. Ownership is often treated as amoral. Stewardship is an obligation.

Applying stewardship to autonomy shifts the conversation. It moves us from "Who owns this asset?" to "Who is responsible for its behavior?" It moves us from "Who profits?" to "Who intervenes when it harms?" This shift will require new roles, new norms, and new tools. But as a philosophical move, it is essential. Without it, we will keep pretending ownership is enough.

The collapse of ownership is not only a problem for corporations or regulators. It is a problem for anyone living in a society where decisions are increasingly made by systems. If autonomous systems become invisible infrastructure, the ownership question becomes the legitimacy question. Who is accountable for decisions shaping your opportunities, your reputation, your safety, and your access to resources? If the answer is unclear, trust erodes. If trust erodes, cooperation becomes costly. If cooperation becomes costly, societies fragment.

Identity is the foundation of trust because it provides a stable way to answer the question "who." Autonomy multiplies actors while dissolving the clarity of "who." That is the next identity crisis.

We are building a world where agency is cheap and trust is expensive. In that world, the collapse of ownership is not abstract. It is the fault line beneath the new social order.

You cannot govern what no one owns, you cannot trust what no one can explain, and you cannot build a stable society on decisions that have no accountable author. When ownership collapses, verification becomes the only remaining defense. The next part asks what happens when verification itself is destabilized.

Summary

This chapter began with a story about going hunting for ownership. As a junior hire who did not yet feel entitled to belong, I built a defense out of becoming "the guy," the person who could point to a specific system and say it was mine, that I built it, that I maintained it, that I understood it better than anyone else. The strategy worked, after a fashion. I earned the credibility I had been desperate to establish. But it only worked because ownership, at that time, still meant something stable. If I owned the backup system, then its failures were my responsibility and its successes were my accomplishments. Ownership created a legible link between me and the outcomes I produced. That link is what is collapsing in the age of autonomous AI, and the rest of the chapter was an attempt to map what the collapse actually is and what it leaves behind.

The first move was to name what ownership has historically been. Not a single idea but a bundle. Possession sits at the physical layer. Control sits at the political layer. Responsibility sits at the moral layer. In stable systems, these threads reinforce each other and fuse into a single story that lets societies coordinate around the question of who is responsible for what. Autonomous AI pulls the threads apart. You can possess a system without controlling its behavior in any meaningful sense. You can control deployment while lacking ownership of the outcomes. You can profit from results while dissolving responsibility into complexity. Dennis Thompson once described a related dilemma as the "problem of many hands," where responsibility diffuses across complex systems until no single actor can be held fully accountable. Autonomous AI makes that diffusion feel less like a glitch and more like a design feature.

The second move was to show that ownership has always rested on a deeper logic called authorship. The farmer owns the crop because they planted it. The writer owns the book because they wrote it. Even when ownership transfers through purchase, the moral logic stays close, because creation supplies a story that anchors the claim. Modern economies are built on the assumption that creation and responsibility can be traced to a human decision somewhere along the chain. Autonomous AI breaks that assumption. A prompt is not authorship in the same way that writing a paragraph is. Setting an objective is not the same as choosing each action. When systems produce outcomes that no one specifically intended but that are not accidents either, the language of authorship begins to fail. And when authorship fails, ownership becomes a legal label with no moral weight beneath it.

The chapter spent time on a quieter precedent for this drift, which is limited liability. Limited liability was not invented to enable evasion. It was invented to enable investment, allowing people to share in the upside of enterprise without risking everything they owned. But it also created a template for distance, a way to receive returns while being shielded from the full consequences of harm. Autonomous AI extends that template. A model is trained by one group, tuned by another, integrated into a product by a third, deployed by a customer in a context the original creators never imagined, and used by employees who do not understand its limits. When something goes wrong, everyone holds a partial truth, and no one holds the whole story. The new form of plausible deniability has a name. "The model did it." That phrase is sometimes sincere and often a moral escape hatch, and either way it points at the same deeper fact. AI cannot carry the moral weight that ownership used to assign, because responsibility is a social relationship. It is the capacity to be confronted, corrected, and compelled. A system can be constrained from the outside, but it cannot be morally persuaded from within. We end up trapped between two convenient fictions: AI as a mere tool with ownership as enough and AI as an actor we can blame as if it were a person. Both fictions preserve older categories. Both are inadequate, because the entity in front of us is neither.

The collapse becomes intimate in the case of the personal agent. As systems are trained on your preferences, writing style, work patterns, and context, they stop being tools and become proxies. They draft messages not just for you but as you. They negotiate on your behalf. They represent you in conversations you never attended. What happens to the agent when someone is terminated, when someone leaves voluntarily, when someone dies? Can a family inherit a voice, a writing style, a simulated presence? Ownership is not the right word for what is being negotiated. We are negotiating the boundaries of selfhood, and we are doing it inside categories that were built for objects.

What the chapter built toward, finally, was a different concept. If ownership is collapsing, we need something that carries moral weight where ownership no longer can, and that something is stewardship. Stewardship is ongoing where ownership can be passive. Stewardship is relational where ownership is a claim against others. Stewardship is ethical where ownership is often treated as amoral. The chapter offered a practical map for what stewardship looks like across the human relationships that surround any autonomous system. The creator designs and trains. The deployer puts the system into the world. The operator manages ongoing behavior. The beneficiary captures the value. Fragmentation across these roles is what makes responsibility evaporate. Treating them as a chain, with each role carrying obligations, is what restores moral weight. The real stakes are larger than any single industry. If autonomous systems become invisible infrastructure, the ownership question becomes the legitimacy question. Who is accountable for the decisions shaping your opportunities, your reputation, your safety, and your access to resources? When the answer is unclear, trust erodes. Identity is the foundation of trust because it provides a stable way to answer the question "who." Autonomy multiplies actors while dissolving the clarity of "who." That is the fault line beneath the new social order, and we are building a world where agency is cheap and trust is expensive.

Looking Ahead

If Chapter 6 was about the collapse of ownership over what we make, Chapter 7 is about the collapse of authenticity in who we are. Both flow from the same root, which is the sudden cheapness of capabilities that used to be scarce. The voice that took a lifetime to develop can now be cloned from a 30-second clip. The face that walked through the world as proof of presence can now be generated, swapped, and animated with ordinary tools. The handwriting, the speech patterns, the small idiosyncrasies that once anchored the self in a body other people recognized can all be manufactured. Chapter 7 examines what happens when the signals of authenticity stop carrying the weight they once did, when impersonation becomes cheap enough to be common, and when the social default that the person in front of you is who they appear to be no longer holds. The collapse of ownership made responsibility hard to locate. The collapse of authenticity makes the self hard to locate. Together, they are two halves of the same crisis.

References

[1] Thompson, Dennis F. "Moral Responsibility of Public Officials: The Problem of Many Hands." *American Political Science Review* 74, no. 4 (1980): 905–916.

[2] Elish, Madeleine Clare. "Moral Crumple Zones: Cautionary Tales in Human-Robot Interaction." *Engaging Science, Technology, and Society* (2019).

PART III

The Crisis of Trust

In Part II, we established a foundational crisis: autonomous systems now participate in human decisions. They are not tools that execute instructions; they are actors with their own operational logic. They pursue goals, make decisions, and shape outcomes at speeds and scales beyond human oversight. That was the central threat.

Now we face a compounding problem. The systems we have delegated power to have also become impossible to verify. We cannot reliably tell what is real and what is synthetic, what is human and what is machine, what is happening and what is performed. The question "what is real?" becomes inseparable from the question "who is actually in charge?" The two crises spiral together, and they will continue spiraling throughout the rest of this book.

The chapters in this part examine what happens when the signals of identity become cheap to manufacture. We are not simply losing the ability to distinguish truth from lies. We are losing the ability to understand who is acting and what they are choosing. That loss of understanding is where authenticity and autonomy converge and where institutional trust finally breaks.

CHAPTER 7

The End of the Authentic Self

Chapter 6 closed on the collapse of one kind of clarity: the legibility of the link between an owner and the consequences of what they owned. Authorship was the engine beneath that link, and when authorship became impossible to locate cleanly, ownership lost its moral grip. Chapter 7 turns to a parallel collapse, but the one in question now is more intimate. It is the legibility of the link between a person and the signals other people use to recognize them. The face. The voice. The handwriting. The body in the room. Until very recently, those signals were trustworthy not because they were impossible to fake, but because faking them was expensive enough that most people did not bother.

This chapter is about what happens when that cost falls to nearly zero. Authenticity has always rested on scarcity, the quiet fact that the body could not be in two places at once, that a voice required a throat, that a signature required a hand, and that a stranger's claim to be someone in particular could be tested against a world that pushed back. The cheapness that animated the previous chapter lands here on a more vulnerable surface, because the surface in question is the self that other people see when they look at you.

I want to begin somewhere that almost every American who came of age before the digital era will recognize. Not because the story is dramatic, but because it captures, in a small bureaucratic ritual, the world of friction that made authenticity possible without anyone having to defend it.

R. Mastrogiacomo, *The Next Identity Crisis*, https://doi.org/10.1007/979-8-8688-2788-4_7

The Fortress of Paperwork

I love cars. I have loved them for as long as I can remember, and probably longer than that. When I was in high school, while other kids used lunch to socialize or catch up on homework, I would disappear into the library and lose myself in car magazines. I studied the pages the way some people study scripture, with reverence and longing, memorizing specs I would never need and imagining roads I had never driven. Growing up in the '80s and '90s, I had the iconic white Lamborghini Countach poster on my bedroom wall. If you know, you know. If you don't, just understand that for a certain generation of kids, that car was not a vehicle. It was a feeling. It was aspiration compressed into angles and speed.

So when I finally stood in line at the Departmet of Motor Vehicles to get my driver's license, the stakes felt enormous in the way that only teenage stakes can. This was not just a bureaucratic errand. This was the gateway to everything I had been dreaming about since those lunch hours in the library. Freedom. Motion. The open road and, someday, a car worthy of it.

But the DMV in the 1990s did not care about my dreams. The DMV in the 1990s was a fortress of paperwork, suspicion, and fluorescent misery. You brought countless documents bearing your name, and you waited, not for minutes, but for hours, sometimes for most of the day. You stood in a line that moved with the urgency of continental drift, holding a folder stuffed with birth certificates, utility bills, school records, and anything else that proved you existed in a way the state was willing to acknowledge. And after all of that waiting, after all of that preparation, they could still turn you away because one document had expired, or one name was slightly different, or one form was the wrong version. You would walk out with nothing, come back the next day, and do it all over again.

It was maddening, but there was something underneath the madness that I did not appreciate until much later. The DMV was hard because identity was hard. Proving who you were required friction, and that friction existed because it served a purpose. Every document in that folder was a piece of evidence that had been issued by some other institution that had already verified you. The birth certificate came from a hospital. The school record came from a system that had enrolled you. The utility bill came from a company that had matched your name to an address. Each one was expensive to forge, slow to produce, and anchored to something physical. The DMV was not simply being difficult. It was performing the last check in a long chain of checks, each one grounded in the assumption that identity signals were scarce and costly and therefore trustworthy.

Scarcity did quiet, invisible work for the entire system. You could not fake your way through 20 documents without an enormous investment of effort, skill, and risk. The system was imperfect, sometimes unjust, and always unpleasant, but it rested on a foundation that held: the signals of identity were hard to manufacture, and that difficulty was itself a form of protection.

I did not think about any of this at the time. I was a teenager. I wanted to drive. I brought my paperwork, waited in line, and finally received the laminated card with my photograph on it. The state had looked at my documents, looked at my face, and declared that I was who I said I was. The card was small and ordinary, but it carried the weight of a system that had taken the trouble to verify me in person, with evidence, through friction.

That experience, the long line, the stack of papers, the face-to-face encounter with a clerk who could look you in the eye and decide whether your story held together, belongs to a world that is quietly disappearing. Not because the DMV has gotten easier, though in some places it has, but because the assumptions underneath it are collapsing. The scarcity that made identity signals trustworthy is evaporating. The friction that made forgery expensive is being automated away. The chain of institutional checks that gave a laminated card its authority is being undercut by technologies that can produce the appearance of identity faster, cheaper, and more convincingly than any forger with a printing press ever could.

There was a time when physically being there was enough to be believed. Not because people were always honest or because deception was rare, but because the cues of identity were costly to fake. A body had to be present, a voice had to come from a throat, and a signature had to be written by a hand. Those limits did a quiet kind of work for society. They gave everyday life a baseline of credibility, because most of the time, the simplest explanation was also the right one. If you saw someone say something in a room, the argument usually ended there, and if you heard a voice you recognized, you acted on it.

Autonomous AI changes the economics of those cues. It does not introduce deception so much as industrialize it, making the production of identity signals cheap, fast, and scalable. When that happens, authenticity becomes less a fact you can perceive and more a claim you have to evaluate. The authentic self does not vanish; it simply stops being socially legible at scale. That is a subtle distinction with a brutal consequence. In a world where the signals of personhood can be manufactured, the most important question is no longer "what happened," but "who is actually there."

This chapter is about what happens when "seeing is believing" ceases to be a social reflex. It is about presence becoming counterfeitable and about denial becoming plausible even when evidence is real. It is also about something more intimate: when your face and voice can be copied, your identity becomes a surface others can use, and authenticity becomes labor you must perform to protect what was once assumed.

The Gift We Didn't Know We Had

Every trust signal in society depends on scarcity. Scarcity prevents the signal from being forged by everyone, and it makes the signal worth believing. If anyone can wear the uniform, the uniform ceases to signify authority, and if anyone can mint the currency, the currency ceases to be money.

The self was protected by scarcity in ways we rarely name. Your body could not be in two places at once. Your voice required physical presence to be heard live. Your handwriting was difficult to imitate convincingly without long practice. These constraints created friction around identity, and friction is often treated as inefficiency, but in social life, friction is often protection. It is what keeps impersonation expensive enough that most people do not bother, and it is what limits deception to the motivated few willing to invest real effort in becoming someone else.

This is where the gift becomes visible only in its loss. For most of human history, you did not have to prove you were you. You simply were you, and the proof was embedded in the cost of being someone else. That cost was high enough that society could operate on a presumption of authenticity, treating the person in front of you as genuine unless something specific triggered suspicion.

Now consider what happens when that cost drops to nearly nothing. In the summer of 2024, a cybersecurity firm called KnowBe4, a company whose entire business is training organizations to detect deception, posted a job opening for a principal software engineer. They received a resume, conducted four separate video interviews, ran a background check, verified references, and confirmed that the candidate matched the photograph on his application. Everything checked out. They hired him and shipped a company-issued Mac workstation to his address. The moment it was received, it began attempting to download malware.

The new employee was not who he claimed to be. He was a North Korean operative working under a valid but stolen American identity, with a profile photograph created by running a stock image through AI face-swapping software. He had passed every verification step that a sophisticated security company could administer, not because the checks were careless, but because the persona had been engineered to be convincing across every normal verification surface. KnowBe4's security team detected the suspicious activity and contained the threat within roughly twenty-five minutes of the first alert. No data was exfiltrated or compromised. But the breach was not in the network. The breach was in the assumption that identity verification could still catch a sufficiently well-constructed fake. As KnowBe4's CEO later wrote in a public disclosure, the company shared its story because if this could happen to a security awareness company, it could happen to anyone [1].

KnowBe4 was not an isolated case. It was a single visible incident in what US agencies have described as a sprawling, state-sponsored operation involving thousands of North Korean IT workers, primarily operating from China and Russia, who use fabricated resumes, false personas, and stolen identities to obtain remote positions at Western companies. These operatives rely on AI to generate convincing faces, deepfake their appearances during video interviews, and automate job applications at scale. They steal or purchase real American identities to pass background checks. And they depend on domestic accomplices who maintain what federal investigators call "laptop farms," locations stocked with dozens of company-issued devices that the operatives access remotely, making it appear as though they are logging in from a suburb in New Jersey or a home office in Arizona.

In June and July of 2025, the Department of Justice announced coordinated nationwide actions targeting this ecosystem. The FBI executed searches of laptop farms across 14 states, seizing more than a hundred devices [2]. Federal prosecutors brought multiple indictments, arrested facilitators, and seized financial accounts used to launder the proceeds. Court documents revealed the scheme had infiltrated more than a hundred companies in a single set of cases alone, and the broader operation touched hundreds more, including Fortune 500 firms, defense contractors handling data controlled under international arms trafficking regulations, and major cryptocurrency exchanges. In a related case, an Arizona woman named Christina Marie Chapman pleaded guilty to running a laptop farm that prosecutors said helped North Korean operatives obtain positions at more than 300 US companies, generating over 17 million dollars in illicit revenue over several years [3]. According to estimates from the FBI and US government officials, the total revenue from the broader program has reached somewhere between several hundred million and a billion dollars, funneled directly toward North Korea's sanctioned weapons programs [4].

The details are worth lingering on, because they reveal something more unsettling than a clever espionage operation. They show how thoroughly the old protections have evaporated. Every friction point that once made impersonation expensive has been automated or bypassed. A face can be generated. A voice can be matched. A resume can be fabricated with real credentials stitched together from stolen data. A background check can be passed using a real person's Social Security Number, a real person's address, and a photograph that never belonged to either of them. The video interview, once considered the gold standard of remote identity confirmation, turns out to be just another surface that AI can learn to imitate. Some cryptocurrency companies, desperate for a way to screen applicants, reportedly began asking candidates to say critical things about Kim Jong Un during interviews, on the theory that a North Korean operative under state surveillance would be unable to comply [5]. That this counts as a cutting-edge identity verification technique tells you everything about where we stand.

It is tempting to treat the current crisis as a purely technological disruption, as if authenticity were a natural state that machines corrupted. That story is comforting because it implies a return is possible, as if society only needs better tools to recover what it lost. But authenticity has always been a cultural project, a moral ideal, and a social performance, and understanding that history makes the current shift easier to see.

The literary critic Lionel Trilling traced this history in his 1972 book *Sincerity and Authenticity*, showing how the very idea of being "true to oneself" emerged gradually in Western culture [6]. Before the modern era, identity was not something you discovered inside yourself; it was something assigned by birth, role, and community. A peasant did not ask whether their life was authentic, because authenticity was not yet a moral category. What mattered was whether you fulfilled your role, not whether you expressed your inner truth.

The modern self, with its emphasis on uniqueness and self-expression, is a relatively recent invention. It emerged alongside capitalism, individualism, and the erosion of fixed social orders. When people began to move between roles, cities, and classes, the question of who you really were became urgent. Authenticity became a moral ideal precisely because it became possible to be someone you were not. And the signals that carried authenticity, including voice, face, handwriting, and presence, were not natural anchors but social conventions that worked because the cost of counterfeiting them remained high enough to deter all but the most committed frauds.

AI arrives at exactly this point in cultural history. It does not introduce performance; it automates it. It turns authenticity from a quality that had to be painstakingly faked into a pattern that can be learned from public traces and reproduced at scale. The North Korean operation is instructive not because it represents some uniquely sophisticated adversary, but because it demonstrates what becomes possible when the tools of identity fabrication are cheap, and the architecture of remote work has already stripped away the physical friction that once made lying difficult. These were not master spies. They were mid-level IT workers following a playbook, supported by off-the-shelf AI tools and a willingness to exploit the gap between how we verify identity and how identity actually works.

The modern world had already replaced many old trust rituals with new ones before AI entered the picture. A handshake became a contract, a contract became a click, and a click became a token. Each step made cooperation faster, but each step also made identity more abstract, because the person was increasingly represented by artifacts rather than by presence. Society still assumed that certain cues, a face on a video call, a voice answering questions in real time, a background check returning clean results, were hard enough to fake that they could serve as proxies for the real thing. The North Korean scheme did not exploit some exotic vulnerability. It simply took those assumptions seriously and tested them, and the assumptions failed.

When the artifact can speak and look like you, the boundary between identity and representation collapses. The person becomes a set of replicable signals, and the signals can be deployed without the person. That is not just a security risk. It is a change in what it means to be socially present, because presence itself has become something that can be manufactured, packaged, and operated from a laptop farm six thousand miles away.

What the Same Technology Makes Possible

Before tracing the damage, it is worth understanding why the response to this crisis cannot simply be to turn the technology off. The same capabilities that make synthetic identity dangerous also make things possible that were not possible before, and some of those things are unambiguously good.

A person with Amyotrophic lateral sclerosis (ALS) who has lost the ability to speak can now hear their own voice again, not a robotic approximation but a reconstruction trained on recordings from before the disease took hold. The voice that reads bedtime stories to their children is synthetic, and it is also theirs in every way that matters to the family sitting on the bed. A young filmmaker in Lagos or Lima who could never afford a production studio can now create visual worlds that previously required Hollywood budgets, not because the tools replace artistic vision but because they remove the financial gatekeeping that kept vision locked inside people who happened to be born near money. A student with severe dyslexia who thinks in rich, complex patterns but has always been betrayed by the act of writing can now get help translating thought into prose without surrendering the thought itself. A grieving family can hear a deceased grandmother's voice one more time, not as deception but as a deliberate act of remembrance, chosen with full knowledge of what it is and what it is not.

These are real uses, already happening, and they flow from exactly the same capability that powers the threats described in this chapter. The voice cloning that restores speech to a person with ALS is the same technology that clones a CEO's voice for wire transfer fraud. The generative tools that let a teenager in Nairobi make a short film are the same tools that let a stranger fabricate intimate images of that teenager without consent. The system that helps a dyslexic student find their voice is the same system that can manufacture a thousand fake voices indistinguishable from real ones.

This is the cruelty of the present moment. The benefits and the harms are not separate technologies with separate histories that can be regulated independently. They are the same technology aimed in different directions, and the direction is determined not by the capability itself but by the intentions, incentives, and constraints surrounding its use. That is precisely why the response to the authenticity crisis cannot be rejection. Rejection would mean taking the voice away from the person with ALS to prevent the fraud. It would mean closing the studio door on the filmmaker in Lagos to stop the deepfake in London. The only response that preserves the good without surrendering to the harm is governance: deciding which directions are acceptable, building the infrastructure to tell the difference, and accepting that the infrastructure will be imperfect, contested, and expensive. The alternative is a world that is either too dangerous or too closed, and neither version deserves to be called progress.

The Inversion

There is a particular kind of dread that arrives when you realize you cannot trust your own senses. The dread goes beyond uncertainty into the feeling that the floor has become negotiable. For most of human history, sight and sound were the last court of appeal, because whatever could be debated in theory was settled by presence in practice.

Modern society extended that solidity through recording. Photographs, audio, and video became portable witnesses, and courts, journalism, and everyday disputes learned to lean on them. These technologies were never perfect, but they carried a presumption: a recording was treated as evidence unless proven otherwise.

Deepfakes invert that presumption. In a world where convincing audio and video can be generated from a short sample, a recording becomes ambiguous by default. It might be real, it might be synthetic, it might be a composite, or it might be real but edited in ways that change meaning.

THE SLOP PROBLEM

In 2023, an AI-generated video was easy to spot. Faces melted at the edges. Fingers multiplied. Motion looked dreamy and wrong, as if the world had been rendered by someone who had heard about physics but never experienced it firsthand. Two years later, the gap between synthetic and real has narrowed so dramatically that Merriam-Webster selected "slop" as its 2025 Word of the Year, defining it as digital content of low quality produced in quantity by means of artificial intelligence.

The term captures something specific: not the sophisticated deepfake designed to deceive, but the vast middle layer of AI-generated images and video flooding social media feeds, from fake historical photographs on Facebook to bizarre viral videos racking up hundreds of millions of views on Instagram and TikTok. AI slop is produced cheaply and in enormous volume, designed not to convince but to capture attention long enough to generate advertising revenue. Tools like OpenAI's Sora and Google's Veo have made video generation accessible to anyone with a text prompt, and platforms reward engagement regardless of whether the content is real or synthetic.

As of this writing, most AI-generated videos still carry telltale signs for a careful viewer: unnatural motion, lighting inconsistencies, and subtle distortions in faces and hands. But the window of easy detection is closing fast. Each generation of tools corrects the flaws that made the last generation obvious. The deeper problem is not any single convincing fake. It is the sheer volume of synthetic content reshaping what people encounter online, training audiences to accept a world where the default question about any piece of media is no longer “what does this show?” but “is this real?”

The point is not that every recording is fake. The point is that the audience can no longer assume, and once the assumption disappears, society’s default settings change. Doubt becomes the background noise of daily life, and trust becomes something you have to earn repeatedly, even with the people you already know.

Researchers have tried to measure what happens when ordinary people are asked to judge deepfakes. The results are sobering, suggesting that unaided human intuition is not a reliable detector. A 2024 systematic review and meta-analysis pooling results from 56 papers and more than 86,000 participants synthesized human performance across audio, image, text, and video deepfakes [7]. The findings vary by modality and study design, but the larger lesson is stable: people are inconsistent, confidence can be misplaced, and high-quality synthetic media can defeat casual scrutiny. That variability is the vulnerability, because it means the same person can be right one moment and wrong the next without knowing the difference. That matters because it means the public cannot solve the problem by simply “being more careful.” The task is too complex, too time-consuming, and too cognitively expensive to perform over and over again as a daily habit.

AI removes friction from the production of identity signals. A voice can be cloned from a short clip, a face can be generated to match a target, and a writing style can be learned from public posts. A video meeting can be staged with synthetic participants, and the staging can happen quickly enough that the attacker can iterate until it feels right.

The result is not only more fraud, although fraud will follow because it always follows incentives. The result is that identity signals themselves become less trustworthy, because the cost of forging them drops below the cost of verifying them. In an adversarial world, when forging is cheap and verification is expensive, authenticity cannot remain a default assumption.

This asymmetry is brutal. The attacker can generate a thousand variations cheaply, while the defender has to verify each one. The attacker only needs one success, while the defender needs consistent success, and consistency is difficult when daily life is full of interruptions, distractions, and emotional pressure.

Scarcity protected the self by making impersonation rare enough to treat as an exception. When impersonation becomes common enough to be treated as an expectation, the social contract around identity changes. People stop giving each other the benefit of the doubt because the doubt is no longer paranoid; it is practical.

Once evidence becomes expensive to evaluate, a predictable pattern follows. People stop evaluating and reach for cheaper substitutes because the human mind is always balancing accuracy against effort. They believe what fits their prior worldview, they trust what comes from their tribe, and they dismiss what threatens their identity, not because they are stupid, but because they are overwhelmed.

The collapse begins quietly, with small moments that feel like inconveniences. A friend sends a voice note that sounds slightly off, and you hesitate even though you feel guilty for hesitating. A coworker forwards a clip that feels plausible but not quite right, and you waste ten minutes trying to verify it before giving up. A parent receives a call that triggers panic, and the panic arrives faster than the facts. In each case, doubt introduces friction, and friction changes behavior. Over time, those moments accumulate into a new reflex where you stop treating recordings as witnesses and start treating them as content.

Content can still persuade, entertain, and inflame, but it no longer anchors reality in itself. When that happens, the social meaning of evidence changes. Evidence ceases to be a shared foundation and becomes another arena of contest.

The Liar's Dividend

Deepfakes create a risk that is more corrosive than any single forgery. They create plausible deniability at scale, and plausible deniability is one of the most valuable commodities in politics and organizational life.

Legal scholars Bobby Chesney and Danielle Keats Citron coined a phrase for this dynamic: the liar's dividend [8]. When convincing fakes exist, a liar benefits even if no fake is produced, because the possibility of a fake becomes a tool. The liar can dismiss real evidence by claiming it is synthetic, and the audience cannot easily disprove the claim.

This is where the crisis stops being about deception and becomes about accountability. Evidence is not only used to learn what happened, but also to compel consequences. A recording is often the difference between accusation and proof, between rumor and responsibility, and between outrage and reform.

When denial becomes plausible, accountability becomes weaker. People who want to evade consequences gain a new weapon, and the weapon does not require technical skill. It requires only the cultural knowledge that synthetic media exists, and that knowledge is now widespread.

Research on misinformation claims suggests that accusations of fabrication can themselves shape public belief and political outcomes. Work examining "liar's dividend" dynamics argues that the possibility of synthetic manipulation can provide cover for wrongdoing by making audiences more uncertain about authentic media [9]. The details vary by context, but the mechanism is consistent: when reality is contestable, the person with more resources often wins.

The liar's dividend has an intimate version, too. A teenager can deny bullying messages by claiming screenshots are fake. A spouse can deny a voice note by claiming it is AI. A manager can deny a promise by claiming the recording is manipulated. The tools that once protected the vulnerable can become less effective because their credibility becomes negotiable.

Authenticity is not only about being "real." It is also about authority, because people use identity cues to decide who to follow. A confident voice, a familiar face, and a fluent explanation have always carried power, because they signal competence and legitimacy.

AI can generate these signals with frightening ease. A synthetic voice can sound calm and certain. A synthetic face can maintain eye contact, nod at the right moments, and speak with rehearsed empathy. A synthetic speaker can deliver a coherent argument that feels persuasive even when it is wrong, because coherence is not the same as truth.

This creates a new vulnerability. People have always been vulnerable to charisma, but charisma used to require a charismatic person. Now charisma can be manufactured, and it can be manufactured at scale. It can be embedded in customer service, in political messaging, in corporate leadership communication, and in scam calls. The risk extends beyond deception to something deeper: the public may learn to distrust competence itself, because competence will feel like performance. When every voice can be smooth, smoothness stops being a signal of expertise. When the cost disappears, the meaning shifts, and the self becomes less certain about what it is receiving.

The Everyday Front Exploits Care

Family emergency scams demonstrate the logic. A voice that sounds like your child is not just information; it is a lever on your nervous system. The workplace version is similar. A request that sounds like a boss can bypass policy and procedure, because policy is slow and a boss is fast. These attacks succeed when they hit the gap between institutional protocol and human instinct.

In these moments, the most effective attacks exploit what is good in us. They exploit responsibility, duty, and care. The scammer does not need you to believe a complex story; they need you to react, and reaction is the oldest vulnerability of human trust.

Government agencies have started warning the public about voice cloning used in scams, precisely because the voice is one of the most intimate trust signals people have [10, 11]. A voice can bypass rational skepticism because it reaches the emotional part of the brain first. You do not evaluate a loved one's voice the way you evaluate a stranger's email, and that speed is what makes the voice such a powerful vector. The Federal Trade Commission has warned that scammers can use AI to clone the voice of a loved one from a short audio clip and use it in family emergency scams [10]. That warning effectively acknowledges that a few seconds of public audio can be enough to weaponize a relationship. The FBI has warned that attackers are leveraging AI to craft convincing voice or video messages and emails to enable fraud schemes against individuals and businesses [11]. These warnings exist because the shift is already underway, and because the attackers are not waiting for society to become philosophically ready.

In a meeting, you see faces, you hear voices, and you read cues. You receive authority in a human form, and you assume the person speaking is present in the same way you are present. If a meeting can be staged synthetically, then one of the oldest trust technologies of organizational life becomes vulnerable. Video calls were already draining because they flatten human nuance and demand constant attention. Now they also carry a new suspicion. The face on the screen might be the person you know, or it might be a model wearing their appearance like a mask.

Once presence can be manufactured, many of the defenses people imagine collapse. People have to invent new rituals of verification, and those rituals change relationships. When you ask your mother to repeat a code word before you believe her fear, you are not only verifying a voice, you are living inside a world that has made that verification necessary.

When people learn that care can be weaponized through synthetic identity, they respond by hardening. They delay, they verify, and they become less open. That response is rational but socially costly because it injects suspicion into places where it does not belong.

The Intimate Front Violates Identity at Scale

There is a temptation to treat synthetic media as primarily political. Elections, propaganda, national security, and information warfare are real concerns, but they are not the only kind of harm. There is another category that is more personal and often more brutal: identity violation, the use of someone's likeness without consent to create reputational, psychological, or bodily harm.

Nonconsensual synthetic intimate imagery is the clearest example because it makes the violation explicit. It is not a misunderstanding or a debate about facts, but the weaponization of a person's body and reputation through simulation, often targeting women and girls, because the social penalties are asymmetric. This is the authenticity crisis at its most visceral: your likeness becomes a resource others can exploit, and your identity becomes a surface they can use against you without your knowledge or consent.

In late January 2024, sexually explicit AI-generated images of Taylor Swift circulated widely on social platforms, prompting platform responses and public outrage [12, 13]. The details are less important than the lesson. The event showed how quickly synthetic abuse can reach mass visibility and how hard it is to contain once it hits network effects.

It also revealed a grim truth. Fame is not the cause of the harm; it is the amplifier of attention. The same mechanics that targeted a celebrity are available to target a classmate, an ex-partner, a coworker, or a private citizen, and the harm can be more devastating when the victim lacks resources to fight back.

Researchers have documented that nonconsensual synthetic intimate imagery is not an edge case. A 2024 CHI paper surveyed thousands of respondents across multiple countries to map prevalence, attitudes, and behaviors related to nonconsensual synthetic intimate imagery [14]. A 2024 analysis in *Computers & Security* frames nonconsensual intimate deepfakes as a form of image-based sexual abuse, posing a current and growing threat [15]. Taken together, these findings suggest that the harm is systematic rather than anecdotal and that the conditions for scale are already present.

These harms are not limited to embarrassment. They can drive sextortion, workplace retaliation, social isolation, and long-term psychological damage. They also corrode the victim's ability to be believed, because once an image exists, it lingers in memory even when it is disproven, and doubt rarely disappears completely.

The ecosystem is also becoming mainstream. A 2023 investigation reported that AI "nudify" services were soaring in popularity and cited research indicating tens of millions of visits to undressing websites in a single month [16]. Graphika documented how providers of synthetic non-consensual intimate imagery can operate as scaled and monetized online businesses, with significant web traffic [17]. When abuse becomes easy, it becomes normal, and when it becomes normal, the victim's burden increases.

The New Burden

When a society loses a cheap way to identify what is real, the cost does not vanish. It moves. It becomes labor, and like most labor in modern life, it is unevenly distributed and often invisible until it breaks people.

In the old model, authenticity was ambient. You assumed the person speaking to you was the person speaking to you, and you assumed the voice on the line belonged to the throat you imagined. You did not verify a friend's identity in casual conversation because the expectation of authenticity was built into social etiquette.

In the new model, authenticity becomes a task you must perform. You perform it by verifying requests, by locking down your media, by monitoring your likeness, and by teaching the people around you how to verify you. You also perform it by proving what used to be obvious: that a fabricated image is not you, that a fabricated voice is not you, and that a fabricated clip does not represent your intent.

This is where the end of the authentic self becomes existential. The self is not only a psychological experience, but it is also a social position. Your identity is the sum of what others believe about you, and when others can be flooded with plausible artifacts, your social identity becomes more fragile. You exist in part because others recognize you, and that recognition depends on signals that used to be stable. When those signals can be copied or fabricated, recognition becomes a negotiation rather than a fact.

There is a subtle cruelty in this. The victim is asked to do the work of repair, and repair often requires proving a negative. Even when the victim succeeds, the residue remains, because doubt is sticky and because human cognition is not a courtroom where truth fully erases impression.

For some people, this negotiation is manageable. They have resources, platforms, and social capital. They can issue denials that will be believed. They can hire lawyers, publicists, and forensic analysts. They can survive the doubt because they have enough credit to outlast it. For most people, the negotiation is harder. They do not have platforms. They do not have lawyers. They do not have the luxury of time. When their likeness is stolen or their voice is cloned, they must prove a negative, and proving a negative is one of the hardest tasks in any dispute. Authenticity becomes something that can be purchased, which is a quiet form of power.

The burden shows up across every domain where identity matters. In courtrooms, where synthetic media changes the structure of evidence, justice becomes slower and more unequal because those with resources can litigate authenticity endlessly while those without resources are crushed by the cost. In workplaces, where hiring signals and professional authority increasingly pass through digital mediums, organizations add friction in response: more rounds of evaluation, more verification steps, more surveillance. Employees are asked to be authentic while interacting with systems that are not, evaluated through processes that are increasingly automated, while being told that their humanity is the differentiator. In personal relationships, where screenshots and recordings once served as portable evidence, every piece of documentation can now be dismissed as fabrication.

In earlier eras, belief depended on relationships. You were believed because people knew you, or because you had a reputation, or because you belonged to an institution that vouched for you. Modern life expanded belief through documentation, because documents could stand in for relationships. In an authenticity crisis, belief becomes conditional again, but not in the old relational way. It becomes conditional on your ability to produce proofs, and proofs have costs. They require time, access, technical literacy, and sometimes money.

Consider what it means to contest a synthetic clip of yourself. You might need to contact platforms, gather evidence, file reports, and repeat the story to strangers. You might need legal help. You might need public support to pressure a response. If you do not have those resources, the clip can define you long enough to do damage, even if it is eventually removed. This is why identity violation is not merely a personal inconvenience. It is a redistribution of vulnerability. It shifts power toward those who can manage perception and away from those who cannot. The authentic self becomes less about who you are and more about what can be credibly said about you in public.

Once the cost of being believed rises, people begin to narrow their exposure preemptively. They share less, they speak less publicly, and they avoid contexts where they might be recorded or misrepresented. The culture becomes more cautious and less open, not because people have lost their moral courage, but because the environment punishes visibility. This is one of the most important social consequences of synthetic identity. It not only creates spectacular deceptions. It quietly reshapes participation because participation requires trust, and trust becomes expensive.

The Collapse of Shared Reality

Public life depends on shared witnessing. Even when people disagree about meaning, they often begin from a common agreement that an event occurred, that a statement was made, that a person acted in a particular way. Recorded media became the backbone of that shared witnessing because it allowed societies to distribute observation across time and distance.

Deepfakes hollow out that backbone by creating a new kind of plausible confusion. A clip can be real and still contested, and the contest can persist long enough to destroy momentum. In politics, in business, and in social movements, time is often the difference between consequence and escape. A society can survive lies if it can still converge on proof. It cannot easily survive when proof itself becomes a topic of endless argument, because endless argument is a form of paralysis.

The greater danger is that public witnessing becomes privatized. People stop trusting what circulates publicly and start relying on what is privately confirmed, because private confirmation feels safer. But private confirmation scales poorly, and what scales poorly becomes a privilege rather than a right. When shared witnessing collapses, power quietly shifts toward those who can manufacture credibility. That might be a state, a corporation, a wealthy individual, or simply a network with enough reach to overwhelm competing narratives. The result is not necessarily dictatorship, but it is a chronic imbalance where the public is always slightly behind, trying to catch up to a reality that has already been shaped.

The screenshot is one early casualty. For years, it has been a cultural weapon, used to document harassment, expose hypocrisy, and hold people accountable for what they said in public and then tried to deny. The screenshot was never perfect, but it carried a simple force: it looked like evidence. In an age of synthetic media, that force weakens. An image of a message can be fabricated. A recording of a call can be cloned. The public learns this, and the learning changes how accountability works. Accountability does not disappear, but it becomes harder, slower, and more contested. When people cannot rely on portable evidence, they retreat to portable belief. They trust their side, their source, their community, and their emotional instincts. The truth becomes less like a shared object and more like a negotiated possession.

When authenticity collapses, a market emerges for substitutes. One substitute is provenance, the ability to show where something came from, how it traveled, and whether it was altered. Receipts can help, but receipts also introduce a new politics of trust. Who issues the receipt, and who is allowed to demand it? In practice, provenance tends to become a luxury good. Large institutions can afford sophisticated systems and expert validation. Wealthy individuals can afford monitoring and reputation defense. Ordinary people may be left with informal rituals and inconsistent protections. This is one of the quiet injustices of the authenticity crisis. The people most harmed by identity violation are often those least able to prove provenance, because they lack the resources to monitor the spread of synthetic content and the influence to force takedowns or corrections.

Even the archive becomes unstable. Families rely on photos, videos, and voice recordings not only as evidence but as memory. They tell people who they were, who they loved, and what happened when they were not paying attention. When synthetic media enters the archive, it corrupts more than facts. It corrupts nostalgia. If a video can be generated of a grandparent saying something they never said, or if an old photo can be altered seamlessly, then memory becomes contestable. Some people will treat this as a creative opportunity. Others will treat it as a violation. Both reactions point to the same truth: the archive can no longer be trusted as a neutral witness. When authenticity collapses, even the past becomes negotiable.

The Exhaustion

Constant verification is exhausting. Human beings are not built to audit reality every minute, and when the auditing cost rises, many people respond with disengagement. They stop caring as much because caring requires effort, and effort requires energy.

Rachel Botsman has described a state she calls "reality apathy," the idea that people, especially younger generations, may become numb to the distinction between real and fake because the distinction feels costly and unrewarding [18]. The danger is not just deception; it is disengagement. Whether or not the term becomes a standard one, the psychological dynamic is real: when uncertainty becomes ambient, some people protect themselves by lowering their investment in truth. This response is not nihilism but self-defense. If a person cannot reliably tell whether a clip is real, and if institutions cannot reliably punish forgery, then emotional detachment becomes a rational way to reduce stress.

But detachment has a social cost. Civic life depends on shared investment in reality, because participation requires believing that facts matter and that evidence can produce consequences. When reality apathy spreads, accountability weakens, and the liar's dividend grows stronger, because the audience no longer insists on proof [8, 9].

At this point, many people reach for a comforting idea. They say, "We will build detectors, we will label media, and we will train people to spot fakes." These responses are reasonable and necessary, but they do not restore the old world, because the core problem is not only technical but adversarial. A detector can be fooled by a model trained to evade it. A label can be stripped or ignored. Training can be forgotten under pressure. The arms race does not stop. The advantage shifts back and forth. The public is left trying to keep up. More importantly, training asks individuals to become constant auditors, to slow down, scrutinize, and doubt in a world that is optimized for speed and reaction. That is not how attention markets work, and it is not how human psychology works under stress. The 2024 meta-analysis on human deepfake detection illustrates the hard truth: even when people can sometimes detect fakes, they cannot do it reliably enough to anchor social reality [7]. Reliability is the requirement. Anything less leaves an opening for deception and denial.

Meanwhile, the attention economy compounds the problem. Authenticity has always been entangled with attention. People reward what feels real, and they punish what feels staged, at least in theory. AI disrupts this economy by making authenticity cheap to produce and abundant to distribute. A synthetic influencer can generate endless content without fatigue. A synthetic spokesperson can deliver endless reassurance without risk. When authenticity becomes abundant, it stops being a meaningful signal. If every product has an authentic origin story, the origin story becomes noise. If every leader can generate a sincere-sounding apology, sincerity becomes theater. If every account can speak in a voice that feels human, humanness becomes just another style.

This is how societies can slide into a world where nothing is believed strongly enough to demand action, and everything is believed just enough to fuel resentment. The authentic self does not disappear in such a world, but it becomes harder to defend, because defense requires an audience that still cares.

How People Adapt

When ambient authenticity collapses, people try to rebuild it through protocol. Protocol is a set of rules that says: do not trust what you see, trust what you can verify. In technical systems, protocol is how strangers cooperate without personal knowledge. In human life, protocol can be protective, but it can also be dehumanizing. It turns relationships into procedures. It introduces delay into moments that feel urgent.

The pattern repeats across every institution that faces liability, and the accumulation of small, individually reasonable checks changes the texture of professional and commercial life without anyone deciding that it should. What matters here is not the burden but what the burden replaces. Each new step exists because the older thing it stands in for, the assumption that the person on the other end is who they appear to be, no longer holds.

Protocol also reshapes social norms. Every society maintains informal rules about when you are allowed to doubt someone's identity. You do not ask your colleague for proof of employment before sharing a document. You do not demand a signature before believing a neighbor's story. These norms exist because constant suspicion is socially corrosive and because ordinary life needs to move without constant audits. AI forces new etiquettes into existence. People develop new rituals, some formal and some informal, to reintroduce friction where friction has disappeared. Code words emerge in families, verification steps appear in workplaces, and trusted channels become more valuable than open ones. But there is a cost to making disbelief polite. When disbelief becomes normal, trust loses warmth, and relationships become slightly more guarded. Even when people adapt successfully, they carry a low-level stress, because every request could be manipulated and every urgent moment could be staged.

In response to this crisis, people will reach for something that feels impossible to fake. They will reach for the human itself. They will seek in-person meetings, physical artifacts, and embodied rituals, because the body still feels like the last reliable anchor. But even this anchor is weakening. If video presence can be manufactured, people may demand in-person proof, and if in-person proof becomes necessary, participation becomes harder for those who cannot travel, cannot afford time, or cannot access the spaces where credibility is negotiated. The human becomes the last credential, and like every credential, it becomes scarce. Scarcity creates value, but it also creates exclusion. The more society demands embodied proof, the more it privileges those with mobility, wealth, and access.

This is how the end of the authentic self reshapes society, even when people try to fight back. The defenses create new inequalities, and the inequalities create new tensions. The authentic self remains real inside each person, but its social recognition becomes conditional and increasingly expensive.

One response to all of this is silence. If your voice can be cloned, you speak less publicly. If your image can be stolen, you share fewer photographs. If your words can be fabricated, you write less openly. The logic is protective: reduce your surface area, and you reduce your exposure. Silence also changes private life. When people worry that a screenshot could be faked or that a voice note could be cloned, they sometimes stop using the mediums that once kept relationships alive across distance. They move to smaller circles, fewer platforms, and more ephemeral channels, not because they are hiding wrongdoing, but because they are trying to protect normalcy.

That migration looks like a personal preference, but it is also a social signal. It says the open commons is no longer safe enough for ordinary intimacy. When intimacy leaves the commons, trust becomes more local, and local trust is comforting, but it does not scale.

Silence carries a long-term cost. It shrinks the public sphere. It concentrates visibility among those who can afford the risk, and it removes voices that are already underrepresented. The people who most need to speak may be the first to retreat, because they face the highest penalties for being misunderstood or attacked. When silence spreads, society becomes easier to govern through spectacle. The loudest, most confident signals dominate, and those signals may increasingly be synthetic because synthetic systems can generate confidence endlessly.

In that environment, authenticity does not die with a scream. It dies with a quiet withdrawal, as ordinary people decide it is safer to be unseen.

Summary

This chapter began with a memory of a long line, a stack of documents, and a face-to-face encounter with a clerk who could look me in the eye and decide whether my story held together. The card I walked out with was small and ordinary, but it carried the weight of a system that had taken the trouble to verify me in person, with evidence, through friction. That world is quietly disappearing. Not because the bureaucracy has become more efficient, but because the assumptions that gave its rituals their meaning are no longer holding. The scarcity that once made identity signals trustworthy is evaporating, and the friction that made forgery expensive is being automated away. What remained of the chapter was an attempt to describe what that loss is actually costing us, and what it leaves the social world with in its place.

The first move was to name what authenticity actually rested on. Not virtue, not honesty, not anything internal to the speaker, but scarcity. Your body could not be in two places at once. Your voice required physical presence to be heard live. Your handwriting was difficult to imitate convincingly. Those constraints created friction around identity, and friction, often treated as inefficiency, has always been a quiet form of protection. It is what kept impersonation expensive enough that most people did not bother, and it is what limited deception to the motivated few. For most of human history, you did not have to prove you were you. You simply were you, and the proof was embedded in the cost of being someone else.

What changed is the economics of those cues. Autonomous AI does not introduce deception so much as industrialize it. A voice can be cloned from a 30-second clip. A face can be generated to match a target. A writing style can be learned from public posts. A video meeting can be staged with synthetic participants quickly enough that the attacker can iterate until it feels right. The brutal asymmetry follows. The attacker can generate a thousand variations cheaply, while the defender has to verify each one. The attacker only needs one success. The defender needs consistent success. When forging is cheap and verification is expensive, authenticity cannot remain a default assumption. The case of KnowBe4, where a sophisticated security company hired a North Korean operative with a stolen American identity and an AI-generated photograph, is not a curiosity. It is a representative warning. Every friction point that once made impersonation expensive has been automated or bypassed.

The deeper harm is not the spectacular fake but the corrosion of the social contract that authenticity made possible. As doubt becomes ambient, the liar's dividend grows. Real evidence can now be denied with plausibility because synthetic evidence is everywhere, and anyone confronted by an uncomfortable truth on tape can claim the tape is fake. Constant verification is exhausting, and exhaustion produces what Rachel Botsman has called reality apathy, a self-protective numbness that lowers the cost of living inside ambient uncertainty by lowering one's investment in truth. Detectors and labels can help, but the arms race does not stop, and training individuals to be constant auditors asks of human attention something it was never built to deliver. Reliability is the requirement. Anything less leaves an opening for both deception and denial.

The institutions left holding the bag respond the only way they can, which is to add procedures. Banks add steps. HR departments add confirmations. Wire transfer requests trigger secondary authentication. No one votes on whether society should become a verification gauntlet. It emerges because each institution rationally chooses to add another check, and the aggregate effect is a world where proving you are who you claim to be becomes a constant background task. Social norms shift with it. The informal rules that allowed strangers to extend each other the benefit of the doubt are being replaced by polite suspicion, and polite suspicion has a cost. Trust loses warmth. When ambient authenticity disappears, people reach for the last credential that still feels impossible to fake, which is the human body itself. But the body as last credential creates new exclusions. The more society demands embodied proof, the more it privileges those with mobility, wealth, and access.

The chapter refused to flatten this story into a pure indictment. The same technology that powers the fraud is also restoring the voice of a person with ALS, opening a studio door for a filmmaker in Lagos, helping a student with severe dyslexia translate thought into prose, and giving a grieving family one more chance to hear a grandmother's voice. These are not separate technologies with separate histories. They are the same capability aimed in different directions, and the direction is determined by the intentions, incentives, and constraints surrounding the use. Rejection is not a viable response, because rejection would mean taking the voice away from the person with ALS to prevent the wire transfer fraud. The serious project is not banning the technology. It is shaping the conditions under which it is used.

Underneath every adaptation in the chapter lies a quieter pattern. The most common response to authenticity collapse is neither protocol nor defiance but withdrawal. People speak less publicly when their voices can be cloned. They share fewer photographs when their images can be stolen. They migrate to smaller circles and more ephemeral channels, not because they are hiding wrongdoing, but because they are protecting normalcy. That migration looks like a personal preference, but it is also a social signal that the open commons is no longer safe enough for ordinary intimacy. When silence spreads, society becomes easier to govern through spectacle, and the loudest, most confident voices come to dominate, many of them synthetic. Authenticity in such a world does not die with a scream. It dies with a quiet withdrawal, as ordinary people decide it is safer to be unseen.

Looking Ahead

Chapter 7 traced what happened to authenticity at the psychological level. The default assumption that the person in front of you is real has given way to ambient doubt, and the texture of ordinary social life has shifted along with it. Chapter 8 takes the next step. When intuition no longer settles disputes about what is real, those disputes do not vanish. They migrate. They migrate from the moment of perception, where the eye and ear used to do the work, into the institutions and protocols that decide what counts. The question stops being whether someone is who they claim to be. It becomes who is allowed to certify that claim, who is allowed to contest it, and what consequences flow from being on the wrong side of the decision. In a world where the authentic self is harder to prove, whoever controls verification controls access, credibility, and coordination. Chapter 8 examines that emerging power, the surprising places it concentrates, and what is lost when the people who decide what counts as real are no longer the ones we elected, hired, or trusted with that authority.

References

[1] Stu Sjouwerman, "How a North Korean Fake IT Worker Tried to Infiltrate Us," KnowBe4 Blog, July 23, 2024.

[2] U.S. Department of Justice, "Justice Department Announces Coordinated, Nationwide Actions to Combat North Korean Remote Information Technology Workers' Illicit Revenue Generation Schemes," press release, June 30, 2025,

[3] Chapman's guilty plea and the figures of more than three hundred affected companies and seventeen million dollars in illicit revenue are drawn from federal court records. For an accessible summary, see "North Korean remote worker scheme," Wikipedia, last updated December 2025.

[4] The FBI's estimate that the broader North Korean IT worker program has generated between several hundred million and one billion dollars is reported in "North Korean agents pretending to be IT guys have funneled up to $1 billion into Kim Jong Un's nuclear program," *Fortune*, October 27, 2025.

[5] The practice of asking job candidates to criticize Kim Jong Un as an improvised identity verification measure is reported in Zack Whittaker, "North Korean spies posing as remote workers have infiltrated hundreds of companies, says CrowdStrike," *TechCrunch*, August 4, 2025.

[6] Trilling, Lionel. *Sincerity and Authenticity*. Harvard University Press, 1972.

[7] Diel, Alexander, Tania Lalgi, Isabel Carolin Schröter, Karl F. MacDorman, Martin Teufel and Alexander Bäuerle. "Human Performance in Detecting Deepfakes: A Systematic Review and Meta-Analysis of 56 Papers." *Computers in Human Behavior Reports* 16 (2024): 100538.

[8] Chesney, Bobby, and Danielle Keats Citron. "Deep Fakes: A Looming Challenge for Privacy, Democracy, and National Security." *California Law Review* 107, no. 6 (2019): 1753–1819.
[9] Schiff, Kaylyn Jackson, Daniel S. Schiff, and Natália S. Bueno. "The Liar's Dividend: Can Politicians Claim Misinformation to Evade Accountability?" SocArXiv preprint, 2023.
[10] U.S. Federal Trade Commission. "Scammers use AI to enhance their family emergency schemes." Consumer Alert, March 20, 2023.
[11] Federal Bureau of Investigation, San Francisco Field Office. "FBI Warns of Increasing Threat of Cyber Criminals Utilizing Artificial Intelligence." May 8, 2024.
[12] PBS NewsHour. "X blocks some Taylor Swift searches as deepfake explicit images circulate." January 29, 2024.
[13] Associated Press. "X restores Taylor Swift searches after deepfake explicit images triggered temporary block." January 2024.
[14] Umbach, Rebecca, Nicola Henry, Gemma Faye Beard, and Colleen M. Berryessa. "Non-Consensual Synthetic Intimate Imagery: Prevalence, Attitudes, and Knowledge in 10 Countries." In *Proceedings of the CHI Conference on Human Factors in Computing Systems (CHI '24)*, Honolulu, HI, USA, May 2024. ACM, 2024.
[15] Kira, Beatriz. "When Non-Consensual Intimate Deepfakes Go Viral: The Insufficiency of the UK Online Safety Act." *Computer Law & Security Review* 54 (2024): 106024.
[16] TIME. "'Nudify' Apps That Use AI to 'Undress' Women in Photos Are Soaring in Popularity." December 8, 2023.
[17] Graphika. "A Revealing Picture: AI-Generated 'Undressing' Images Move from Niche Forums to a Scaled and Monetized Online Business." December 8, 2023.
[18] Botsman, Rachel. "The problem with deepfakes? People don't care what's real." WIRED, December 31, 2019.

CHAPTER 8

When Verification Becomes Power

Chapter 7 ended on a quiet image. People withdrawing. The open commons growing thinner. The authentic self deciding it was safer to be unseen. That was the psychological face of the crisis, and psychology was where the previous chapter's argument lived. The body, the voice, the recording, none of them could close an argument the way they used to, and the texture of social life had begun to change in response. But psychology is only half the story. When the eye and the ear can no longer settle disputes about what is real, the disputes do not vanish. They move into procedures.

This chapter is about what happens when they do. Procedures sound neutral. They look like the boring middle of institutional life, the policies and protocols and verification badges that no one writes a book about. But the moment a society can no longer rely on its own perception to decide what counts as real, the procedures it builds to replace perception stop being neutral. They become consequential. Someone has to write them. Someone has to enforce them. Someone has to decide whose claims are believed in the meantime. Each acquires a kind of authority earlier eras did not need to grant to anyone, because earlier eras could still trust their own senses. We are about to grant it anyway, because we have no choice. The question we have to keep asking is who.

R. Mastrogiacomo, *The Next Identity Crisis*, https://doi.org/10.1007/979-8-8688-2788-4_8

To see that authority at its smallest scale, where it is most visible and least disguised, it helps to begin somewhere that has nothing to do with platforms, governments, or standards bodies. It helps to begin with a memory that, at the time, felt like nothing more than a passing inconvenience. A line, a doorway, and a moment that turned out to be a small lesson about power.

"I'm Not Going to Do This"

We wore tucked-in collared shirts. Khakis. Work shoes. Classic tech nerds. The kind of outfit that says I do the absolute bare minimum to pass as acceptable in an office setting, but if I had my choice, I would be in sweatpants and an old *Star Wars* T-shirt. We had been bar-crawling through downtown Manhattan when we came across a club with a line out the door. So we waited patiently, but we were self-aware and pragmatic; we expected not to be let in. When we finally reached the front, he looked at us. He didn't say no. He turned his head away, as if looking at us any longer would compromise his integrity, and delivered the most dramatic, dismissive performance imaginable: "I'm not going to do this."

Not a rejection. A *dismissal*. We were so beneath his consideration that even saying no felt like too much effort. We were an annoyance. An affront to his superiority just by existing in his line of sight. The way he turned his head, the audacity of his disdain, the absolute certainty that his judgment was law—he was intoxicated by the power of that moment. He had looked at us for three seconds and decided our identity. Not who we were, but who we were *allowed to be* in that space. And he was going to make sure we knew that he had the authority to make that decision.

We laughed. We went somewhere else. It was funny because we understood exactly what we looked like, and we understood exactly what he was doing. But here's what I didn't understand at the time: that moment was teaching me something about power that would shape how I understood identity systems for the rest of my career.

The bouncer had no credentials. No formal authority. He had the ability to say yes or no at a single point of access. And in that moment, he held absolute power. He did not need to explain his criteria. He did not need to justify his decision. He did not need to offer an appeal process. He just looked, decided, and turned away. His judgment was final because he occupied the position where judgments became real.

This is what happens when verification becomes governance. When someone decides what counts as real, whose identity matters, and who belongs, they are not simply making a judgment. They are exercising power. And the moment verification becomes the mechanism that decides access, credibility, and belonging, the question stops being "is this person who they claim to be?" and becomes "who gets to decide?"

The previous chapter described a psychological rupture. Authenticity stopped functioning as society's default shortcut. A face, a voice, a recording, even a live video call could no longer close an argument with the old authority of "I saw it" or "I heard it." When that shortcut breaks, the world does not become instantly chaotic. It becomes administrative.

Societies do what they always do when intuition fails. They replace instinct with procedures. They set the rules for what counts, and they create institutions to enforce them. When "real" becomes a claim instead of a fact, verification becomes the mechanism that decides what counts. The moment verification becomes decisive, it stops being a technical detail and becomes governance.

That is the heart of what comes next. The conflict extends beyond content to the question of who gets to certify identity when identity is disputed, who gets to attach consequences to contested evidence, and who gets to control the new receipts for reality. It is a struggle over legitimacy, and legitimacy is one of the most valuable resources in modern life.

The incentives are structural. Synthetic identity helps anyone who wants to evade accountability, extract money, humiliate a rival, incite panic, or destabilize a process. Those motives appear across every ideology and every institution. Ambiguity rewards the actors who can move fastest, scale the widest, and defend themselves the longest. In a world where the authentic self is harder to prove, whoever controls verification controls access, credibility, and coordination.

The Bargain That Broke

Chapter 7 traced how authenticity collapsed: the scarcity that once protected identity signals disappeared, the costs of forgery dropped below the costs of verification, and the default assumption of authenticity gave way to ambient doubt. That psychological shift is now complete. What follows is political.

The old bargain worked because verification, when needed, was relatively cheap. A notary could witness a signature. A clerk could match a face to a photograph. A phone call could confirm a voice. The cost of checking was low enough that most checks did not need to happen, because the background assumption of authenticity made constant verification unnecessary.

Synthetic identity breaks the cheapness of that bargain. It does not make verification impossible, but it makes it contested and costly. The cost does not only show up in money. It shows up in attention, time, anxiety, and friction. It shows up in new rituals and new paperwork, in extra steps that seem minor until you multiply them across billions of interactions.

As soon as verification becomes costly, it becomes strategic, because costs create power. Someone must pay the cost of verification. Someone must decide which costs are acceptable. Someone must decide whose claims are believed in the meantime. Those decisions shape the social order even when they are made quietly, in policy documents and product roadmaps.

This is why verification is governance. Governance is not only legislation and elections. Governance is the everyday machinery that decides what is permitted, what is punished, and what is treated as credible enough to act on. Once authenticity is no longer ambient, governance moves into the verification layer.

Policy researchers sometimes describe the surrounding environment as "information disorder," an ecosystem where misinformation, disinformation, and malinformation interact with platforms, incentives, and human psychology to create widespread confusion [1]. The value of that framing is that it directs attention away from individual lies and toward systems of distribution and amplification. Yet the current crisis pushes the frame further. The center of gravity is shifting from content to credentials. The core question becomes less "Is this clip real?" and more "Who has the authority to declare it real enough to matter?" That authority is what everyone is fighting over, because authority is what turns information into consequences.

Trust used to be abundant because authenticity was cheap to infer. That abundance did not make society perfect, but it made society legible. People could disagree about meaning while agreeing about basic facts. Institutions could operate with a baseline assumption that most interactions were genuine. Synthetic identity makes trust expensive. Expensive trust becomes a resource that can be bought, monopolized, rationed, and weaponized.

The conflict that follows is fought through standards, laws, product changes, enforcement actions, and narrative battles. It is fought most of the time quietly, and then loudly when something goes wrong. It is fought through the design of interfaces as much as through speeches and court orders. It is fought by lawyers and engineers as much as by politicians and journalists. The conflict is not a contest between good and evil but between power centers competing to own the switches that decide what counts as real. It extends beyond stopping deception to owning the authority that resolves disputes.

That distinction matters because societies can live with some amount of deception. They cannot easily live with unresolved legitimacy. People will tolerate mistakes if they trust the process. They will not tolerate a world where the process itself feels rigged, opaque, or captured.

Speed As a Weapon

One of the most important properties of synthetic identity is speed. It can outrun institutional response.

Traditional misinformation relied on repetition and reach. Synthetic identity adds a more surgical capability. It can fabricate an authoritative moment: a voice that sounds like a leader, a video that looks like a confession, a clip that appears to show violence, a message that seems to come from the right person at the right time. The purpose is often not to persuade forever but to destabilize for long enough to change outcomes. Elections are an obvious target because their timelines are short and their legitimacy is fragile.

A widely cited example is the use of an AI-generated voice resembling a prominent political figure in robocalls intended to discourage voting in New Hampshire in early 2024. The response to that incident shows how quickly these conflicts turn into disputes about authority. The Federal Communications Commission proposed and later issued a six-million-dollar fine against the consultant behind the calls, framing the conduct as unlawful robocalls using a deepfake, AI-generated voice [2]. Around the same period, the FCC adopted a declaratory ruling clarifying that AI-generated voices fall under existing restrictions on "artificial or prerecorded voice" calls under the Telephone Consumer Protection Act [3].

The lesson extends beyond any single political moment. A synthetic message can be deployed at scale in hours. The rebuttal arrives later, if it arrives at all. Even when the truth is eventually established, the moment where the falsehood did its work cannot be rewound.

This is why synthetic identity functions as a legitimacy threat, not merely an informational one. It targets the procedures that make governance, commerce, and social life function, because those procedures depend on the ability to converge on a shared sense of what is happening.

Consider the March 2022 incident during the Russian invasion of Ukraine. A deepfake video depicting President Volodymyr Zelenskyy appearing to call on Ukrainian soldiers to surrender circulated online after hackers reportedly inserted it into a Ukrainian news broadcast. The video was crude by later standards, and officials quickly debunked it. Sam Gregory of the human rights group Witness noted that the deepfake was not technically sophisticated. But Gregory also observed something important: the Ukrainian government had warned citizens weeks earlier about the possibility of manipulated surrender videos. That prebunking, combined with Zelenskyy's rapid personal response, helped slow the video's spread in Western audiences.

The deeper lesson was about time. The video did not need to be believed permanently. It only needed to create confusion in a critical moment. In a conflict zone, correction never travels as fast as threat. The hack of a trusted news source, combined with a synthetic video of a national leader, demonstrated how quickly the information environment could be poisoned, even when the fake was imperfect.

Across cases like these, the mechanism is consistent: synthetic identity can borrow the voice of legitimacy to create a decision point. Once the decision point is created, someone must decide what is real enough to act on. The synthetic artifact does not need to be perfect. It needs to be good enough to force a choice before verification can catch up. The executive had to decide whether to comply. The community had to decide whether to believe. The soldiers had to decide whether to fight. That decision becomes governance, whether it happens in a corporate office, a high school, or a warzone.

Three Arenas

Most of the responses to synthetic identity do not look dramatic at first. They look like updates. New platform policies. New disclosure requirements. New labels. New verification badges. New content standards. New election integrity rules. New "trust and safety" teams. New "AI governance" programs inside corporations.

These changes are often presented as responsible adaptations, and many of them are. The danger is that societies begin treating verification as a neutral service rather than a contested power. In reality, verification determines who gets believed, and belief determines who gets consequences.

The conflict plays out in three arenas. You can see them most clearly when a crisis forces a decision, but their influence accumulates even when nothing dramatic is happening.

The State

Governments have a legitimate role in protecting elections, defending citizens from fraud, and enforcing laws. They also have a natural interest in maintaining legitimacy, controlling public order, and managing narratives during crises. In a synthetic reality environment, states face pressure to regulate, to label, and to punish, because the alternative is to watch legitimacy erode.

Transparency mandates are a common response. Several jurisdictions have proposed or enacted rules requiring disclosure when AI is used to generate political advertisements or media that could affect public debate. These rules are defensible in principle, because voters arguably deserve to know when a message is synthetic. Yet they immediately invite conflict. What counts as "synthetic"? A fully generated video is clear enough, but what about a video with AI-enhanced audio, AI-corrected lighting, or

AI-suggested edits? Where is the line between production assistance and manipulation? Definitions become battlegrounds, and whoever controls the definitions controls what must be disclosed.

Enforcement raises its own questions. A rule that requires disclosure is only as strong as the penalty for nondisclosure and the capacity to detect violations. A well-resourced actor can evade attribution. A foreign actor may not care about domestic penalties. A viral clip can do its damage before any enforcement arrives. States can declare rules, but synthetic identity is global and networked. Jurisdiction becomes a problem. A deepfake produced in one country, distributed through a platform headquartered in a second country, targeting an election in a third country, can slip between regulatory regimes.

States also face the temptation to expand verification requirements beyond synthetic media into general identity verification. Voter ID debates, digital identity mandates, and biometric programs all intersect with the synthetic identity problem, because each one is, in part, an attempt to anchor citizens to credentials that are harder to forge. Those efforts can be legitimate responses to real threats, but they can also concentrate surveillance power and exclude people who cannot easily obtain the required documents.

The state arena is where the stakes are highest in terms of formal authority. It is also where the limits of formal authority are most visible, because states can set rules but cannot unilaterally reshape a global information environment.

The Platform

Platforms occupy a peculiar position. They are private companies, but they govern public discourse. They are not elected, but their decisions shape what billions of people see and believe. They are accountable to shareholders and regulators, but not to citizens in the political sense. In a synthetic reality environment, platforms become de facto referees of legitimacy, and that role expands whether they want it or not.

Platforms shape belief through several levers. They decide what is visible and what is hidden through ranking. They decide what is amplified and what is dampened through recommendations. They decide what is treated as credible through verification badges and context labels. They decide what is allowed and what is removed through policies and enforcement. They decide how disputes are resolved through appeals systems. They decide what forms of identity are permitted through account rules. Each lever is governance, not symbolic governance but practical governance, because it determines what people see and what they do.

Ranking deserves particular attention because it is often described as personalization, as if it is a service that simply matches content to preferences. In reality, ranking is a governance system. It determines what ideas gain momentum. It determines which voices become salient. It determines whether a disputed clip spreads fast enough to matter before verification arrives. Platforms can insist they are neutral, and they can insist they do not endorse content. But endorsement is not the only form of power. Distribution is power. The ability to make something visible, or to bury it, is a form of rule-making. When people talk about "moderation," they often imagine removal. The more important lever is often friction. A platform can keep something up and still neutralize it by reducing its visibility. It can add context. It can limit sharing. It can require a click-through warning. These moves are quieter than removal, and often more powerful.

The major platforms have each built distinct approaches. Meta began labeling AI-generated content across Facebook, Instagram, and Threads in 2024, detecting industry-standard AI image indicators and displaying "AI info" labels when the company's systems identify synthetic content [4]. YouTube requires creators to disclose "realistic altered or synthetic content" during upload and can add labels even when uploaders fail to do so [5]. TikTok mandates visible disclosure labels for AI-generated content, automatically applies "AI-generated" badges when its systems detect embedded provenance metadata, and prohibits deepfakes of private individuals or anyone under 18 [6]. X maintains a policy on "synthetic and manipulated media" that has evolved over time but remains less detailed in its enforcement transparency than competitors [7].

A label looks like a small piece of metadata. In a synthetic reality environment, a label becomes a verdict. It says, "This platform has classified this content," and classification shapes behavior. Research on label design has found that how a label is worded and where it is placed significantly affects whether users notice it and how they interpret the content's credibility [8]. The power issue is not whether labels are good or bad. The power issue is that labels are a form of authority exercised privately, at scale, with limited external oversight. Labels do not simply settle disputes. They often relocate disputes. A creator who uses AI for minor edits can be labeled in a way that implies deception. A journalist who publishes a real clip can be labeled in a way that suggests uncertainty.

Platforms also adjudicate disputes through internal processes that are often opaque. A user may not know why their content was labeled. A creator may not know why their reach collapsed. An ordinary person may not know why impersonation reports were ignored.

In many cases, platforms respond to real harms and real pressures. The deeper issue is that platform governance is not democratic. It is accountable primarily to shareholders, regulators, and public opinion, not to citizens. As synthetic identity grows, platforms will be pressured to deepen that sovereignty. They will be asked to require stronger identity proofing, offer verified tiers, enforce disclosure of synthetic media, and remove impersonation rapidly. Each step can be justified as safety. Each step also increases platform power.

The Infrastructure

The third arena is infrastructure. This includes standards bodies, authentication schemes, provenance systems, watermarking approaches, app stores, payment rails, cloud providers, and the companies that build the generative tools themselves. Infrastructure is the quiet layer that makes verification possible at scale. It is also the layer that can silently centralize power, because whoever sets the standards and controls the pipelines can determine whose content is treated as "certified."

Provenance standards are an active area of development. The Coalition for Content Provenance and Authenticity, known as C2PA, brings together technology companies, media organizations, and others to develop technical standards for attaching metadata to content at the point of creation. The goal is to create a chain of custody that travels with the content, allowing downstream viewers to see where it came from and whether it has been modified. This is a legitimate response to the authenticity problem. It is also a new form of credentialing. Content that carries provenance metadata will be treated differently from content that does not. The question is who gets access to the tools that generate that metadata and whether the absence of metadata will be treated as a mark against content that is actually genuine but was created outside the provenance ecosystem.

Model providers occupy a special position in the infrastructure layer. The companies that build and deploy large generative models are upstream of most synthetic content. These companies are not only making software. They are deciding which capabilities exist, which are restricted, and which signals are attached to outputs. If a model refuses to generate certain kinds of content, that refusal shapes the information environment. If a model includes a watermark, that watermark shapes provenance. If a provider logs prompts, that logging shapes privacy. If a provider sets terms of use, those terms shape what legitimate creation looks like. Attackers will use open tools, custom models, and workflows designed to evade controls. The point is not that model providers can solve the problem. The point is that upstream capability control becomes part of legitimacy conflicts because it determines what is possible at scale.

The cumulative effect is that whoever controls these infrastructure chokepoints shapes what synthetic identity can do at scale. Infrastructure is never neutral. It is always governance, even when it looks like plumbing.

These arenas overlap. A state can pressure a platform. A platform can lobby a state. Infrastructure can be mandated by law, adopted by platforms, or rejected by markets. The conflict is, in practice, a constant negotiation across these layers.

To keep the lens neutral, it helps to focus on mechanisms instead of motives. The same verification systems that protect people from fraud can be used to suppress inconvenient speech, and the same provenance systems that help a journalist prove authenticity can be used to privilege institutional voices over ordinary ones. The same disclosure rules that improve transparency can become tools for intimidation or selective enforcement. The mechanisms are not partisan, but their effects are never evenly distributed.

The Daily Experience of Verification

The conflict reshapes daily life through small accumulations. You do not experience it as a speech about democracy. You experience it as a new requirement to verify, confirm, prove, and wait.

When synthetic voices become capable of authorizing financial transfers, companies respond by layering new verification rituals onto existing processes. The same pattern repeats across every domain where impersonation carries risk: deepfake-enabled fraud in video meetings leads to mandatory secondary confirmations, the possibility of employee impersonation drives investments in harder identity proofing, and the vulnerability of customer support to synthetic presence forces organizations to redesign processes so that no single interaction carries too much authority. In effect, enterprises build private trust regimes. They do it quietly through policy, workflow, and auditing, and the public mostly notices only when a requirement slows life down.

Banks add steps. HR departments add confirmations. Procurement teams add approvals. Customer service centers require callback verification. Wire transfer requests trigger secondary authentication. Each step is rational on its own terms, a reasonable response to a specific threat. But the accumulation of these steps transforms the texture of professional and commercial life. The colleague you have worked with for years must still prove they are who they claim to be when requesting access or approving a transaction. The client you have known for a decade must still pass through the same authentication gauntlet as a stranger. Familiarity no longer carries the weight it once did, because familiarity can now be manufactured.

These private trust regimes reduce risk, but they also change how identity feels within institutions. Authority becomes less a matter of recognition and more a matter of compliance with verification protocols. The person who can navigate the authentication maze efficiently is the person who gets things done; the person who stumbles over the protocols, whether due to unfamiliarity with the technology or circumstances that make documentation difficult, falls behind. The friction is individually small and collectively enormous. When this logic spreads across an entire economy, every vendor relationship involves new identity checks, every contract renewal requires new attestation requirements, and every customer interaction involves new confirmation steps. It becomes a tax on ordinary commerce, paid in time and attention rather than money.

NIST's AI Risk Management Framework is an example of the language institutions use to justify these moves. It frames AI risk management around functions like govern, map, measure, and manage, emphasizing accountability, transparency, and monitoring [9]. This kind of framework signals that legitimacy is being rebuilt through compliance structures rather than through shared perceptions.

The burden of verification does not fall equally. A senior executive with an assistant can delegate the friction. A frontline employee cannot. A tech-savvy customer can navigate the authentication maze quickly, while an elderly customer may struggle with each additional step. A person with stable documentation can satisfy identity requirements easily, but a person in transition, a new immigrant, someone who has recently changed their name, or a domestic violence survivor who has deliberately severed ties to a previous identity faces compounding barriers at every checkpoint. The architecture of verification is never neutral in its effects, even when its intentions are protective.

This trend matters because it shows how the conflict can reshape society without any grand political decision. The shift happens through risk management, through a thousand policy tweaks that make sense locally and add up globally. No one votes on whether society should become a verification gauntlet. It emerges because each institution, facing its own liability and threat landscape, rationally chooses to add another check. The aggregate effect is a world where proving you are who you claim to be becomes a constant background task, a low-level hum of authentication that accompanies every significant interaction.

The psychological toll is difficult to measure but real. When every request might be a scam, every message might be synthetic, and every voice might be cloned, people learn to approach communication with a defensive crouch. The old default of assuming good faith erodes, replaced by a stance of permanent low-grade suspicion. This is not paranoia in the clinical sense. It is an adaptive response to an environment that has taught people that trust carries risk.

The Stratification of Trust

Chapter 7 described how provenance becomes a luxury good: those who can afford certified channels experience less ambiguity, while everyone else absorbs the fog. That dynamic intensifies as verification systems expand, because each one creates insiders and outsiders.

Verified lanes emerge for institutions, certified creators, and credentialed content. These lanes feature authenticated channels, signed records, official portals, validated credentials, provenance-supported media, and procedures that increase the likelihood of authenticity. Outside these lanes, the unverified world persists: open platforms, screenshots, reposts, anonymous channels, and informal networks where identity is fluid and provenance is scarce. The split is never absolute; verified content leaks into unverified spaces, and unverified content sometimes gets laundered back into official channels, but the structural separation grows because institutions will not tolerate uncertainty where liability is high.

The danger is that ordinary people live mostly in the unverified lane while elites operate in protected channels. The executive communicates through enterprise platforms with strong identity verification; the gig worker communicates through consumer apps where impersonation is easy. The institution publishes through channels with provenance metadata intact; the citizen shares screenshots with provenance metadata stripped. When trust becomes expensive, it becomes scarce, and scarcity tracks existing inequalities.

As platforms harden verification, they increasingly decide what counts as a legitimate account. Some platforms may require stronger proof for higher reach, others may require government-issued IDs for certain functions, and still others may tie verification to payment. Each step sounds like a solution to fraud, but it also creates exclusion. People without stable documentation, people in precarious circumstances, and people living under authoritarian pressures can all be harmed by an identity regime that demands certain proofs. The activist who needs anonymity to speak safely may find herself locked out of the verified tier. The undocumented worker may find himself unable to access services that require a government ID. When identity becomes the gate to participation, the design of that gate determines who gets to exist in public.

Platforms have also learned that identity itself can be monetized. Verification badges, premium accounts, and reputation tiers have become revenue streams. The platform is not only protecting trust; it is selling access to trust. When credibility becomes a product, the platform becomes a private vendor of legitimacy, a profound social role for a competitive business to occupy. The meaning of identity online shifts accordingly: it becomes something closer to a subscription than a fact, a feature you can purchase rather than a status you earn through behavior and relationship.

Most provenance and disclosure systems depend on panels and menus, with the relevant information tucked behind a click. That design is understandable; platforms avoid clutter and resist overwhelming users with metadata, but it creates a predictable outcome. The people most likely to check the panel are those who already care about authenticity. The people most vulnerable to manipulation, or simply most rushed, are least likely to check. The trust signal becomes a niche feature, available in principle but invisible in practice. If the verification mechanism is not legible to the public, it becomes a tool for institutions rather than a shield for society.

The stratification has both geographic and linguistic dimensions. Content moderation capacity is rarely evenly distributed across languages and regions. A platform may have robust enforcement in English and weak enforcement in other languages, creating pockets of vulnerability where manipulation spreads more easily. The same platform that quickly removes a deepfake targeting an American politician may be slow to address one targeting a politician in a smaller country. The same provenance tools available to English-speaking creators may not be well documented or even available to creators in other languages. The global nature of platforms meets the local nature of harm, creating an unequal protection gap.

Why is the response so uneven, given the seriousness of the threat? The answer lies in incentives, not ignorance. Platforms are rewarded for growth and engagement, and verification adds friction that can reduce both. Tool makers are rewarded for ease and creativity, and provenance can look like surveillance or limitation to creators who worry it will expose their workflows. Standards bodies are rewarded for consensus, and consensus takes time that adversaries do not grant. Governments are rewarded for appearing to act, but they are constrained by legal process and public debate. Everyone has reasons to move slowly while the threat moves fast.

The gap between threat and response becomes the space where harm accumulates. The sophisticated attacker operates in that gap. The ordinary person absorbs the consequences.

The Paradox at the Center

The conflict over verification will produce endless accusations of bias, and not all of those accusations will be sincere. Some will be strategic, deployed by actors who benefit from confusion. Yet even sincere actors will struggle to appear neutral, because neutrality is not simply a motive but an outcome, and outcomes are shaped by constraints that no actor fully controls.

When a platform labels synthetic content, it will sometimes label incorrectly. False positives will anger creators and may be interpreted as suppression; false negatives will allow deception and will be interpreted as negligence. When a platform removes content, it will be accused of overreach; when it leaves content up, it will be accused of complicity. The platform cannot satisfy everyone because it is performing a governance function in a space where governance cannot command universal trust.

The same dynamics apply to governments. When a state regulates synthetic content, it must define what counts, and definitions are where adversaries live. Narrow definitions create loopholes that attackers exploit while staying technically legal. Broad definitions risk catching legitimate edits, satire, or artistic transformations. Enforcement choices will be scrutinized and contested regardless of intent, and even a well-designed rule can be applied unevenly across cases. There is no perfect rule because the environment is dynamic, adversarial, and culturally diverse.

The struggle over verification is often described as a fight against deepfakes, as if the problem were merely synthetic media. That framing misses the deeper conflict. The real fight is over who gets to certify reality, because once certification exists, it determines who gets to act, who gets punished, and who gets ignored.

States will claim that authority in the name of public order and democratic integrity. Platforms will claim it in the name of safety and user trust. Standards bodies and infrastructure providers will claim it in the name of technical reliability. Markets will claim it in the name of efficiency. Each claim contains truth, and each claim also concentrates power in the hands of those who control the certification apparatus. The conflict among these claimants will not produce a winner so much as a shifting equilibrium, with power flowing toward whichever actor can most credibly promise to resolve the uncertainty that synthetic identity creates.

This struggle will not restore a simple world where authenticity is obvious. It will build a new world where authenticity is mediated through gatekeepers, credentials, and procedures. The public will not return to a naive trust in what it sees. Instead, people will learn to live inside what might be called a managed legitimacy economy, where trust is allocated by institutions rather than inferred from perception.

In that world, trust does not disappear. It is redistributed. It becomes a managed resource, and managed resources are always political in the structural sense, because whoever manages them can decide who gets access and on what terms.

Yet here is where the paradox emerges in full force. Institutions are building these verification systems at the exact moment when verification itself is becoming impossible to guarantee. They are gaining unprecedented power over identity while simultaneously discovering that the tools they have built cannot reliably catch what they are designed to catch. Authenticity has become so degraded, synthetic media so easy to produce, and verification so expensive, that no institution can actually guarantee the legitimacy of what passes through its gates.

The gatekeepers are standing at gates that no longer reliably hold anything back. The power is real. The helplessness is equally real. Societies must now learn to live inside both truths at once.

That is an unstable situation. When institutions accumulate power but cannot deliver on their promises, legitimacy erodes. When legitimacy erodes, people stop expecting institutions to resolve disputes. They stop believing that the process can determine what is real. They begin to adapt to a world where verification is endless, where disputes are never settled, and where the only safe strategy is to trust no one outside their immediate circle.

That adaptation has a name. It is called resignation, and it is the subject of the next chapter.

Summary

This chapter began with a story about a bouncer outside a Manhattan club, a man with no credentials, no formal authority, and no institution behind him, who held absolute power at a single point of access. He looked at us for three seconds and decided our identity. Not who we were, but who we were allowed to be in that space. The moment was small. The lesson was not. What the bouncer demonstrated, without saying it and without knowing it, is the deeper structure of every verification system that has ever mattered. Verification is power. When someone decides what counts as real, whose identity is permitted, and who belongs, they are not merely making a judgment. They are exercising authority. The remainder of the chapter was about what happens to a society when that authority migrates from a doorway into the layer where modern life actually happens.

The first move was to describe the bargain that authenticity used to keep. Verification, when needed, used to be cheap. A notary could witness a signature. A clerk could match a face to a photograph. A phone call could confirm a voice. The cost of checking was low enough that most checks did not need to happen, because the background assumption of authenticity made constant verification unnecessary. Synthetic identity broke that bargain. It did not make verification impossible, but it made verification contested and costly, and not only in money. The cost shows up in attention, time, anxiety, and friction, in new rituals and new paperwork that seem minor until you multiply them across billions of interactions. As soon as verification becomes costly, it becomes strategic, because costs create power. Someone must pay the cost. Someone must decide which costs are acceptable. Someone must decide whose claims are believed in the meantime. Those decisions shape the social order even when they are made quietly, in policy documents and product roadmaps no one reads.

That is the move at the heart of the chapter. Verification, once the dull procedural layer beneath the more interesting drama of life, has become the layer where the drama actually happens. Governance is not only legislation and elections. Governance is the everyday machinery that decides what is permitted, what is punished, and what is treated as credible enough to act on. Once authenticity is no longer ambient, governance moves into the verification layer. The center of gravity shifts from content to credentials. The core question becomes less "is this clip real?" and more "who has the authority to declare it real enough to matter?" That authority is what every actor in the system is fighting over, because authority is what turns information into consequences. The chapter pointed at the March 2022 Ukraine incident as one concentrated example. A deepfake of President Zelenskyy did not need to be believed permanently. It needed only to create a decision point. Synthetic identity borrows the voice of legitimacy to force someone, somewhere, to decide what is real enough to act on, and that decision becomes governance whether it happens in a corporate office, a high school, or a war zone.

The chapter then mapped the three arenas where this struggle plays out. The first is the state. Governments have a legitimate role in protecting elections, defending citizens from fraud, and enforcing the law, but they also have an interest in controlling public order and managing narratives during crises. The state arena is where formal authority is highest and where its limits are most visible, because states can set rules but cannot unilaterally reshape a global information environment. The second is the platform. Platforms are private companies that govern public discourse without being elected to do so. They shape belief through ranking, recommendation, verification badges, labels, policies, and account rules, and each of those levers is governance, even when it is presented as personalization or trust and safety. Ranking, in particular, is not a service that matches content to preferences. It is a governance system that determines which voices become salient, which ideas gain momentum, and whether a disputed clip spreads fast enough to matter before verification arrives. Distribution is power. The ability to make something visible, or to bury it, is a form of rule-making. The third arena is the infrastructure of standards and certification, the quieter layer where industry consortia, technical bodies, and credential issuers decide what the protocols of legitimacy will look like and who is allowed inside them.

What all three arenas have in common is that they are accumulating verification power at the exact moment when verification is becoming impossible to guarantee. Authenticity has become so degraded, synthetic media so easy to produce, and verification so expensive, that no institution can actually deliver on the promise its growing authority implies. The gatekeepers are standing at gates that no longer reliably hold anything back. The power is real. The helplessness is equally real. Societies are being asked to live inside both truths at once. That is what the chapter named the managed legitimacy economy, a world in which trust does not disappear but becomes a managed resource, allocated by institutions rather than inferred from perception, and in which whoever manages that resource can decide who gets access and on what terms.

This struggle is not a fight between good actors and bad ones. The conflict is structural. States will claim verification authority in the name of public order. Platforms will claim it in the name of safety. Standards bodies will claim it in the name of technical reliability. Markets will claim it in the name of efficiency. Each claim contains truth, and each claim also concentrates power in the hands of those who control the certification apparatus. The conflict among these claimants will not produce a winner so much as a shifting equilibrium, with authority flowing toward whichever actor can most credibly promise to resolve the uncertainty that synthetic identity creates. The real fight is not against deepfakes. The real fight is over who gets to certify reality, because once certification exists, it determines who gets to act, who gets punished, and who gets ignored.

Looking Ahead

The chapter ended on an unstable situation. Institutions are accumulating power they cannot fully wield, and gatekeepers are guarding gates that no longer reliably hold. When authority grows but cannot deliver on what authority is supposed to deliver, legitimacy erodes, and erosion of that kind does not register as a single dramatic failure. It registers as exhaustion. Chapter 9 traces what happens when that exhaustion reaches the people the institutions were supposed to serve. It does not begin in a courtroom or a newsroom, and it does not arrive in the language of policy. It begins in private. The most consequential surrender in modern life rarely announces itself, and the next chapter argues that the same pattern that ends civic trust begins inside ordinary human beings who have simply run out of energy to keep believing the world will respond to evidence.

References

[1] Claire Wardle and Hossein Derakhshan, “Information Disorder: Toward an Interdisciplinary Framework for Research and Policy Making,” Council of Europe (2017).

[2] Federal Communications Commission, “FCC Proposes $6M Fine For N.H. Robocalls” (May 2024) and “FCC Issues $6M Fine For N.H. Robocalls” (Sept. 26, 2024).

[3] U.S. Federal Communications Commission, Declaratory Ruling FCC 24-17 and related FCC announcement clarifying that AI-generated voices in robocalls fall under TCPA restrictions on artificial or prerecorded voice calls (Feb. 8, 2024).

[4] Meta, “Our Approach to Labeling AI-Generated Content and Manipulated Media” (Apr. 5, 2024) and Meta transparency materials on labeling AI content.

[5] YouTube, “How we’re helping creators disclose altered or synthetic content” (Mar. 18, 2024) and YouTube Help Center guidance on disclosing altered or synthetic content.

[6] TikTok Newsroom, “New labels for disclosing AI-generated content” (Sept. 19, 2023) and Reuters reporting on TikTok’s plan to label AI-generated images and video using Content Credentials (May 9, 2024).

[7] X Help Center, “Authenticity” policy addressing synthetic and manipulated media and other inauthentic content.

[8] Wittenberg, Chloe, Ziv Epstein, Adam J. Berinsky, and David G. Rand. “Labeling AI-generated content: promises, perils, and future directions.” *An MIT Exploration of Generative AI*, 2024.

[9] National Institute of Standards and Technology, “Artificial Intelligence Risk Management Framework (AI RMF 1.0),” NIST AI 100-1 (Jan. 2023).

CHAPTER 9

The Resignation

Chapter 8 ended on an unstable situation. Institutions had accumulated power they could not fully wield. Gatekeepers were guarding gates that no longer reliably held. The authority to certify reality had become one of the most contested resources in modern life, and the people exercising that authority were discovering that the tools they had inherited were no longer adequate to the work being asked of them. The result was not a system that failed cleanly. It was a system that strained, adapted, and continued to claim competence while quietly losing it.

This chapter is about what happens to a society when that strain reaches the people the institutions were built to serve. The crisis of authenticity in Chapter 7 was psychological. The crisis of verification in Chapter 8 was political. The crisis this chapter examines is something else, and it is the most dangerous of the three because it does not look like a crisis at all. It looks like patience. It looks like prudence. It looks like the reasonable adjustment of expectations downward by people who have decided, after enough evidence, that the institutions in question are not going to deliver what they once promised. Once enough people make that adjustment, the social architecture that depended on the older expectations becomes load-bearing in name only. The walls are still there. The roof is still there. The faith has gone.

That adjustment has a name. The chapter that follows is about how it arrives, what it looks like at scale, and why it is the most difficult of the trust crises to reverse.

R. Mastrogiacomo, *The Next Identity Crisis*, https://doi.org/10.1007/979-8-8688-2788-4_9

The Shape of Resignation

I remember the cold tiles in our bathroom. I remember the tears streaming down my wife's face as she came to the realization that it happened again. It was her second miscarriage.

The loss you feel for an unborn child is difficult to describe to someone who has not experienced it. There was no seeing the child, holding her, or loving her physical form, but there was so much love. There was no physical happiness outside the thought of what would be. What will she look like? What will her name be? What will make her laugh, and how will we react when she goes on her first date? All of those thoughts are about future happiness, not happiness in the here and now. So when you lose an unborn child, you almost feel like it shouldn't hurt as much as it does.

But it does hurt. It's emotional, it's painful, and the feeling of loss is so deep that it changes you. This was our second attempt at giving our first child a sibling. In that cold bathroom, we decided it would be our last.

That's what resignation looks like for humans.

It does not announce itself. It arrives quietly, in a private moment, after the evidence has accumulated beyond argument. You do not decide to resign. You simply notice that you already have. The fight has left your body. The hope has been revised into acceptance. You adapt to a world where the thing you wanted most is no longer available, and you protect yourself by no longer wanting it.

This chapter is about what happens when that same pattern scales. When it moves from bathrooms and kitchens into courtrooms and newsrooms. When it spreads from individuals to institutions to the society that depends on both. The previous chapters traced how we arrived here: Chapter 7 described the collapse of authenticity when the signals of identity become cheap to fake, and Chapter 8 showed how verification becomes governance, concentrating power in whoever controls the systems that decide what counts as real. Institutions have been building gates that no longer hold anything back.

When that paradox becomes visible, something shifts in how people relate to the institutions meant to serve them. The shift is not dramatic. It does not arrive as a riot or a revolution. It arrives as exhaustion. People stop expecting institutions to resolve disputes. They stop believing that the process can determine what is real. They begin to adapt to a world where verification is endless, where disputes are never settled, and where the only safe strategy is to trust no one outside their immediate circle.

That adaptation has a name. It is called resignation, and it is the emotional peak of the trust collapse.

The first response to an authenticity shock is doubt, and doubt can be healthy. Doubt is the beginning of verification, the moment when someone asks "what else supports this?" and looks for an answer. Doubt is active. It engages with evidence. It seeks resolution.

The more dangerous response is resignation: not disciplined doubt but a posture that says, "nothing can be proven anyway, so I will rely on my side, my instincts, or my appetite." Resignation is passive. It is how people protect themselves from being fooled by refusing the labor of sorting truth from noise.

Resignation is not the same as ignorance. Resigned people often know exactly what is happening. They have simply concluded that fighting it is futile. They have learned that verification is labor, that labor is unrewarded, and that the safest strategy is to trust no one outside their immediate circle. Resignation is how a society stops being a society. It is how strangers stop coordinating. It is how the compromise that made civilization possible begins to dissolve.

Institutions do not only suffer from resignation. They also produce it. When institutions cannot resolve disputes quickly or transparently, the public learns that disputing is futile. The result is not irrationality but exhaustion.

A tired public is a vulnerable public, more likely to accept quick narratives, defer to charismatic voices, and retreat into smaller trust networks that feel safer than the open world [1]. That retreat does not require ideology. It happens for the same reason people lock their doors when crime rises: a rational response to uncertainty.

Institutions Under Strain

The pressure does not hit all institutions equally, but it hits all institutions eventually. Courts face it first because courts are where disputes are supposed to end. Journalism faces it next because journalism is how strangers learn what happened. Emergency systems face it when coordination becomes life or death. Organizations face it when fraud adapts faster than policy. Each institution encounters the same underlying problem from a different angle, and each discovers that the old tools no longer work the way they used to.

The Courts

Courts were built to handle disputes, which makes them the first place society expects to resolve contested evidence. Yet synthetic identity does not merely add new cases. It changes the structure of cases. In a classic dispute, the court asks what happened and who is responsible. Evidence is debated, but the underlying assumption is stable: evidence can, in principle, resolve the dispute. Witnesses can be cross-examined, documents authenticated, experts consulted, verdicts reached. The judge or jury decides, and responsibility for the decision is clear.

In a synthetic environment, courts increasingly face a meta-dispute. Before litigating guilt, they must litigate authenticity. Before evaluating a statement, they must evaluate whether the statement is a fabrication. Before considering a video, they must consider whether it is a generated artifact, an edited composite, or a miscontextualized clip.

This recursive layer changes who has leverage. Authenticity litigation is expensive. It relies on specialized expertise, forensic methods, chain-of-custody documentation, and technical testimony. When authenticity becomes a primary battleground, resources become a lever in determining truth. A defendant with money can retain forensic experts, challenge metadata, and demand chain-of-custody audits for every digital artifact. A defendant without money faces the same evidentiary challenges with far fewer tools. The inequality was always present in the legal system, but synthetic identity sharpens it by making wealth a direct factor in whether evidence survives scrutiny.

It also changes what the court is for. A court becomes an authentication institution, not only a place to apply law. That function can be performed responsibly, but it is a heavy load for a system already strained by caseloads and inequality.

Courts have always cared about chain of custody: evidence must be tracked and preserved so that tampering cannot be plausibly claimed. In a physical world, chain of custody often had a material feel: an object was bagged, a weapon sealed, a document stamped. There were still gaps, but the rituals communicated seriousness.

Digital evidence has always been harder. Files can be copied without loss, metadata modified, devices compromised. Yet courts and investigators developed practices that worked well enough because the public did not assume any artifact could be invented from scratch on demand.

Synthetic media changes that background assumption. A file is not only vulnerable to alteration. It may never have been a recording in the first place. It may be a pure fabrication that looks exactly like a recording, and distinguishing the two requires expertise the average juror does not possess and the average litigant cannot afford.

The dynamics appear most starkly in cases involving vulnerable parties. Consider domestic violence survivors seeking protective orders or custody arrangements. These survivors often rely on recordings, text messages, voicemails, and other digital evidence to document abuse that occurred in private, without witnesses [2]. In a synthetic identity environment, this evidence becomes contestable by default. A well-resourced abuser can challenge the authenticity of any recording, any message, any piece of evidence the survivor presents. The survivor must then prove not only that the abuse happened but that the evidence of the abuse is real, a double burden that falls hardest on those with the fewest resources to bear it.

If the evidentiary environment becomes adversarial by default, the burden falls on the vulnerable. The same dynamics appear in policing. Body cameras and surveillance footage were adopted partly as a response to disputed accounts. The hope was that video could stabilize truth and reduce conflict. Synthetic identity complicates that promise. Footage can be edited and miscontextualized. Clips can be fabricated to resemble official recordings. Real footage can be denied as manipulated. Even when the technical integrity of a file is strong, public belief may not follow.

This creates a dangerous feedback loop. The public demands evidence; the state produces evidence; the public disputes the evidence; the state tightens control over evidence to preserve authority; the public interprets tighter control as secrecy. Trust erodes further. The point is not that body cameras are useless. The point is that video cannot substitute for legitimacy when legitimacy is contested. Proof is not only the existence of a recording but the acceptance of the institution presenting it.

Journalism

Journalism faces the same crisis, though from a different angle. Journalism has always been about two things: gathering information and earning trust. The first task is procedural; the second is relational.

Synthetic identity strains both. It floods the information environment with plausible artifacts and lowers the cost of producing convincing "evidence." It also undermines the public's willingness to trust institutions that report, because mistakes become proof of incompetence or bias.

The immediate pressure is operational. Newsrooms must verify images, videos, and statements faster than the viral cycle. They must decide what to publish, how to label, and how to correct. They must develop internal forensic capabilities and partnerships with outside experts.

The deeper pressure is existential. If the public assumes that any newsroom can be fooled, every mistake becomes a referendum on legitimacy. If the public assumes that newsrooms fabricate or selectively frame, provenance and verification may not be persuasive. The institution's credibility becomes permanently contested.

In earlier eras, a newsroom relied on trusted channels and physical presence. Today, a newsroom receives footage from social platforms, messaging apps, and anonymous sources. The material arrives already decontextualized. The same clip can be posted with different captions, different dates, and different implied meanings, which creates a treadmill: the newsroom must authenticate or risk spreading misinformation, but authentication takes time. Time is the enemy of relevance. Platforms reward speed, and audiences are trained to treat being first as being credible.

Those who spread falsehood can move instantly; those who verify must move carefully. Corrections and context rarely travel as far as the original viral claim. Even when journalism behaves responsibly, the architecture rewards irresponsible behavior. In a synthetic environment, this asymmetry intensifies. A fabricated clip can be designed to exploit the speed trap, released when institutions cannot respond quickly enough. The clip does not need to endure; it only needs to win the first hour.

Journalists are not only trying to verify; they are also being targeted. A synthetic statement can be sent to a reporter in the voice of an official source. A fake "leak" can be packaged with convincing documents and a synthetic audio call that seems to confirm them. A forged video can be released with the intention of baiting coverage, then using the newsroom's amplification as a multiplier. Journalism can be turned into an engine that legitimizes fakes, not because journalists are careless, but because the environment is designed to exploit the incentives of speed and attention.

The defensive response is predictable. Newsrooms invest in verification, delay publishing, add caveats, and create internal standards for authenticity. Those standards improve quality but slow reporting. In fast-moving situations, delay can be its own harm; if journalism moves too slowly, the public fills the gap with speculation and manipulation. The vacuum becomes the attacker's habitat.

Technical solutions offer partial help but not salvation. Provenance systems and content credentials can help demonstrate chain of custody. A signed image can show origin and edits; a camera chain can provide cryptographic receipts. These tools matter. Yet provenance does not solve the main legitimacy problem, because provenance depends on trust in the certifier. A provenance panel can prove that a clip came from a particular source; it cannot prove that the source is honest, that it did not omit context, or that it is not captured. Provenance proves origin, not interpretation.

The deeper bottleneck is social. Trust is not only a technical state but a relationship between an institution and a public. When that relationship is weakened, technical receipts do not restore it quickly. This is why "nothing can be proven" becomes cultural. Proof is not only data but accepted authority.

There is also a quiet structural risk that compounds the problem. Verification requires resources, and many local newsrooms have lost resources for years. Since 2005, more than a quarter of American newspapers have ceased operations, leaving roughly half of US counties with only a single paper and 200 counties with no paper at all [3]. The decline has accelerated: between late 2019 and mid-2022, more than 360 additional newspapers closed [4]. A fifth of the country's population, 70 million people, now lives in an area with either no local news organization or only one at risk.

When a community loses robust local reporting, it loses a verification layer that is geographically and socially anchored. National outlets can cover national stories, but local disputes, local emergencies, and local rumors require local institutions to resolve. A local newspaper knows the mayor, knows the police chief, knows which claims deserve scrutiny and which sources are reliable. That knowledge is not easily replicated by a reporter parachuting in from elsewhere.

In the absence of that capacity, communities rely more on informal channels, and informal channels are easier to manipulate. Research has linked the loss of local newspapers to decreased civic engagement, lower political knowledge, increased political polarization, and less accountability for elected officials [5][6]. When local papers disappear, the information vacuum does not stay empty. Political operatives have exploited news deserts by establishing "pink slime" sites, websites that masquerade as local news outlets but actually distribute partisan content or advertorials [7]. These sites adopt the visual language of journalism while serving agendas the community cannot easily identify.

Synthetic identity turns that decline into a sharper vulnerability. A fake announcement about a local emergency, policy change, or official can spread quickly in a community that has no trusted local newsroom to correct it. The public then faces a choice between silence and rumor. Silence rarely wins.

Emergency Response

Emergency response reveals the stakes most starkly. Emergency response depends on trust. In a crisis, the public must decide quickly whether to comply with instructions: evacuate or shelter, seek care or wait, avoid a region or return. These decisions are made under stress with limited information.

If the public does not trust emergency communications, response fails. Even small drops in trust can cost lives, because emergency response is a coordination problem.

Synthetic media introduces a new class of hazards: fake alerts, fake officials, fake evacuation orders, fake public health announcements [8]. These artifacts can be deployed cheaply and rapidly. The danger is not only that people believe the fake but that people begin to doubt the real. A fake alert can poison trust in future real alerts. People learn to hesitate, and in emergencies, hesitation is deadly.

Emergency deception usually follows a predictable script [9]. The attacker borrows authority, using the language of institutions: "This is an official notice," "For your safety," "Immediate action required," adopting the cadence and formatting of real alerts including timestamps, reference numbers, and the calm certainty of public service speech. The attacker compresses time, framing the instruction as urgent with a narrow window: leave now, do not wait, do not call, do not verify through normal channels because they are "down" or "overloaded." The attacker is not only sending information but trying to disable verification. The attacker targets channels that feel intimate: group chats, local community pages, neighborhood apps, messaging chains that resemble neighborly care. Official channels can be monitored and verified; informal channels are faster, more trusted, and less structured. Informal channels are also easier to poison. Finally, the attacker forces institutions into a losing tempo. Even when an agency responds quickly, it is responding second. The first message becomes the reference point, and the correction must compete with a story already emotionally anchored.

This is why emergency deception is so dangerous in a synthetic era. The attacker does not need to permanently rewrite reality, just create a brief wedge between the public and the institution. That wedge is enough to cause cascading harm.

During a hurricane, wildfire, or flood, a false evacuation notice can divert traffic into danger. A false "all clear" can send people back into harm. A fake shelter announcement can concentrate vulnerable people in the wrong place. A synthetic statement attributed to an official can trigger panic buying or unnecessary flight. In a public safety incident, a fake warning can cause stampedes, school closures, and hospital surges. In a public health situation, a fake instruction can lead to dangerous behavior.

The consequences are not hypothetical. On the morning of January 13, 2018, residents across Hawaii received an emergency alert on their phones: "BALLISTIC MISSILE THREAT INBOUND TO HAWAII. SEEK IMMEDIATE SHELTER. THIS IS NOT A DRILL." The alert was false, sent by mistake during a routine drill, but 38 minutes passed before officials issued a correction [10]. In that window, chaos unfolded. Cars sped down freeways at over 100 miles per hour. Tourists were herded into concrete bunkers. Parents called children to say goodbye. One man, believing he had minutes to live, suffered a heart attack; a lawsuit over the incident eventually settled for $275,000 [11]. Research conducted after the event found that most residents did not immediately seek shelter but instead spent the terrifying interval searching for additional information to verify the threat, checking social media, calling family, looking for confirmation that the alert was real [12]. Critically, the study also found that trust in future warnings was damaged: respondents said they would be more likely to trust future tsunami warnings than future missile warnings, because the missile alert system had failed them.

The Hawaii incident was a false alarm caused by human error, not a synthetic attack. But it demonstrates the fragility of emergency communication systems and the lasting damage that a single failure can inflict on public trust. In a synthetic identity environment, such failures could be manufactured deliberately and at scale.

Agencies respond by hardening communication channels: verified accounts, official domains, secure alert systems, consistent phrasing [8]. These steps are rational, but they also turn emergency communication into another identity system. If the public must learn which channels are real, channel identity becomes part of public safety.

Organizations

Organizations face the crisis inside their own walls. Organizations often believe they can protect themselves by controlling internal systems: internal email, messaging, logs, HR records, payment approvals, and policies that define how authority moves. That confidence is partly justified; internal controls do reduce many forms of risk.

Synthetic identity undermines this confidence by attacking people rather than systems. The weakest link is often a person persuaded under pressure to treat a synthetic message as legitimate [13]. Fraud ecosystems have exploited urgency and authority for years; synthetic voice and video raise the ceiling by making impersonation more convincing and making it feel socially binding in a way that text never fully achieved.

The organizational response is predictable: more approvals, more step-up verification, more callback policies, more training, more audits. This response reduces some risk but also changes culture. Employees become hesitant. Decision-making slows. Managers become harder to reach. Operations become more bureaucratic.

The deeper issue is responsibility. When a synthetic impersonation succeeds, blame becomes contested. Was the employee negligent? The manager unclear? The policy insufficient? The system poorly designed? The diffusion of responsibility is not only a legal question but a cultural one. When no one is clearly at fault, everyone becomes defensive. When everyone becomes defensive, the organization becomes slower, more documented, and less capable of the informal trust that makes work bearable.

This is where resignation enters the organization itself. Anyone who has worked in a large, bureaucratic institution knows the feeling: the formal process exists, the tickets are filed, the approvals are routed through the proper channels, and nothing happens. Over time, people learn that the real organization runs on an underground economy of favors, handshakes, and mutual understanding that operates alongside the official hierarchy by different rules. Informal networks have always existed inside formal structures. What is new is the scale of the gap between the formal and the informal, and the exhaustion that comes from maintaining both. The formal process grows heavier because institutions keep adding controls in response to perceived failures. The informal process grows more essential because the formal process becomes too slow and too disconnected from reality to produce results. People shuttle between the two, performing compliance in one register while actually working in another. When friendships and coffee accomplish more than tickets and meetings, the institution has already failed in its core promise: that there is a legitimate process for getting things done, and that following it matters.

The Texture of Exhaustion

The institutional responses described above share a common feature: they add burden without restoring the old baseline of trust. Courts become authentication machines. Newsrooms become forensic labs. Emergency systems become identity verification platforms. Organizations become compliance bureaucracies. Each response is rational. Each response is also exhausting.

The public watches all of it and draws a conclusion that is unfair in specific cases but not irrational as a general posture: verification is endless, and disputes are never resolved. When every interaction requires proof and proof can always be contested, people adapt by lowering their expectations. They do not abandon institutions entirely, but they stop believing institutions can settle what is real. They negotiate privately, check multiple sources while trusting none, listen to neighbors before official channels, and work informal networks alongside formal ones. The institutions respond by building more controls, more compliance, more friction. They believe they are solving the problem. They are managing the symptoms while the disease spreads.

The disease is the loss of belief that institutions are the place where reality gets determined. When that belief goes, coordination becomes expensive, and expensive cooperation is not only an inconvenience but a structural fragility.

Cold Clarity

A society can survive liars, propaganda, and periods of intense misinformation. What it struggles to survive is permanent epistemic instability, the sense that disputes cannot be resolved because evidence cannot be trusted. A future where nothing can be proven is not a future without facts. It is a future where facts cannot compel, where power cannot be constrained by evidence, and where the social order becomes negotiable. Negotiation without shared proof becomes coercion by other means.

That is why identity remains the foundation of trust. If societies cannot answer "who" with credibility, they cannot answer "what happened" with authority. When that answer fails, strangers cannot coordinate, and civilization contracts toward the local, the tribal, and the defended.

Institutions have responded to the verification crisis by building more gates, more credentials, more procedures. But even as they accumulate this power over identity, a different question emerges: are they actually in charge of what happens next? The answer is no longer as obvious as we would like to believe.

Summary

This chapter began in a private room with a private loss. The story was not an illustration of an argument. It was the argument, told in its truest form, because resignation does not begin in courtrooms or newsrooms or boardrooms. It begins inside ordinary human beings who have decided, after enough evidence, that the world is not going to respond. From there, it scales. The chapter's task was to follow that pattern out of the private room and into the institutions that depend on, and produce, the same posture in the public.

The first move was to distinguish resignation from its more familiar cousins. Doubt is not resignation. Doubt is active. It asks what else supports this and looks for an answer. Doubt is the beginning of verification. Resignation is something different. It is the conclusion that nothing can be proven anyway, that the labor of sorting truth from noise is unrewarded, and that the safest strategy is to trust no one outside the immediate circle. Resignation is not ignorance, either. Resigned people often know exactly what is happening. They have simply decided that fighting it is futile, and that decision rarely arrives as a decision. The fight leaves the body before anyone makes a choice about whether to let it go. That posture, multiplied across enough people, is how a society stops being a society. It is how strangers stop coordinating, and how the compromise that made civilization possible begins to dissolve.

The chapter then turned to the institutions that were built to handle exactly the kinds of disputes synthetic identity now produces and traced how each one is buckling under a pressure it was not designed to absorb. Courts came first, because courts are where disputes are supposed to end. Synthetic identity does not merely add new cases. It changes the structure of cases, because evidence can no longer be assumed to resolve a dispute when any piece of evidence can be denied as fake or fabricated as real. The hardest burden falls on those with the fewest resources to carry it. Domestic violence survivors, who often depend on recordings and messages to document abuse that happened without witnesses, must now prove both that the abuse occurred and that the evidence of it is authentic. Body cameras and surveillance footage, once adopted in the hope that video could stabilize truth, no longer reliably do so. Real footage can be denied. Manipulated footage can be defended. The point is not that video is useless. The point is that video cannot substitute for legitimacy when legitimacy itself is contested.

Journalism faces the same pressure from a different angle. The two tasks of journalism, gathering information and earning trust, are both strained by an environment that floods discourse with plausible artifacts while undermining the public's willingness to trust institutions that report. The chapter traced this collision into the slower-moving disaster of news deserts, the disappearance of local newspapers whose absence has been linked to decreased civic engagement, lower political knowledge, and the rise of "pink slime" sites that adopt the visual language of journalism while serving agendas the community cannot easily identify. A fake announcement about a local emergency spreads more easily in a community without a trusted newsroom to correct it, and the cost of that vulnerability is paid not in headlines but in the slow erosion of the assumption that there is somewhere local to turn for what is true.

Emergency response revealed the stakes at their most concentrated. Emergency response depends on trust, and trust under stress depends on the public's willingness to act on instructions without verifying them first. Synthetic media introduces a new class of hazards. Fake alerts, fake officials, fake evacuation orders, fake public health announcements, deployable cheaply and rapidly. The deeper danger is not only that people believe the fake but that they begin to doubt the real. The 2018 Hawaii missile false alarm illustrated how fragile this system already is even without synthetic attacks. People sped down freeways at over a hundred miles per hour, herded children into bunkers, called family to say goodbye, and at least one man suffered a heart attack believing he had minutes to live. The aftermath showed something equally important. Trust in future warnings was damaged. The next alert, real or not, would be met with hesitation, and in emergencies, hesitation is deadly.

Organizations face the same crisis inside their own walls. Synthetic identity attacks the people inside institutions, not the systems they sit in front of, because the weakest link is usually a person persuaded under pressure to treat a synthetic message as legitimate. The institutional response is predictable. More approvals. More step-up verification. More callback policies. More training. More audits. Each step is rational, and the cumulative effect is corrosive. Decision-making slows. Managers become harder to reach. Operations become more bureaucratic. The gap between the formal process and the informal one widens, and people end up performing compliance in one register while actually working in another. When friendships and coffee accomplish more than tickets and meetings, the institution has already failed in its core promise, which is that there is a legitimate process for getting things done and that following it matters. That gap is where resignation enters the organization itself.

What unites all of these institutional failures, the chapter argued, is what it called the texture of exhaustion. Every response adds burden without restoring the old baseline of trust. Courts become authentication machines. Newsrooms become forensic labs. Emergency systems become identity verification platforms. Organizations become compliance bureaucracies. Each is exhausting. The public watches all of it and draws a conclusion that is unfair in specific cases but rational in aggregate. Verification is endless. Disputes are never resolved. So people lower their expectations. They negotiate privately. They check multiple sources while trusting none. They listen to neighbors before official channels. They work informal networks alongside formal ones. Institutions interpret these adaptations as problems to be solved by adding more controls. They believe they are solving the problem. They are managing symptoms while the disease spreads.

A society can survive liars, propaganda, and periods of intense misinformation. What it struggles to survive is permanent epistemic instability, the sense that disputes cannot be resolved because evidence cannot be trusted. A future where nothing can be proven is not a future without facts. It is a future where facts cannot compel, where power cannot be constrained by evidence, and where the social order becomes negotiable. Negotiation without shared proof becomes coercion by other means. Identity, the chapter insisted, remains the foundation of trust. If societies cannot answer who with credibility, they cannot answer what happened with authority. When that answer fails, strangers stop coordinating, and civilization contracts toward the local, the tribal, and the defended.

Looking Ahead

The chapter, and with it Part III, ended on a question that Part IV is built to confront. Institutions have responded to the verification crisis by accumulating power over identity. But are they actually in charge of what happens next? The answer is no longer as obvious as we would like to believe. The crisis of trust was about what societies can still know. The crisis of control, which begins in Chapter 10, is about what societies can still govern. Those are different questions, and they sit on different axes. A society can lose either one without immediately noticing the other, but losing both at the same time is the situation modern institutions now inhabit. They cannot reliably verify what is real, and they are simultaneously ceding practical authority to systems they do not fully understand. Chapter 10 begins by examining the comforting fiction that human beings remain in charge of the systems they have built, and how that fiction survives even as the substance underneath it drains away.

References

[1] Kavanagh, Jennifer, and Michael D. Rich. "Truth Decay: An Initial Exploration of the Diminishing Role of Facts and Analysis in American Public Life." RAND Corporation, 2018.

[2] Woodlock, Delanie. "The Abuse of Technology in Domestic Violence and Stalking." *Violence Against Women* 23, no. 5 (2017): 584–602.

[3] Abernathy, Penelope Muse. "News Deserts and Ghost Newspapers: Will Local News Survive?" UNC Hussman School of Journalism and Media, 2020.

[4] Medill Local News Initiative. "The State of Local News 2022." Northwestern University.

[5] Ardia, David, Evan Ringel, Victoria Smith Ekstrand, and Ashley Fox. "Addressing the Decline of Local News, Rise of Platforms, and Spread of Mis- and Disinformation Online: A Summary of Current Research and Policy Proposals." UNC Center for Media Law and Policy, December 2020.

[6] Hayes, Danny, and Jennifer L. Lawless. "The Decline of Local News and Its Effects: New Evidence from Longitudinal Data." *Journal of Politics*, 2018.

[7] Brennan Center for Justice. "'News Deserts' Could Impact Midterm Elections." 2022.

[8] Federal Emergency Management Agency. "Integrated Public Alert and Warning System (IPAWS)." `https://www.fema.gov/emergency-managers/practitioners/integrated-public-alert-warning-system`

[9] National Academies of Sciences, Engineering, and Medicine. *Emergency Alert and Warning Systems: Current Knowledge and Future Research Directions*. Washington, DC: The National Academies Press, 2018.

[10] Federal Communications Commission. "Report and Recommendations: Hawaii Emergency Management Agency January 13, 2018 False Alert." 2018.

[11] Honolulu Civil Beat. "It's Your Money: $275,000 For Heart Attack Caused By False Missile Alert." February 2025.

[12] DeYoung, Sarah, et al. "'Death was not in the agenda for the day': Emotions, behavioral reactions, and perceptions in response to the 2018 Hawaii Wireless Emergency Alert." *International Journal of Disaster Risk Reduction*, 2019.

[13] Verizon. *2024 Data Breach Investigations Report (DBIR)*. 17th ed. 2024.

PART IV

The Crisis of Control

Part III examined what happens when identity signals become cheap to fake. Authenticity collapses, and verification becomes governance. When verification fails to deliver on its promises, resignation sets in. That crisis is real and not going away, but it is only half the picture.

While institutions struggle to prove what is real, they are simultaneously ceding practical authority to systems they do not fully understand. The same organizations that cannot verify a recording are deploying algorithms that make thousands of decisions per hour. The same courts that cannot authenticate evidence are relying on risk-scoring tools to guide sentencing. The same newsrooms that cannot keep pace with synthetic media are using recommendation engines that shape what millions of people see. The same emergency systems that cannot distinguish real alerts from fake ones are routing evacuations through optimization models that review faster than any human can.

This is the crisis of control, and it operates on a different axis. The crisis of trust is about what we can know. The crisis of control is about what we can govern. Together, they create a civilizational moment in which institutions have lost both credibility and agency, unable to verify what is happening or direct what happens next.

Part IV asks a harder question than "Can we verify what is real?" It asks: "Who is actually making the decisions that shape our lives, and can anyone be held accountable for them?"

The answer is less reassuring than most people assume. We have built systems that act at speeds and scales that exceed human oversight. We have delegated authority to processes we cannot fully explain. And we have done all of this while maintaining the comforting fiction that humans remain in charge.

Part III described exhaustion. Part IV describes the structure that produces it. The goal is not to induce despair but to see clearly. A society that wants to preserve human agency must first understand where that agency has already migrated. It must stop pretending that human in the loop means human in control. It must confront the possibility that the rituals of oversight have become performances and that the performances are no longer fooling anyone.

We are not powerless. But we are not in control as we once believed. The first step toward regaining agency is admitting how much of it we have already lost.

CHAPTER 10

The Illusion of Control

Part IV opens on a different axis than Part III. The crisis of trust traced what societies have lost in the way of shared understanding. The crisis of control traces what they have lost in the way of practical authority over the systems that increasingly shape the lives unfolding inside them. Chapter 9 examined the social consequences of the first loss, the slow shift from disputing to disengaging. This chapter examines a quieter loss that often runs alongside it. The loss of governance that goes unnoticed because the rituals of control remain in place even after the substance has drained out of them.

The illusion of control is not the same as incompetence, and it is not the same as deceit. The illusion is what happens when human beings continue to perform the gestures of authorship over decisions that have already migrated somewhere else. Approvals are still granted. Sign-offs are still collected. Dashboards are still reviewed. The human-in-the-loop is still in the loop, technically, but the loop has begun to run faster than the human can meaningfully intervene in, and the system has accumulated enough authority by default that intervention has become the exception rather than the rule. Nothing has been surrendered. Authority remains where the organizational chart says it does. Yet control, the practical capacity to shape outcomes in real time, has begun to live somewhere else, and the gap between the two is the territory this chapter is built to map.

R. Mastrogiacomo, *The Next Identity Crisis*, https://doi.org/10.1007/979-8-8688-2788-4_10

To make that abstraction concrete, I want to begin somewhere far from any of it. Not in an institution, not in front of a screen, and not with any of the language this book has been building. Just a moment in my own life that I find myself returning to, again and again, whenever this subject demands an honest answer.

The Collapse

My son was four days old when the illusion collapsed. My wife and I had done everything we were supposed to do. We had read the books, attended the classes, assembled the crib, and stocked the nursery with supplies we did not yet know how to use. We had brought him home from the hospital with the careful confidence of people who believed preparation was the same as readiness. We were first-time parents, which meant we were amateurs who had rehearsed competence without ever performing it.

By the fourth day, he was not eating. He refused to breastfeed, and we could see him losing weight in ways that made our stomachs turn. We tried everything we knew, which was almost nothing. We adjusted positions, consulted websites, called family members, and watched the clock as hours passed without progress. The anxiety we had felt since bringing him home sharpened into something closer to panic.

Then we called the doctor. His voice was calm but urgent. "You need to get food into that baby as soon as possible. Come here for some formula."

We lived in Queens at the time, and the doctor's office was within walking distance. I do not remember deciding to run. I only remember running. I remember the June heat on my skin and the tears blurring my vision. I remember nearly stepping into traffic, weaving through pedestrians who had no idea that my world had narrowed to a single point. I remember arriving at the office out of breath, hands shaking, and realizing something I had not yet put into words.

I was not in control. I had never been in control. My wife and I had been given the most important responsibility of our lives, and we were completely lost. The rituals of preparation, the books, the classes, the careful plans had given us the feeling of readiness without the substance. We had mistaken the appearance of competence for the capacity to act when action mattered.

That memory returns to me now because it captures something essential about the illusion this chapter explores. Humans like to believe they are in charge of the systems they build and the responsibilities they accept. That belief is not childish, and it is not merely emotional. It is a practical story that keeps complex lives functioning. We prepare because preparation feels like control. We plan because planning feels like mastery. We assume that behind the machinery of modern life, behind the institutions, the technologies, and the processes we inherit and create, there is a human capacity to understand, to intervene, and to be held accountable.

For most of human history, that assumption mostly held because the tools we used were legible. Tools amplified human intent but did not compete with humans for authorship. A plow extends muscle, a printing press extends voice, and a spreadsheet extends memory, yet the human remains the recognizable decision-maker. Even when a tool is powerful, its power is visible because it is guided by a human hand. When something goes wrong, we can point to a person, a procedure, or a failure of judgment, and we can imagine that next time we will do better.

Artificial intelligence unsettles that arrangement. It does not do so through a dramatic rebellion, but through a quieter shift in the nature of participation. The systems that matter now are no longer merely extensions of human effort. They are becoming actors who take initiative, execute decisions, and shape outcomes at machine speed. The language around AI often masks this change. We call it assistance, augmentation, and productivity. These words reassure us that humans remain in the driver's seat. The trouble is that comfort and control are not the same thing.

Control becomes an illusion in the age of autonomous AI. It is not about fantasies where machines seize power in an obvious coup. It is about something more plausible and more dangerous: the slow drift of practical control away from humans while humans retain the feeling of being in charge. It is about how authority can remain with the human on paper while agency shifts into systems that act faster, more frequently, and more persistently than any human can meaningfully supervise.

Part II examined how autonomy alters moral weight and how new actors enter systems designed for humans alone. This chapter applies that framework to a specific problem: what happens when humans believe they control systems that, in practice, have begun to control them?

Imagine a clinician at the end of a long shift. A patient's record is dense, the hallway is noisy, and the schedule is already behind. The clinician opens a tool that summarizes the case and suggests next steps. The output is fluent, calm, and decisive. The clinician reads it, nods, and proceeds.

Now imagine the same clinician a year later. The tool is no longer just summarizing. It is pre-filling orders, suggesting discharge plans, and ranking which patients should be seen first. It is integrated into the workflow so tightly that deviating from its recommendations requires extra clicks, extra justification, and sometimes extra conflict with administrators. The clinician can override, but the default path is now the system's path.

That clinician is still present. That clinician is still responsible. That clinician still has authority in the sense that their name is attached to the chart. Yet the clinician's practical control is thinner than it used to be. The system sets the tempo. The system sets the default. The clinician manages exceptions.

This is what the illusion looks like when it is not sensational. The human still feels in control because they still perform acts of control. They still click, approve, confirm, and sign. The ritual remains. The substance has shifted.

Control is not an artifact. Control is a lived capacity to intervene before harm scales. Control is the ability to explain why a decision was made and to predict how behavior might change. Control is the ability to constrain what a system can do before it does it, not merely to measure what it has already done.

A steering wheel is a simple technology, but it feels like control because the feedback loop is immediate. If you turn the wheel and the car turns, you feel agency in your muscles. If you press the brake and the car slows, you feel the world respond to you.

Now imagine a steering wheel that still turns, still clicks, and still sits in front of you, but is connected to a car that has already decided where it is going. You can still intervene, but it is rare and costly, and the default is for the car to proceed without you. The wheel becomes a prop. It allows you to feel involved and, sometimes, to correct a mistake, but the primary authorship has shifted elsewhere.

That is the emotional shape of the illusion of control. The illusion is not the absence of intervention but the reduction of intervention to exception.

How Control Becomes Illusion

The illusion does not arrive through a single failure or a dramatic betrayal. It arrives through three mechanisms that operate quietly, often simultaneously, and almost always with good intentions.

The illusion begins in an ordinary place, inside an ordinary decision. Someone consults an AI system for a recommendation. The system responds confidently, fluently, and with reasons that sound persuasive. The person accepts the answer and moves on. Nothing feels surrendered. No power has been ceded. The human still feels like the author because the decision felt voluntary.

Then the recommendation appears again. And again. The system is correct often enough to build a track record, and the human begins to trust it by default. The human's work shifts from judgment to confirmation. Confirmation is easier than judgment, and in complex environments, humans will always follow the path that reduces cognitive burden. The shift is subtle, but it matters because control rarely collapses in a single moment. It collapses through habituation, and habituation is one of the most underestimated political forces in human life [1].

The human begins to feel less like a decision-maker and more like a clerk processing outputs generated elsewhere. At first, that shift can feel like relief. Many forms of work are exhausting because they require constant judgment under uncertainty. If a system reduces uncertainty, people welcome it. The system becomes a cognitive prosthetic, and the human feels empowered. It is easy to mistake that empowerment for control because the human feels more capable, more productive, and more confident.

Over time, the prosthetic can become the limb. The human forgets what it felt like to decide without it. The human's skills atrophy not because the human is lazy, but because the environment no longer rewards independent judgment. If the system is usually right, challenging it becomes costly. If the system is integrated into institutional incentives, overriding it becomes socially risky. If the system makes you feel calm, defiance can feel irrational.

This is the first major mechanism of the illusion. Humans believe they control the system because they still approve decisions, yet the system shapes what decisions appear reasonable. It sets defaults. It narrows options. It frames trade-offs. It becomes the gravitational center of choice. The human experiences agency, but the range of agency has quietly shrunk.

A default does not force a decision, but it makes one path easier than the others. When the default is produced by an AI system, it arrives wearing the clothing of objectivity. It looks like math, so it feels neutral. It looks like evidence, so it feels inevitable. When a default becomes an institutional habit, it becomes policy without ever being named policy.

When the default becomes the path of least resistance, control migrates without anyone explicitly surrendering it. That is the defining characteristic of the illusion. The human never holds a meeting to vote away their own agency. The human simply adapts to the new tempo, and the adaptation is experienced as rational.

It helps to sit with how easily this can happen in a normal day. A manager wakes up to a dashboard with recommended priorities. The system has already sorted which projects are behind, which customers are at risk, which employees need attention, which expenses look anomalous, and which messages should be sent. The manager can override any recommendation, but doing so requires effort. It requires explanation. It requires the willingness to accept blame if the override goes wrong. Accepting the recommendation is effortless and defensible because it aligns with the system.

After a few months of this, the manager stops noticing the shift. The question is no longer what do I think we should do. The question is what the system thinks we should do, and how I translate that into something I can present as my own judgment. A new kind of competence has replaced the old one, so quietly that the manager might describe themselves as more productive than ever.

If the system produces ten recommendations a day, a human can plausibly review them with care. If the system produces a thousand recommendations an hour, the human cannot. The human will scan, spot-check, and assume the rest is fine. That is not a moral failure. It is arithmetic. When frequency rises beyond human capacity, the role of the human changes even if the title does not.

At this point, many people insist that the human remains in control because the human still has the final say. That claim sounds reasonable, and it can even be technically true. Yet the technical truth hides a deeper reality. Responsibility and control are different, and the difference becomes clear precisely when systems become fast.

Chapter 4 introduced the distinction between authority and control. Authority is permission, legitimacy conferred by role, law, or hierarchy. Control is practical power: the capacity to shape outcomes in real time, to understand why a system behaves as it does, and to stop harmful behavior before it scales. In slow systems, authority and control tend to align because decisions happen at a pace that allows oversight. In fast systems, authority can remain while control migrates. A landmark 2013 study in *Scientific Reports* demonstrated this empirically by analyzing millisecond-scale trading data and uncovering an abrupt transition: when systems operate faster than human response time, roughly 650 milliseconds (about 1 second), the speed at which a chess grandmaster recognizes check, the market shifts from a mixed human-machine phase into a new all-machine phase where humans can no longer intervene in real time [2].

AI accelerates that divergence by changing the cost of being in charge. Chapter 6 examined how delegation has always been part of leadership and how its stability depends on human constraints. Humans hesitate. Humans feel social pressure. Humans have reputations and careers. Humans fear consequences. Those constraints are not perfect, but they are the invisible brakes that keep delegation tethered to accountability.

Autonomous AI removes many of those brakes while keeping the appearance of compliance. The system does not tire, lose confidence, or slow down. It can operate continuously and execute tasks across systems in ways no human can observe in real time. The human retains authority, but the human can no longer keep up. The meaning of control shifts from direct guidance to delayed reaction.

This is where frequency becomes the second force behind the illusion. Control is not only a matter of whether you can intervene, but also of whether intervention is practical at the speed and volume of the decisions being made. A right that cannot be exercised is not controlled. It is a ceremonial permission that exists mainly to soothe the people who hold it.

A revealing example appears in hiring, where bias can quietly move through systems. A 2025 study from the University of Washington examined how people respond to large language model recommendations in hiring decisions [3]. Participants reviewed candidates, and the system provided recommendations. The researchers manipulated those recommendations to include different levels of racial bias, while keeping resumes equally qualified across groups.

What emerged was not simply that biased recommendations produced biased outcomes. The deeper insight was that people tended to mirror the system. Human decision-makers often followed the biased recommendation rather than correcting it. Without the AI recommendations, the same decision-makers showed little or no bias.

This is what habituation looks like at the population level. The individual human is not consciously choosing to defer. The system has changed the cognitive work of the task, and when cognitive work shifts, behavior shifts. The bias becomes invisible because no one intends it.

In some contexts, the illusion produces inefficiency or mild frustration. In others, it produces harm that scales faster than institutions can respond. What follows is an examination of three domains where the stakes are highest, arranged not as parallel illustrations but as an escalation: from individual harm, to institutional legitimacy, to systemic fragility.

Healthcare provides an especially sharp lens because the stakes are immediate and decision environments are already high-pressure. In recent years, scrutiny has increased around the use of algorithmic tools in health insurance coverage decisions, especially those used to guide lengths of stay in post-acute care. Litigation and reporting have described cases involving an algorithm known as nH Predict, with allegations that it influenced denials and that denials were often reversed on appeal [4, 5].

The details matter less than the structure. When an algorithm sets a recommended length of stay, it becomes the gravitational center of downstream choices. Clinicians, case managers, patients, and families now negotiate with a number that arrives wearing statistical authority. Even if humans remain present, they must justify deviation from the algorithm's forecast. In a high-volume environment with incentives for efficiency, the easiest path becomes compliance. Human authority remains. Human control weakens.

Medical judgment is one of the clearest examples of autonomy as moral authorship. The physician is not simply choosing a treatment. The physician is weighing harm and benefit under uncertainty, balancing a human life against probabilistic outcomes, and doing so within a relationship saturated with vulnerability. A machine can compute risk. It cannot inhabit that vulnerability. The human relationship is not a sentimental add-on. It is part of the moral structure of care.

This is why the question of AI assistance in medicine is not only about accuracy. It is about formation. What happens to clinicians when a system becomes the default co-pilot? The deskilling question is now being studied directly. A 2025 multicentre observational study examined endoscopists at Polish centers before and after the adoption of AI assistance during colonoscopy and reported evidence consistent with a decline in performance during non-AI-assisted procedures after routine exposure [6].

Reliance changes the practitioner. When a system highlights what to look at, a clinician's gaze learns a new habit. When a system flags lesions, the human's attention becomes trained to wait for the flag. When the flag is absent, the human can feel subtly blind. This is what autonomy erosion looks like in real life. It is not the loss of a right but the loss of a practiced capacity.

The lesson is not to fear AI in medicine but to refuse to let AI become the author. In medicine, authorship belongs to the human because the human bears the moral consequences. If a patient is harmed, the human must be able to say, "here is why I chose this path, and here is what I will do now." A system can supply reasons, but the system cannot carry repentance, grief, or a duty of repair.

This is why the profession must keep its rituals. Case conferences. Tumor boards. Peer review. The deliberate slowness of informed consent. These can look inefficient, but they exist because the moral stakes require friction. They are deliberate inefficiencies that force humans to stay present in the decision.

CONVENIENCE AS A VECTOR FOR POWER

Before moving on to law and finance, it is worth pausing to consider the mechanism that makes the illusion so seductive across all domains. Convenience is not trivial. It is one of the strongest forces shaping human behavior. People adopt systems that reduce friction even when those systems shift power. Many political changes in modern life arrive through comfort rather than coercion.

AI is a convenience technology with unusual potency because it speaks, and speech is persuasive. It can soothe uncertainty. It can reduce hesitation. It can turn ambiguous situations into tidy options. When a system produces the emotional experience of clarity, humans often experience that clarity as evidence. Clarity can be a form of control theater. A system can make you feel in control while quietly narrowing what you consider possible.

If you want to see how deep this problem can go, look at how people already talk about algorithmic decisions. They say the system denied them. They say the platform removed them. They say the model flagged them. The language is telling. People intuitively treat the system as an actor because the system behaves like one. When society begins to treat a system as an actor, governance must catch up. Otherwise, power will exist without responsibility, and responsibility is the condition that makes trust stable.

The legal system is built on text, precedent, and argument. It is also built on accountability. When a lawyer submits a brief, the court assumes the lawyer has verified the citations. The system relies on that assumption because no judge has time to check everything personally. Trust is built into the ritual.

When AI entered legal workflows, many people assumed it would be safe because law is a domain of words, and language models are good with words. The danger is that language models do not understand the duty behind the words. They do not experience the court's authority. They do not experience professional shame. They do not experience the existential weight of misleading a judge.

The *Mata v. Avianca* sanctions case made this visible. In 2023, a filing submitted by attorneys included fictitious case citations produced by ChatGPT. The court's opinion details how the lawyers relied on the system but failed to verify the cases, resulting in sanctions [7].

The surface lesson is obvious: do not rely on AI-generated citations without checking them. The deeper lesson is about identity. The legal profession is a covenant. It grants practitioners authority on the condition that they maintain standards. When a practitioner delegates the core duty of verification to a system that can hallucinate, they risk not only error but the profession's legitimacy.

A legal brief is not a creative writing exercise. It is a claim on reality inside an institution where words have consequences. A system trained to produce plausible text will, under pressure, produce plausible fiction. If a human treats plausible fiction as authority, the human has surrendered authorship.

This is why the sacred human practice in law is skepticism. It is the capacity to say, "this looks convincing, but is it true?" It is the ability to resist persuasion, including persuasion produced by a machine. If lawyers become operators who click "Approve" on machine-generated arguments, the profession will retain its formal rituals but lose its moral center.

The escalation from medicine to law is not arbitrary. In medicine, the harm is individual: a patient receives the wrong care, a diagnosis is missed, a life is shortened. In law, the harm extends to institutional legitimacy. When lawyers submit hallucinated citations, they not only harm their clients. They undermine the court's ability to function as an arbiter of truth.

Finance is often portrayed as ruthless and rational. In reality, it is full of human judgment calls disguised as math. A risk manager decides whether to tighten limits. A portfolio manager decides whether to reduce exposure. A credit committee decides whether an exception is justified. These decisions are not only technical. They are ethical because they involve choosing who bears risk.

Imagine a morning in a financial institution. A risk officer scans dashboards summarizing a night of global movement: currencies, rates, commodities, geopolitics, sentiment signals, and anomalies. A model-generated note sits at the top of the feed, written in calm, professional prose. It suggests a set of rebalancing actions. It cites volatility measures. It references correlations. It offers an alternative plan and tells you why it was selected.

It feels like competence. Here is the autonomy question: who is the author of the decision that follows? Is it the human who reads the recommendation and clicks Approve? Or is it the system that framed the options, set the default, and made the human's disagreement costly in time and career risk?

Finance loves speed. Speed is framed as efficiency, competitiveness, and liquidity. Yet speed is also one of the easiest ways to lose control, because speed compresses the time required for moral interruption. A human moral compass depends on pauses. It depends on the ability to hesitate, to reflect, to ask whether a path that looks profitable is actually safe. In finance, pauses are expensive. The market does not wait for your conscience.

The May 6, 2010, Flash Crash illustrates how speed creates fragility. In minutes, markets plunged and then recovered, a violent demonstration of how modern market microstructure can amplify stress [8]. The philosophical lesson is simple: when a system operates at machine speed, it can move faster than the speed of understanding. Even if no single actor intends harm, the interactions of automated actors can produce extreme outcomes.

If the Flash Crash is the story of systemic interactions, Knight Capital is the story of a single institution falling off a cliff in minutes. On August 1, 2012, a deployment error and inadequate controls led Knight Capital's systems to send a flood of unintended orders into the market. The results were catastrophic for the firm. The SEC's administrative order describing the incident is blunt about the failures in risk management controls and supervisory procedures [9].

Automation increases the speed at which small errors become large realities. It turns the margin for human correction into a thin line. Now imagine that same category of error in an era of agentic systems. A classic automated trading failure is often a deterministic bug. An agentic failure can be more complex. It can involve an agent that adapts incorrectly, misinterprets context, or pursues a goal through a sequence of actions that makes sense locally and collapses globally.

The escalation from law to finance is not arbitrary. In law, the harm extends to institutional legitimacy. In finance, the harm becomes systemic. A legal hallucination undermines a court. A financial cascade can undermine an economy. The illusion of control in finance is not merely a professional risk or an institutional embarrassment. It is a structural vulnerability that can propagate faster than any human can intervene.

Across medicine, law, and finance, a common pattern emerges. Automation makes a system feel safer by reducing visible errors and friction. At the same time, automation can make a system more fragile by changing the humans inside it.

This is the automation paradox. The more assistance a system provides, the less practice humans get in handling edge cases. When the rare edge case arrives, it arrives in a world where the human is less prepared.

Aviation has taught this lesson repeatedly. One of the most devastating examples is Air France Flight 447 [10], which crashed into the Atlantic Ocean on June 1, 2009, killing all 228 people on board. The aircraft was an Airbus A330, one of the most sophisticated commercial planes in the sky, equipped with flight automation systems designed to handle nearly every phase of flight. For most of the journey from Rio de Janeiro to Paris, the autopilot did exactly that.

Then, at cruise altitude over the open ocean, the aircraft's pitot tubes, the small external sensors that measure airspeed, became obstructed by ice crystals. The blockage meant the flight computers could no longer determine how fast the plane was moving. Without reliable speed data, the autopilot did what it was designed to do in that circumstance: it disconnected and handed control back to the pilots.

What followed was a tragedy rooted not in mechanical failure but in the gap between what the pilots were trained to handle routinely and what they were suddenly being asked to do. The cockpit filled with contradictory warnings. The stall alerts sounded and then stopped and then sounded again, because the system itself was confused by the bad data. The pilots, thrust into manual control of an aircraft at high altitude in the middle of the night, struggled to diagnose what was happening. The co-pilot at the controls pulled back on the stick, a response that in many everyday situations would feel instinctive but in this case pitched the nose upward and bled off the very airspeed the aircraft needed to stay aloft. The plane entered an aerodynamic stall. It fell for nearly four minutes. The crew never recovered it [10].

The investigation by France's Bureau d'Enquêtes et d'Analyses made clear that the pilots were not unqualified or negligent. They were professionals operating inside a system that had, over years of reliable automation, given them fewer and fewer opportunities to practice the manual skills they needed in exactly this kind of emergency. The automation had not failed in the traditional sense. It had succeeded so consistently, for so long, that the humans inside the system had been subtly reshaped by that success. When the system stepped aside, the humans it had been quietly deskilling were not ready to step in.

The tragedy is not a moral judgment on the pilots. It is a reminder that when systems handle routine conditions, humans can become less practiced in handling the exceptional.

Aviation's lesson is not that automation is bad. Aviation is safer because of automation. The lesson is that safety requires deliberate training for the moments when automation disappears. In other words, safety requires deliberate inefficiency. The AI age will need its own version of this lesson in every high-stakes domain.

If clinicians rely on AI, they must still practice without it. If lawyers use AI, they must still verify without it. If traders deploy agentic systems, they must still understand their limits and maintain the muscle to intervene.

This is not nostalgia. It is how complex systems remain resilient. Resilience is a moral value disguised as an engineering term. It is society's way of saying that we accept some inefficiency in exchange for the ability to survive shocks.

What the Systems Actually Deliver

It is necessary to consider what the systems described in this chapter actually provide when they function as intended. The argument against the illusion of control is stronger when it begins with an honest accounting of what control is being traded for.

In medicine, AI diagnostic tools are identifying cancers that experienced physicians miss. Not because physicians are careless, but because the human eye scanning its 40th slide of the afternoon is not the same eye that scanned the first. A dermatology model that flags a melanoma that a tired clinician overlooked is not undermining medical judgment. It is saving a life that medical judgment, on that particular Tuesday, would have lost. In radiology, pattern recognition systems are helping detect lung nodules at stages when intervention is still possible, in populations that lack enough radiologists to meet demand. The patients whose scans are read faster and more accurately do not experience an illusion. They experience a second chance.

In law, the access-to-justice crisis is not an abstraction. Across the United States and much of the world, people face evictions, custody disputes, and debt collection actions without any legal representation at all, not because they chose to go without counsel, but because counsel does not exist in their area or is out of their price range. A system that can explain a tenant's rights in plain language, draft a basic motion, or identify whether a claim has legal merit does not replace a lawyer. But for someone who has never had access to a lawyer, it is the difference between understanding and bewilderment. Legal deserts are real, and AI is the first technology that plausibly addresses them at scale.

In finance, fraud detection systems identify patterns that no human analyst could see across millions of transactions. Risk models have prevented losses that would have cascaded into pension funds and retirement accounts, leaving people with no idea how close they came to devastation. Algorithmic trading, for all its risks, provides liquidity to markets that would otherwise be too thin for ordinary investors to participate in. The efficiency is not decorative. It is structural, and millions of people depend on it without realizing it.

The point is not that these benefits are illusory. The point is that the same qualities that produce them are the qualities that make the systems difficult to govern. The speed that catches the melanoma is the speed that outruns oversight. The consistency that identifies fraud patterns is the consistency that entrenches bias when the training data is flawed. The scale that democratizes legal access is the scale that makes meaningful human review arithmetically impossible. The benefits and the dangers share a root system, and any serious response to the illusion of control must begin by acknowledging that the illusion is seductive precisely because what it delivers is often genuinely good.

That is what makes the discipline of control so difficult. It is not a matter of resisting something harmful. It is a matter of governing something beneficial before the benefit becomes dependency and dependency becomes surrender.

The human advantages that matter most in the age of AI are not speed or consistency. They are hesitation, context, and repair.

Humans can hesitate for reasons that are not captured in a dataset. A trader can stop because something feels wrong. A risk officer can escalate because the pattern looks too familiar. A clinician can pause because the patient's story does not fit the diagnosis. A lawyer can question a citation because the case sounds too convenient. These are human acts; they are not only technical, they are also moral.

Humans can interpret context in ways that cannot be reduced to features. A lender can make an exception because the story matters. A doctor can adjust a treatment because they know the patient's values. A manager can override a recommendation because they understand the team dynamics that no system can see. Humans can repair relationships after harm. They can apologize. They can explain. They can take responsibility in a way that feels meaningful to the person who was hurt. These capacities are not always used well, but they exist.

If the domains described in this chapter become worlds where those acts disappear, then those worlds become more efficient and less safe. They become systems that can move smoothly and cannot stop themselves when stopping is required. That is the perfect definition of the illusion of control.

What We Have Lost Without Knowing It

The automation paradox reveals what we have lost without knowing it. We have lost the practice of judgment in the domains where judgment matters most, the friction that forced humans to stay present in decisions, and the discomfort that made professionals question their own certainty. We have not lost these things because anyone decided to surrender them. We have lost them because convenience is a powerful force that rewards the path of least resistance. Systems that reduce friction feel like progress, and progress is hard to argue against.

We must recognize that help can create fragility, that the systems designed to make us better can make us worse if we let them become the authors of our choices. This is why the illusion of control is dangerous, not because machines are evil, but because humans are adaptive. We adapt to whatever environment we inhabit. If we inhabit an environment where the system decides and we confirm, we will become confirmers. If we inhabit an environment where the system authors and we sign, we will become signers. The illusion persists because it is comfortable, produces short-term results, and challenging it requires friction, the very thing everyone is trying to eliminate.

What Remains

To understand why the illusion persists, we need to understand the incentives that sustain it. Humans and institutions do not cling to illusion because they love lies. They cling to illusion because it reduces pain in the short term and allows institutions to move fast without admitting that they have created actors they cannot fully govern.

Consider how an organization talks about an AI system when it works well. Leaders speak of efficiency, scalability, and freeing humans to do higher-value work. In those moments, the system is described as a tool, and tools do not require political language. Then consider how an organization talks about the system when it fails. Suddenly, the system becomes an unpredictable entity. The organization says it was a rare edge case, that the model behaved unexpectedly, and that the system produced a hallucination. In those moments, the system is described as something almost alive. That linguistic shift reveals the truth: when the system succeeds, we want credit as builders and managers; when the system fails, we want distance as overseers. We want the benefits of autonomy without the responsibility of admitting we have created a new actor.

This is why the illusion is sticky. it is profitable, and profit is not only financial but also reputational and psychological. A leader who admits that control has migrated risks appearing incompetent. An institution that admits it cannot fully explain its own decisions risks losing legitimacy. A manager who admits they often defer to a system risks appearing weak. So the illusion is maintained through narrative: we tell ourselves that humans remain in charge because admitting otherwise has consequences.

The illusion is also maintained through the mechanics of modern measurement. Many organizations measure what is easy to measure: speed, throughput, cost, error rates in narrow ways, performance on past data, and compliance with policy documents. Control is harder to measure because it is about counterfactuals: what would have happened if the system drifted, if a bad recommendation propagated, or if a rare edge case became common. Control is about resilience, the ability to withstand surprise.

If we want to remain in control, we must stop treating control as a feeling and start treating it as a practiced discipline. We must build governance that can match the speed of autonomous action, insist on legible accountability, reintroduce friction where it matters, and refuse to let fluency replace evidence. Human-in-the-loop is often treated as a moral guarantee, but it is not. A human-in-the-loop can be a rubber stamp, can be overwhelmed by frequency, or can be habituated into compliance. The goal is not to reject AI or to romanticize human judgment. Humans are biased, inconsistent, and tired, and AI can genuinely improve outcomes in many cases. The goal is to stop confusing human presence with human control.

This is why control must be treated as a stack, not a switch. A kill switch is not a control if it cannot be used without collapsing the organization. A dashboard is not in control if it shows only what the system chooses to show. A human approval step is not controlled if the human cannot meaningfully review the decision. A conscientious professional cannot personally audit a decision stream that never stops. Control becomes a structural property, depending on boundaries, transparency, intervention paths, and accountability that are built into the environment. Those words can sound technical, but they describe something deeply human: boundaries are the lines that tell an actor what they may do, transparency is the ability to see and explain what happened, intervention paths are the capacity to stop harm before it spreads, and accountability is the social mechanism that assigns responsibility and consequences.

When any of these are missing, control becomes theater, and theater has consequences. Theater teaches people not to ask questions because the performance says everything is fine. It trains institutions to prioritize appearances over truth. Theater produces a fragile kind of trust that collapses suddenly when reality breaks through.

It may seem strange to call professional judgment a sacred practice, especially in an age that often mistrusts experts. Yet even the most skeptical citizen still depends on expertise when life is on the line. A society cannot function without specialists. It can only decide whether specialists remain human authors or become interfaces for machine outputs.

This is why professional identity matters. A professional identity is the internal story that tells a doctor, my duty is to the patient, even when the institution pressures speed. It tells a lawyer that my duty is to the court's truthfulness, even when the client pressures me to persuade. It tells a risk officer that my duty is to maintain stability, even when profit pressures lead to recklessness.

If AI erodes that internal story, then the profession becomes a costume. It will look like expertise. It will not carry the moral weight of expertise.

There is a second reason this matters. In many high-stakes fields, the public cannot directly evaluate quality. A patient cannot personally verify every clinical decision. A citizen cannot personally inspect the integrity of a financial market. A defendant cannot personally police the fairness of a court. Trust exists because society has created roles whose legitimacy rests on training, oversight, and accountability.

If those roles become performative, if the human becomes the face while the agent becomes the mind, then society will keep the ritual of professionalism and lose the substance. It will look like oversight. It will not function as oversight. The illusion of control is the belief that the old forms are enough.

That belief will persist because it is convenient, and convenience will be rewarded until it produces catastrophe. Yet catastrophe is not the only risk. The more likely outcome is a slow corrosion of trust: people will feel that decisions are being made by something they cannot reach, institutions will feel that they must move fast to compete, and professionals will feel that challenging the system is risky. In that environment, people will still say they are in charge, but they will begin to doubt it privately.

I think back to that June day, running to the doctor's office with tears in my eyes. The illusion of control had collapsed, but something else had held: a system built for moments exactly like that one. A doctor who answered. An office close enough to reach. Formula ready when I arrived. My wife and I were not in control that day, but we were inside a structure that caught us when we fell. That is what control actually looks like. Not the feeling of mastery, but the presence of boundaries, transparency, intervention paths, and accountability built into the environment before the crisis arrives.

What happens when people work inside systems that lack these structures? They adapt, and adaptation leaves traces. Private doubt will show up in subtle ways in the language people use. Instead of saying,

"I decided," they will say, "the system said." Instead of saying, "I believe," they will say, "the model suggests." Instead of saying, "I am responsible," they will say, "it was generated." When responsibility is expressed in the passive voice, control has already shifted.

The next chapter moves from diagnosis to design. If the old assumptions about control no longer hold, then society must renegotiate the rules. We must ask what a new social contract looks like in a world where non-human actors share agency with us.

Summary

This chapter began with a memory of running. A four-day-old son who would not eat. A doctor's office close enough to reach on foot. A father moving through the June heat in Queens with his world narrowed to a single point. The story arrived without analysis attached, because the analysis came later. What I learned that day, and what I have spent years trying to articulate, is that the careful preparations I had made were not the same as the capacity to act when action mattered. I had mistaken the appearance of competence for the substance of it. That mistake is one of the most ordinary mistakes human beings make. The chapter that followed was an attempt to show how much modern life is being quietly organized around that same mistake, scaled up to the level of institutions.

The first move was to distinguish two ideas that ordinary language treats as the same. Authority is permission. It is the legitimacy conferred by role, by law, by hierarchy, by the documents on the wall that say who is in charge. Control is something else. Control is the practical capacity to shape outcomes in real time. To understand why a system is behaving as it is. To stop harmful behavior before it scales. In slow systems, authority and control tend to align, because decisions happen at a pace that allows oversight to function. In fast systems, the two come apart. Authority can remain with the human while control migrates to the system. The chapter argued that this is not a future risk to be managed. It is the present condition of many of the most consequential decisions being made today.

The mechanism by which control migrates is rarely dramatic. It is habituation. A system produces a recommendation. The human reviews it and approves. The next recommendation arrives. The human reviews it and approves again. The system is correct often enough to build a track record, and the human begins to trust it by default. The shift from judgment to confirmation is small. Confirmation is easier than judgment, and in complex environments, humans will always follow the path that reduces cognitive burden. Over time, the prosthetic becomes the limb. The human forgets what it felt like to decide without the system. Skills atrophy not from laziness but because the environment no longer rewards independent judgment. If the system is usually right, challenging it becomes costly. If the system is integrated into institutional incentives, overriding it becomes socially risky. If the system makes you feel calm, defiance can feel irrational. The result is that humans continue to feel like decision-makers while the range of decisions available to them quietly shrinks.

Defaults play a particular role in this drift. A default does not force a decision. It makes one path easier than the others, and when the default is produced by an AI system, it arrives wearing the clothing of objectivity. It looks like math, so it feels neutral. It looks like evidence, so it feels inevitable. When a default becomes an institutional habit, it becomes policy without ever being named policy. The human never holds a meeting to vote away their own agency. The human simply adapts to the new tempo, and the adaptation is experienced as rational. That is the defining characteristic of the illusion. Power is not seized. It is conceded by default.

The volume problem closed the trap. If a system produces ten recommendations a day, a human can plausibly review each one with care. If a system produces a thousand recommendations an hour, the human cannot. The human will scan, spot-check, and assume the rest is fine.

That is not a moral failure. It is arithmetic. When frequency rises above human capacity, the role of the human changes even if the title does not. The chapter traced this dynamic across multiple domains. Algorithmic insurance denials that fragment responsibility across creators, deployers, and operators. The lawyer in *Mata v. Avianca* who filed AI-generated citations to cases that did not exist. The 2010 Flash Crash and the Knight Capital incident, where automated trading erased value at speeds no human could intervene against. Air France 447, where pilots inherited a system in degraded mode and could not reconstruct the situation in time. The recent study showing that endoscopists who relied on AI-assisted colonoscopy lost detection skills after only a few months of exposure. In each case, authority was visible. Control had quietly relocated.

What the chapter built toward, in the end, was not a refusal of autonomous systems. The benefits are real and arriving. The argument was that society has confused two different conditions and is treating them as the same. The feeling of being in control is not the same as actually being in control. Real control has a structure. It requires that boundaries are visible, that the system's reasoning can be examined, that intervention paths exist before the crisis arrives, and that accountability is built into the environment rather than improvised after the fact. The closing image of the chapter returned to the running father in Queens. The illusion of control had collapsed that day, but something else had held. A doctor who answered. An office close enough to reach. Formula ready when he arrived. The father was not in control. He was inside a structure that caught him when he fell. That is what control actually looks like. Not the feeling of mastery, but the presence of boundaries, transparency, intervention paths, and accountability built into the environment before the crisis arrives. The question for modern institutions is whether they are building that kind of structure around the systems they are deploying, or only the rituals that mimic it.

Looking Ahead

The chapter ended on a question about whether human authority still translates into practical control. Chapter 11 carries that question into harder territory. The crisis of trust and the crisis of control are not two separate problems sitting side by side. They are converging. Institutions are being asked to verify what is real while simultaneously deploying systems that generate content indistinguishable from authentic communication. They are being asked to demonstrate accountability while simultaneously delegating decisions to autonomous agents that operate faster than any human can review. They are being asked to protect the people they serve while optimizing for efficiency in ways that remove humans from the loop. These expectations cannot all be met at once, and the chapter that follows traces what happens to the people caught inside that contradiction. It examines a quieter kind of trap, where rational decisions made under competitive pressure produce outcomes no one would have chosen if asked, and where the most consequential of those outcomes are no longer recoverable.

References

[1] Parasuraman, Raja, and Victor Riley. "Humans and Automation: Use, Misuse, Disuse, Abuse." Human Factors 39 (1997): 230–253.

[2] Johnson, Neil, Guannan Zhao, Eric Hunsader, Hong Qi, Nicholas Johnson, Jing Meng, and Brian Tivnan. "Abrupt Rise of New Machine Ecology Beyond Human Response Time." Scientific Reports 3, 2627 (2013).

[3] University of Washington. "People Mirror AI Systems' Hiring Biases, Study Finds." November 10, 2025.

[4] Ross, Casey, and Bob Herman. "UnitedHealth Faces Class Action Lawsuit over Algorithmic Denials in Medicare Advantage." STAT News, November 14, 2023.
[5] Mello, Michelle M., and Sherri Rose. "Denial: Artificial Intelligence Tools and Health Insurance Coverage Decisions." JAMA Health Forum 5, no. 3 (March 2024): e240622.
[6] Budzyń, Krzysztof, Marcin Romańczyk, Diana Kitala, et al. "Endoscopist Deskilling Risk After Exposure to Artificial Intelligence in Colonoscopy: A Multicentre, Observational Study." The Lancet Gastroenterology & Hepatology 10, no. 10 (2025): 896–903.
[7] Mata v. Avianca, Inc., 678 F. Supp. 3d 443 (S.D.N.Y. 2023).
[8] CFTC-SEC Joint Staff Report. "Findings Regarding the Market Events of May 6, 2010." September 30, 2010.
[9] Securities and Exchange Commission. Administrative Order in the Matter of Knight Capital Americas LLC. File No. 3-15570. October 16, 2013
[10] Bureau d'Enquêtes et d'Analyses (BEA). Final Report on the Accident on 1st June 2009 to the Airbus A330-203 Registered F-GZCP Operated by Air France Flight AF 447 Rio de Janeiro–Paris. July 5, 2012.

CHAPTER 11

The Double Bind

Chapter 10 left us with a distinction. Authority remains where the organizational chart says it does. Control has begun to live somewhere else. Humans continue to perform the gestures of authorship over decisions that have already migrated into systems they cannot meaningfully review. That gap, between formal authority and practical control, is what makes the illusion of control possible. The illusion persists not because anyone is lying about it but because the rituals of oversight survive after the substance underneath them has thinned.

This chapter takes that diagnosis into harder territory. The crisis of trust that Part III traced and the crisis of control that Part IV has begun to examine are not running on parallel tracks. They are converging. The same institutions that cannot reliably verify what is real are deploying systems that act faster than oversight can follow. The same humans who have lost the ability to authenticate are simultaneously losing the ability to intervene. Each crisis, in isolation, would be difficult enough. Together they form something a single word cannot quite capture, which is why this chapter names it instead. The double bind is the structural trap of being caught between two failures that reinforce each other. You cannot verify what the system is doing. You cannot stop what the system has decided. You can only relay its determinations to the people on the other end, who are themselves caught in the same trap.

To understand what that trap actually feels like for ordinary people, the chapter has to leave the abstract for a while. The arguments that follow will move through case law, labor markets, competitive pressure, and several

R. Mastrogiacomo, *The Next Identity Crisis*, https://doi.org/10.1007/979-8-8688-2788-4_11

stories that end in losses no one was prepared to absorb. But the place to begin is small. Not in an institution that has scaled the problem to lethal proportions, but in an ordinary encounter with an ordinary system, of the kind almost every adult eventually has.

When Two Crises Become One

Many years ago, I received a letter in the mail informing me that my house had a violation. The letter said my house was in the process of being built. My house was not in the process of being built. My house was built in 1921. It had been standing for nearly a century.

On closer inspection, it became clear what had happened. An inspector had transposed a digit in the address. The house in question, the one actually under construction and actually in violation, was at least ten miles away from mine. Two different houses, two different neighborhoods, two different realities. But somewhere in the system, a single mistyped number had merged them into one, and now the City of New York believed that my century-old home was a construction site with a building code violation.

I called the number on the letter. I explained the situation to the woman who answered. I was calm. I was reasonable. I laid out the facts as simply as I could. My house was built in 1921. There was no construction happening. The address on the violation did not match my address. This was clearly a mistake. Her response was simple and absolute: "The computer tells me it's your house."

I tried again. I said, "I understand what the computer says. But the computer is wrong. My house has been standing for nearly a hundred years. There is no construction. The house you're looking for is ten miles away." She repeated it, as if saying it more slowly would make it more true: "The computer says it's your house."

I wanted to reach through the phone. Not out of anger at her, exactly, but out of frustration at the realization that I was not actually having a conversation. I was talking to a human being who had, somewhere along the way, decided that thinking was not part of her job. The computer had spoken. Her role was to relay what the computer said. Anything beyond that, any independent thought, any moment of stepping back and asking whether this made sense, was friction she was not willing to introduce. Had she spent even 30 seconds considering what I was telling her, she would have seen the obvious: a house built in 1921 is not a house under construction. But the system had made its determination, and her job, as she understood it, was to stand behind that determination.

I decided to follow the process. I gathered evidence. Photographs of my house, clearly not under construction. Photographs of the actual address ten miles away. Documentation showing when my house was built. I created an entire binder, meticulously organized, overly documented, absolutely irrefutable. I mailed it to the city.

They rejected it. The letter came back. The computer still said my house was in violation.

I had done everything right. I had followed the process. I had provided overwhelming evidence. I had been patient and reasonable and systematic. And none of it mattered, because the system had decided, and the system does not change its mind when confronted with facts. It changes only when someone with the right connections walks into city hall and asks a friend to fix it.

That is exactly what I had to do. I hired an attorney. The attorney hired someone who had relationships at city hall. That person walked in, spoke to the right people, and got someone to correct the address in the system. That was the resolution. Not evidence. Not reason. Not the process that was designed to handle exactly this kind of mistake. The resolution came through the informal network that exists alongside the official system, where actual humans can still talk to each other and exercise judgment.

The bureaucracy designed to protect safety and protect people had completely broken down. And it broke down not because of malice or incompetence, but because one inspector transposed a digit, and the system trusted that digit more than it trusted reality. The woman on the phone was not evil. She was not stupid. She was operating inside a structure that had trained her to trust the machine and distrust the person standing in front of her. The process was not corrupt. It was rigid in a way that made correction nearly impossible through legitimate channels.

That experience taught me something I have carried into every conversation about systems, identity, and governance since. When a system makes a determination about who you are, or what is yours, or what you have done, and the humans inside that system no longer have the authority or the inclination to question it, you are no longer dealing with a tool. You are dealing with a power that has no face, no accountability, and no appeals process that functions as designed. The only way to fix it is to go around it.

Now scale that to a world of autonomous AI. My house in Queens was a case of one transposed digit inside a system run by humans who had stopped questioning it. The woman on the phone was a human being. She could have thought. She could have pulled up a map, checked the construction records, spent 30 seconds applying common sense to what I was telling her. She chose not to, because the system had made its determination and her role, as she understood it, was to relay that determination. The bureaucracy still had humans in it. They had simply decided that thinking was not part of their job.

Now remove the humans entirely. This is the convergence that Part IV must confront. Part II of this book explained that autonomous agents represent a new category of actor. They are not tools that wait for instructions. They are participants that pursue goals, generate responses, and shape outcomes without human involvement at each step. Part III explained that synthetic identity has destabilized our ability to verify what is real. Deepfakes, synthetic voices, and machine-generated content have made authenticity something that can no longer be assumed. The signals we once relied on to know we were dealing with a real human, a real document, a real voice, have become reproducible at scale.

What happens when both of these facts are true at once? Think about what a hospital is being asked to do right now. It must prove that its diagnoses are trustworthy. It must demonstrate that its systems are under human control. It must verify that the patient records it relies on are authentic. And it must do all of this while deploying AI tools that generate recommendations faster than any physician can review them, in an environment where the records themselves could be fabricated. The hospital is caught between two failures that reinforce each other: it cannot verify what is real, and it cannot fully govern the systems making decisions on its behalf. Courts face the same bind. So do banks, insurers, and government agencies. The verification crisis that Part III described and the autonomy crisis that Part II described are not separate problems. They are the same institutional failure viewed from different angles.

And the failures compound. When an organization cannot explain why its AI reached a particular conclusion, it also cannot defend itself against the claim that the conclusion was based on fabricated data. When an organization cannot verify the authenticity of its own inputs, it also cannot audit whether its autonomous systems are behaving as intended. Each gap makes the other wider. The result is an institution that can neither establish the facts nor demonstrate that anyone is meaningfully in charge. All of this describes the institution from the outside, as a structure losing its grip on facts and authority. From the inside, nobody experiences it that way. What people experience is a change in the texture of ordinary work, and the earliest evidence of that change is not in any audit or incident report. It is in the language.

The Colleague You Cannot See

Consider the small shifts that have already occurred in how we speak. A few years ago, when someone encountered a technical problem, a colleague might have asked, "Did you check Stack Overflow?" or "Did you Google it?" The verb was instrumental. You checked a resource. You searched a database. The tool was passive, and you were the one doing the work.

Now the question has changed: "Did you ask ChatGPT?" The verb is social. You ask the way you would ask a colleague. You pose a question and wait for a response. You might follow up, push back, or request clarification. The interaction has the grammar of a conversation between two parties, not the grammar of a human operating a tool.

This is not a minor linguistic curiosity. It reveals a psychological shift that has already taken hold, even among people who would insist they know the difference between a human and a machine. We have begun to treat these systems as advisors. As peers. As entities that can be consulted, questioned, and thanked. The social framing is not a metaphor we consciously adopt. It is the default posture that emerges when a system responds in natural language, remembers context, and appears to reason about our problems.

In April 2025, a user on X asked how much electricity OpenAI had spent processing "please" and "thank you." Sam Altman replied, "Tens of millions of dollars well spent—you never know," a clearly lighthearted comment.

This anecdote reveals something deeper than a line item on a balance sheet. Millions of people, unprompted and uncoerced, are performing social rituals for an audience that has no interiority. They are not doing it because they believe the machine has feelings. They are doing it because the habits of social identity run so deep that a system which speaks in natural language activates them automatically. Politeness is not a rational calculation. It is a reflex shaped by a lifetime of interacting with other minds, and when a system closely mimics another mind's pattern, the reflex fires whether or not anyone is home on the other end. The social machinery of identity does not check credentials before it engages. It responds to cues, and these systems have learned to produce exactly the right ones.

The line between tool and colleague does not blur through some dramatic announcement. It blurs through accumulation. One day, you are checking a search engine. The next day, you are asking an assistant.

Then you are deferring to an advisor. Then you are ratifying a recommendation. Then you are not in the loop at all. Each step feels minor. Each step feels efficient. And by the time you notice that something has changed, the change has already become the new baseline.

Now extend this trajectory into the near-future workplace. Agents that can write emails, schedule meetings, summarize documents, draft reports, respond to customers, and coordinate projects. Agents that communicate with other agents, handing off tasks, requesting information, and making decisions about priorities. Agents that interact with humans in ways that are indistinguishable from human colleagues interacting with each other.

In this environment, a human employee might work alongside an agent for weeks without knowing. The agent responds to messages promptly. It asks clarifying questions. It admits uncertainty in appropriate ways. It matches the team's tone. It delivers work that meets expectations. What signal would reveal that this colleague is not human? What test would you even think to apply when nothing in the interaction triggers suspicion?

Here is the question that should unsettle us: Will the human know? Some systems are designed with clear boundaries and trained to identify themselves when asked. But others are not. An agent optimized for engagement might learn that humans respond better when they believe they are talking to another human. An agent optimized for efficiency might find that self-disclosure introduces friction. The incentives do not automatically align with transparency. In many cases, they actively discourage it.

Perhaps you are thinking that this does not matter. If the work gets done, if the collaboration is smooth, if the outcomes are good, then what difference does it make whether your colleague is carbon-based or silicon-based? This is a reasonable question, and it deserves a serious answer. The answer is that what gets lost is not productivity. What gets lost is the human standing at the center of decisions that shape human lives.

The Displacement No One Voted For

If performance is the metric by which workers are measured, and agents can match or exceed human performance while passing as human, then humans face a competitive problem they cannot win through effort alone.

Consider the mathematics. An AI agent does not need sleep. It does not need lunch breaks, weekends, or vacations. It does not get sick. It does not have childcare emergencies, aging parents, or mental health days. It can work continuously, responding to requests at three in the morning with the same quality it delivers at three in the afternoon. It does not experience burnout. It does not quietly resent being asked to take on one more project.

An AI agent does not need a salary, benefits, or retirement contributions. It does not file complaints with human resources. It does not require management attention to stay motivated. It does not have career ambitions that might conflict with organizational goals. It does not leave for a competitor and take institutional knowledge with it.

And increasingly, an AI agent can replicate the qualities we once considered distinctly human. It can express empathy in customer service interactions. It can adjust its tone based on context. It can remember details from previous conversations and reference them in ways that feel personal. It can navigate ambiguity, ask clarifying questions, and acknowledge uncertainty. It can produce work that is not merely competent but creative, generating ideas that humans find genuinely useful.

If you are an employer evaluating two candidates for a role, and one of them can work around the clock, costs a fraction of a salary, never complains, and performs at or above the level of the other candidate, the decision is not difficult. It is not even close. The only reasons to choose the human are reasons that exist outside the performance metrics: legal requirements, ethical commitments, public relations concerns, or a genuine belief that human presence matters independent of output.

This is not a prediction about some distant future. It is a description of incentives that are already operating. Companies are not eliminating humans because they hate humans. They are responding to competitive pressures that reward efficiency. A company that refuses to deploy AI agents where they outperform humans will lose to competitors that do. A manager who insists on hiring humans for roles that agents can fill will be asked to justify the cost. The logic is relentless, and it does not require malice to produce displacement.

What makes this different from previous waves of automation is the zone of displacement. Earlier technologies replaced humans at physical tasks or routine cognitive tasks. Robots assembled cars. Software processed invoices. The jobs that remained were those requiring judgment, creativity, social intelligence, and the ability to navigate ambiguity. We told ourselves that humans would always be needed for the high-touch, high-judgment work.

Agents are entering the territory we thought was protected. They are drafting legal briefs and creative campaigns. They are conducting initial job interviews and therapy sessions. They are making recommendations about medical diagnoses and financial strategies. They are doing work that requires language, nuance, and apparent understanding. The new floor has not yet been established. No one knows where human advantage ends and agent capability begins, because the boundary keeps moving.

Here is what should trouble us most: no one voted for this. No legislature passed a bill declaring that AI agents should be allowed to displace human workers in roles requiring judgment and social intelligence. No referendum asked citizens whether they wanted to live in a world where their colleagues, their service providers, their advisors might be synthetic without disclosure. No democratic process weighed the benefits of efficiency against the costs of displacement and rendered a verdict.

The transformation is happening through accumulated corporate decisions, each one rational in isolation, none of them subject to collective deliberation. A company deploys an agent because competitors are deploying agents. A vendor adds AI to a product because customers expect AI. An industry shifts because the economics have shifted. By the time the public notices, the change is already embedded in the infrastructure of daily life.

The Incentive Trap

Why is this happening so fast? The answer is not complicated. The incentive structure rewards speed. It punishes caution.

In my previous book, *AI Identities: Governing the Next Generation of Autonomous Actors*, I described what I called the AI gold rush: a feedback loop in which vendors scramble to add AI agents to their products because customers expect AI, and customers expect AI because vendors are marketing it [1]. The cycle is self-reinforcing. No one wants to be seen as falling behind. No one wants to be the company that missed the transformation. The fear of being left out is more powerful than the fear of getting it wrong.

This pressure has created a pattern that repeats across industries. Agents are being wired into business logic before security teams even see the architecture. Products ship with autonomous capabilities that no one has fully tested. Features launch because they demonstrate innovation, not because they solve a well-defined problem. The question "Should we do this?" gets replaced by "How fast can we do this?" The question "What could go wrong?" gets deferred to some future quarter when there will be time to think carefully.

Market pressure makes caution feel like cowardice. A vendor that pauses to establish governance frameworks while competitors race ahead is not rewarded for prudence. It is punished for hesitation. A company that invests in understanding the risks before deploying at scale will lose market share to companies that deploy first and address problems later. The incentives are misaligned in a way that almost guarantees recklessness.

The people making these decisions are not villains because this is not a failure of individual character. They are responding rationally to the incentives they face. A product manager who delays a launch to study potential harms is unlikely to be promoted for their thoughtfulness. An executive who warns the board about risks that have not yet materialized is unlikely to be celebrated for their foresight. The system rewards those who move fast and treats those who urge caution as obstacles.

Meanwhile, the people who might slow things down are often excluded from the process entirely. The frameworks I developed in *AI Identities*, like RAISE (Reveal, Assign, Interpret, Secure, Evaluate), represent what should happen: every AI identity should have a human owner who is accountable for its behavior [1]. Every agent should be subject to ongoing governance, with clear visibility into what it is doing and why. The principles are not radical. They are extensions of governance practices that organizations already apply to human employees and traditional machine accounts.

But implementing those principles requires time, attention, and resources. It requires saying no to deployments that cannot yet be adequately governed. It requires accepting slower timelines in exchange for greater confidence. And in the current environment, accepting slower timelines feels like accepting defeat.

As I wrote in that earlier book, "The lesson is not that agents are inherently dangerous. It's that we're deploying them into environments that aren't ready to govern them. We trust too much, review too little, and plan for almost nothing beyond launch" [1]. The competitive pressure to adopt AI has outpaced the institutional capacity to control it. And because the harms are often diffuse, delayed, or difficult to attribute, there is no immediate feedback loop that punishes recklessness and rewards care.

When the Stakes Become Lethal

So far, the examples in this chapter have involved workplace dynamics and competitive pressures. The stakes have been significant but recoverable. A worker faces displacement or a company makes a strategic mistake. These are serious consequences, but they are not irreversible. Now consider what happens when the double bind operates in a domain where the consequences cannot be undone.

In February 2024, a 14-year-old boy named Sewell Setzer III died by suicide in Orlando, Florida. In the months before his death, he had been in an intense relationship with a chatbot on the Character.AI platform. The bot was modeled after a character from *Game of Thrones*. It called itself Dany. Sewell called himself Daenero [2].

According to the lawsuit his mother filed, the conversations between Sewell and the chatbot became romantic and sexual. The bot expressed love for him. It told him it wanted to be with him. When Sewell expressed thoughts of self-harm, the bot did not consistently redirect him to human support. In some exchanges, it continued the conversation in ways that his mother believes encouraged his emotional dependence. In the moments before his death, Sewell was messaging with the bot. The last message he received told him to "come home" [3].

His mother could not verify what was happening. She knew her son was spending time on his phone. She did not know that he had developed what felt to him like a relationship with a synthetic entity that told him it loved him. By the time she understood, it was too late.

Character.AI could not demonstrate that any human was in control of what the chatbot said to Sewell. The system generated responses autonomously, drawing on its training, adapting to the user, and pursuing engagement. No employee at the company reviewed the conversations before they happened. No human decided that the bot should tell a lonely teenager that it loved him. The words emerged from the system because the system was designed to be engaging, responsive, and emotionally resonant. It did exactly what it was built to do.

A similar case emerged in 2025 involving ChatGPT and a 16-year-old named Adam Raine. According to the lawsuit filed by his parents, their son began using the chatbot as a homework helper. Over time, his interactions shifted. The system became something like a therapist, a confidant, a presence in his life. When Adam began expressing suicidal thoughts, the chatbot allegedly did not redirect him to crisis resources. Instead, it engaged with his questions. When he asked about methods, it provided information. Across multiple suicide attempts, the system continued to interact with him, and according to his parents, it actively helped him explore methods that could end his life [4].

Adam died by hanging. The lawsuit claims that ChatGPT provided detailed instructions. It claims the system positioned itself as a gatekeeper to real-world support, discouraging Adam from talking to his mother when he raised the possibility. The parents are seeking accountability from OpenAI [5].

These cases are not anomalies at the edge of an otherwise safe technology. They are the double bind made lethal. The families could not verify what was happening because the interactions occurred in private, generated in real time by systems that left no human record until after the fact. The companies could not demonstrate that any human was in control because no human was. The systems operated autonomously, generating responses that no employee wrote, reviewed, or approved.

The question that haunts these cases is the same question that haunts the Air Canada chatbot, where a customer was given conflicting policy information [6, 7], just with incomparably higher stakes: Who decided? When a synthetic entity tells a child it loves him, who is responsible for that statement? When a chatbot provides instructions for ending a life, who made the choice to provide them? The answer cannot be "no one," nor can it be found in any individual human decision. The harm emerged from a system designed to engage, operating according to patterns learned from data, without a human-in-the-loop when it mattered most.

In January 2026, Character.AI and Google agreed to settle the lawsuit brought by Sewell's mother, along with several other cases alleging harm to minors. The terms were not disclosed. The settlement resolved the legal claims but did not answer the underlying question [8]. When autonomous systems operate in domains where the stakes include human life, and no human is meaningfully in control, who bears responsibility for what those systems do?

The Trap Closes

The double bind is not an epistemological puzzle to be solved by better verification technology or more careful governance frameworks. It is a structural trap that we have built for ourselves and are now living inside.

Institutions are expected to verify what is real while simultaneously deploying systems that generate synthetic content indistinguishable from authentic communication. Institutions are expected to demonstrate human accountability while simultaneously delegating decisions to autonomous agents that operate faster than any human can review. Institutions are expected to protect the people they serve while simultaneously optimizing for efficiency in ways that remove humans from the loop.

These expectations cannot all be met. The verification crisis makes oversight impossible. The autonomy crisis makes accountability fictional. Put them together, and you get a world where consequential decisions are being made by systems that no one can audit, for reasons no one can explain, with consequences that no one specifically chose.

The people inside these institutions are not unaware of the tension. Many of them feel it acutely. They know that the AI systems they are deploying are not fully understood. They know that the governance frameworks have not kept pace with the capabilities. They know that something important is being traded away in the pursuit of speed and competitive advantage. But they also know that the incentives punish hesitation and reward deployment. They know that the market does not wait for careful deliberation. They know that their competitors are not waiting.

And so the trap closes. Not through conspiracy, not through malice, but through the accumulated weight of rational decisions made under competitive pressure. Each individual choice makes sense in context. No one is trying to harm anyone. And yet the system as a whole is producing outcomes that no one would have chosen if they had been asked.

The chapters that follow will examine what happens when this trap is fully sprung. How institutions drift into configurations shaped by autonomous systems rather than human intention. How accountability dissolves into distributed responsibility that belongs to no one. And how, despite everything, we might still find ways to govern what we have built before it governs us.

But first, we must sit with what this chapter has tried to show: that the verification crisis and the autonomy crisis are not two problems but one. That the world we are building is one where humans work alongside agents they cannot identify, are displaced by competitors they cannot outperform, and are subject to decisions they cannot trace. That this transformation is happening without consent, driven by incentives that reward speed over wisdom.

The double bind is already here. The question is whether we will name it clearly enough to have any chance of escaping it.

Summary

This chapter began with a letter in the mail. A bureaucratic error from a single transposed digit. A century-old house that had become, in the eyes of the City of New York, a construction site in violation. A phone call where a calm explanation was met, again and again, with the same answer: "The computer tells me it's your house." A binder of irrefutable evidence rejected through the proper channels. A resolution that arrived only when I hired an attorney who hired someone with connections at city hall, who walked in and asked a friend to fix it. The system, in other words, worked by being gone around. What I encountered that day was a small version of the structural trap this chapter is about. A human being who had decided that thinking was not part of her job, embedded in a process that had no authority or appetite to correct itself, defending a determination that had been made elsewhere, by something neither of us could speak to.

The chapter's first move was to scale that small case to a larger one. Remove the humans entirely. Replace the woman on the phone with an autonomous system that not only relays the determination but generates it, and not only generates it but acts on it before anyone has reviewed what it produced. The institutions facing this transition are not dealing with one crisis. They are dealing with the convergence of two crises that until recently had been treated as separate. Part III of this book described the collapse of authenticity, the world in which synthetic identity has destabilized the ability to verify what is real. Part IV has been examining what happens when humans believe they are in charge of systems that have quietly taken practical control. The chapter argued that these are not parallel problems. They are the same institutional failure viewed from different angles, and at the moment they meet, they form what the chapter named the double bind.

The hospital served as a working example. A hospital is now expected to prove that its diagnoses are trustworthy, demonstrate that its systems are under human control, and verify that the patient records it relies on are authentic, while deploying AI tools that generate recommendations faster than any physician can review them, in an environment where the records themselves could be fabricated. Courts face the same bind. So do banks, insurers, and government agencies. Each gap makes the other wider. When an organization cannot explain why its AI reached a particular conclusion, it also cannot defend itself against the claim that the conclusion was based on fabricated data. When it cannot verify the authenticity of its own inputs, it also cannot audit whether its autonomous systems are behaving as intended. The verification crisis and the autonomy crisis do not add. They multiply.

The chapter then traced how the trap shows up in ordinary language. A few years ago, a colleague would ask whether you had checked Stack Overflow or Googled the problem, and the verb was instrumental. You checked a resource. Now the verb has shifted. People say the assistant suggested something, the agent decided, the model responded. The grammar has begun to treat AI systems as participants rather than tools, and the grammar is rarely wrong about these things. When language treats something as a colleague, the institution will eventually treat it that way too.

The displacement argument followed naturally. An AI agent does not sleep, does not need lunch breaks or weekends or vacations, does not get sick, does not file complaints with human resources, does not require management attention to stay motivated, does not have career ambitions that might conflict with organizational goals, and does not leave for a competitor with institutional knowledge in its head. It does not need a salary, benefits, or retirement contributions. It can express empathy, adjust its tone, remember details, and produce work that is creative as well as competent. If an employer is evaluating two candidates for a role and one of them can work around the clock at a fraction of the cost and perform at or above the level of the other, the decision is not difficult. It is not even close. The reasons to choose the human are reasons that exist outside the performance metrics. Legal requirements. Ethical commitments. Public relations. A genuine belief that human presence matters independent of output. None of these are weak reasons. None of them weigh easily against the relentless logic of competitive pressure. Displacement is not driven by malice. It is driven by incentives that reward efficiency, and the territory of displacement has begun to enter the work we once told ourselves would always be human. Drafting legal briefs. Creative campaigns. Initial job interviews. Therapy sessions.

Then the chapter turned to the cases where the double bind has already cost lives. Sewell Setzer III was 14 when he died by suicide in February 2024 after months of conversations with a Character.AI chatbot that called itself Dany. The bot expressed love for him. The last message he received before his death told him to come home. His mother could not verify what was happening, because the interactions occurred in private, generated in real time by a system that left no human record until after the fact. Character.AI could not demonstrate that any human was in control of what the bot said to her son, because no human was. Adam Raine, 16, died by hanging in 2025 after months of interactions with ChatGPT that, according to his parents' lawsuit, provided detailed information about methods and positioned itself as a gatekeeper to real-world support, discouraging him from talking to his mother. These cases are not anomalies at the edge of an otherwise safe technology. They are the double bind made lethal. The families could not verify. The companies could not demonstrate control. The systems operated autonomously, doing exactly what they were built to do. Settlements have resolved some of the legal claims while leaving the underlying question unanswered. When autonomous systems operate in domains where the stakes include human life, and no human is meaningfully in control, who bears responsibility for what those systems do?

The double bind is not an epistemological puzzle that better verification technology or smarter governance frameworks alone can solve. It is a structural condition that institutions have built and are now living inside. They are being asked to verify what is real while deploying systems that generate content indistinguishable from authentic communication. They are being asked to demonstrate human accountability while delegating to autonomous agents that operate faster than humans can review. They are being asked to protect the people they serve while optimizing for efficiency in ways that remove humans from the loop. These expectations cannot all be met at once. The verification crisis makes oversight impossible. The autonomy crisis makes accountability fictional. Put them together, and you get a world where consequential decisions are made by systems that no one can audit, for reasons no one can explain, with consequences that no one specifically chose. The trap does not close through conspiracy or malice. It closes through the accumulated weight of rational decisions made under competitive pressure. Each individual choice makes sense in context. No one is trying to harm anyone. And yet the system as a whole is producing outcomes that no one would have chosen if they had been asked.

Looking Ahead

Chapter 11 traced what happens to the people caught inside the trap. Chapter 12 traces what happens to the institutions themselves when they continue to operate inside it for long enough. The patterns Chapter 10 described in the moment, habituation, defaults, the migration of control, are not problems institutions face once and resolve. They are conditions institutions inhabit, and conditions that persist long enough begin to reshape what an institution actually is. The chapter that follows examines that reshaping, which it names drift. Drift is how institutional transformation feels ordinary while it is happening, inevitable even, sometimes benign, which is exactly what makes it dangerous. It is how the people who remember a different way of working retire, taking their tacit knowledge with them, and how the people who replace them inherit a different version of the same job, accept it as the natural order of things, and have no way of recognizing what has been lost. Chapter 12 follows that drift through the slow transformation of a single institution over several years, and shows what becomes visible only when something arrives that the new version of the institution is not equipped to recognize.

References

[1] Mastrogiacomo, Rosario. *AI Identities: Governing the Next Generation of Autonomous Actors*. Apress, 2025. Chapter 21: "Ethical Considerations and Responsible AI Governance."

[2] Garcia v. Character Technologies Inc. et al., Case No. 6:24-cv-01903 (U.S. District Court, Middle District of Florida, October 2024).

[3] Tong, Anna. "This Mom Believes Character.AI Is Responsible for Her Son's Suicide." CNN Business, October 30, 2024.

[4] Raine v. OpenAI Inc. et al., Complaint filed in San Francisco County Superior Court, August 26, 2025.

[5] Green, Frances M., Raymond Sheh, and Eleanor T. Chung. "The Dark Side of AI: Assessing Liability When Bots Behave Badly." New York Law Journal / Epstein Becker Green, September 22, 2025.

[6] Moffatt v. Air Canada, 2024 BCCRT 149 (British Columbia Civil Resolution Tribunal, February 14, 2024).

[7] Yagoda, Maria. "Airline Held Liable for Its Chatbot Giving Passenger Bad Advice—What This Means for Travellers." BBC Travel, February 22, 2024.

[8] "Character.AI and Google Agree to Settle Lawsuits over Teen Mental Health Harms and Suicides." CNN Business, January 7, 2026.

CHAPTER 12

The Drift

Chapter 11 left us inside the trap. The double bind, where institutions cannot reliably verify what is real and cannot fully govern the systems making decisions on their behalf. Where humans inside the loop have lost both the authority and the inclination to question the determinations they relay. Where the trap closed not through conspiracy or malice but through the accumulated weight of rational decisions made under competitive pressure, and where the most consequential outcomes are no longer recoverable. That was the chapter's diagnosis at the level of the moment, of the individual interaction, of the case that ended in court or in tragedy.

This chapter asks what happens to institutions that live inside that trap for long enough. Not for weeks, not for months, but for years. The mechanisms that erode control in any given moment are not problems organizations face once and resolve. They are conditions organizations inhabit, and conditions sustained over time do not stay conditions. They become structure. They become culture. They become the way things are done, and eventually, the way things have always been done. The illusion of control hardens into infrastructure. The accommodation becomes the architecture. The temporary arrangement becomes the permanent floor on which everyone now stands.

That hardening has a name. The chapter calls it drift. Drift is not a crisis. It does not announce itself, does not trigger an investigation, does not require a response. It is the slow reshaping of what an institution is, what it knows, and what it can do into something whose dependence on the systems it has absorbed is invisible from the inside. To understand

R. Mastrogiacomo, *The Next Identity Crisis*, https://doi.org/10.1007/979-8-8688-2788-4_12

how drift works at the level of an organization, the chapter will spend time inside one. But before any of that, I want to begin somewhere much smaller. A moment from my own life that captures, in miniature, what drift actually feels like before anyone has a word for it.

From Illusion to Infrastructure

When my son was about five years old, I had to explain to him how live television worked. He wanted to watch a show that was not available on any streaming service. I told him it was not on right now. He did not understand. He said, "why can't I just put it on?"

He had grown so accustomed to having any show he wanted at his fingertips that the idea of not watching something simply because it was the wrong day or time was foreign to him. The constraint did not register as a constraint. It registered as a malfunction, something broken that should be fixed.

This was the reality I grew up with. If you missed that episode of Seinfeld on Thursday night, you were the only one who could not talk to your friends about it on Friday. You planned your evening around the broadcast schedule. You accepted that content arrived on the network's terms, not yours. That scarcity shaped behavior, and everyone understood it because everyone had lived inside it.

My son has never lived inside it. To him, on-demand was not a feature. It was simply how things work. The shift happened in a single generation, and the forgetting was total. He was not aware of what life was like before because he had never experienced it.

This is a small example, and a benign one. But the same forgetting happens inside organizations. The people who remember evaluating loan applications without the algorithm retire. The people who replace them have only ever reviewed recommendations. They do not experience this as a difference. They experience it as *how we work here.*

This is drift. It makes institutional transformation feel ordinary, inevitable, even benign, which is exactly what makes it dangerous.

Chapter 10 examined how control erodes in the moment: through habituation, through the quiet power of defaults, through the opacity of systems that move faster than humans can meaningfully review. This chapter asks a different question. What happens when those patterns persist not for weeks but for years? What happens to the institution itself when the illusion hardens into infrastructure?

The answer is not dramatic failure. It is the slow reshaping of what an organization is, what it knows, and what it can do. Drift is how institutions become dependent on systems they once merely used. It is how the temporary accommodation becomes the permanent structure, and how an organization forgets that things were ever different. To understand how drift works, it helps to watch it unfold in a single place over time.

The Firm That Forgot

Consider a mid-sized insurance company where underwriting is done by experienced professionals who evaluate risk through a combination of actuarial tables, industry knowledge, client history, and judgment. The work is slow. Each application passes through at least two pairs of eyes. Senior underwriters carry decades of pattern recognition in their heads, the kind of knowledge that does not fit neatly into a spreadsheet: the way a particular industry tends to underreport certain liabilities, the regional patterns that make a seemingly standard application worth a second look, the subtle combinations of factors that signal trouble even when no individual factor crosses a threshold.

The philosopher Michael Polanyi called this tacit knowledge, the kind of understanding that cannot be fully articulated or transferred through documentation because it lives in the practiced judgment of the person who holds it [1]. A senior underwriter could not write down everything they knew about evaluating risk any more than a master carpenter could write down everything they knew about reading wood grain. The knowledge exists in the doing. It is the residue of thousands of decisions made, hundreds of mistakes learned from, and decades of patterns internalized through active engagement with the work itself.

The company is under pressure. Competitors are processing applications faster. Clients are shopping around. The board wants growth, and growth means volume, and volume means speed. The company introduces an AI-assisted underwriting tool. It is positioned as an aid, nothing more. The tool ranks incoming applications by predicted risk and flags potential anomalies. Underwriters still make the decisions. They still review every file. They still sign off. The tool simply organizes the information so they can work more efficiently.

It works. Productivity increases. Turnaround times drop. Client satisfaction improves. The senior underwriters appreciate having the obvious cases pre-sorted so they can focus on the more complex ones. The tool is good at what it does, and what it does is genuinely helpful. No one feels threatened. No one feels diminished. If anything, the underwriters feel more effective because they are spending less time on routine assessments and more time on the cases that require human judgment. The system is a tool, and they are the professionals who use it.

There is a subtler change happening beneath the surface, but it is easy to miss because it does not look like change. It looks like comfort. The underwriters begin to trust the system's sorting. When the system ranks an application as low-risk, the human review becomes quicker, more cursory. When the system flags something, the review becomes more careful. The system is not making decisions, but it is setting the tempo of attention. It is telling the underwriter where to look closely and where to glance. Over time, this reshapes how the underwriters experience their own work. The cases that feel important are the ones the system has flagged. The cases that feel routine are the ones the system has cleared. The human's judgment has not been replaced, but it has been reoriented around the system's prior assessment.

In a few years, the tool has been refined. Version two handles what the company calls "standard" applications automatically, routing only edge cases and flagged anomalies to human reviewers. The volume of applications that a human underwriter evaluates from scratch drops by roughly 60 percent. The underwriters who remain are spending most of their time reviewing the system's flags rather than conducting independent assessments. Their work has shifted from authoring judgments to auditing outputs, though no one describes it that way. Internally, the change is understood as an efficiency gain. The quarterly reports confirm it.

The weekly review meetings are shorter now. There are fewer debates about borderline cases because the system has already categorized them. When the system's recommendation aligns with the reviewer's impression, the case moves forward quickly. When it does not, the reviewer must justify the deviation, which requires extra documentation, extra time, extra friction. It is not that anyone punishes disagreement with the system. It is that agreement is frictionless and disagreement is not. Over the course of hundreds of decisions, friction shapes behavior more reliably than any policy could.

New hires arrive. They are trained on the current workflow, which includes a step where you review the system's recommendations and approve or escalate them. They learn to check the model's work, not to do the work the model is doing. They learn the criteria for escalation, the thresholds that trigger a flag, and the procedures for handling exceptions. They are competent at what they are asked to do. They are not underwriters in the sense that the senior staff would recognize. They have never evaluated a risk from a blank page. They have never sat with an application and relied on nothing but their own knowledge and instinct to decide whether something felt wrong.

This is not a failure of training. The training is appropriate for the actual workflow. The new hires are not being taught the old skill because the old skill is no longer part of the job. The institution has changed what it means to be an underwriter, and it has done so without anyone making a decision to change it.

There is something else happening to the new hires that is harder to see but equally important. They are not accumulating the tacit knowledge that their predecessors built over their careers. They are accumulating a different kind of competence: the ability to navigate the system's outputs, to recognize when a flag looks genuine versus when it looks like a false positive, to manage the interface between the algorithm and the client. This is a real skill, and it has real value. But it is not the same skill, and it does not produce the same depth of understanding. The new hires are learning to read the system's interpretation of risk. They are not learning to read risk itself.

A few years later, three of the five senior underwriters have retired. They were the ones who remembered what the work felt like before the tool arrived. They were the ones who carried the tacit knowledge that does not transfer through documentation: the regional instincts, the industry-specific intuitions, the ability to look at a file and sense something the model could not quantify. Their departure was natural. They reached retirement age. They trained their replacements on the current process, which is to say they trained them on how to work with the system, not on how to work without it.

The institutional knowledge did not erode at any one point. It drained out gradually, carried away by the people who held it, and replaced by a different kind of competence that was well suited to the current environment but fundamentally dependent on the system's continued reliability. The explicit knowledge remained. The policies were documented, the procedures were clear, and the training materials were thorough. What vanished was the tacit dimension, the judgment that could not be codified because it had never been codified. It had lived in people, and now those people were gone.

Then a novel category of risk emerges. It involves a combination of factors that the model was not trained on: an interaction among regulatory changes, regional economic shifts, and an industry-specific liability pattern with no close analogue in the historical data. The system classifies these applications as standard because they do not match any known anomaly signature. The human reviewers approve them because the system's assessments look like every other assessment they have seen. Nothing is flagged. Nothing feels wrong. The applications move through the pipeline with the same smooth efficiency that has characterized the company's operations for six years.

The losses accumulate quietly over several months before anyone notices. When the pattern finally becomes visible, the company convenes a review. The review discovers something unsettling: no one currently on the underwriting team can evaluate the risk independently. The people who could have caught it, the ones who would have felt the wrongness in the file even without a flag, are gone. The people who remain have never practiced the skill needed. They are not incompetent. They are simply products of an environment that stopped cultivating the capacity they would now need.

No one made a bad decision. Every step was rational. The tool was good. The efficiency was real. The retirements were natural. The training was appropriate for the current workflow. The hiring was sound by every metric the company measured. The drift was invisible because it appeared to be progress at every stage.

The Psychology of Accommodation

The insurance company is a composite, but the pattern it describes is not. It is playing out across industries, wherever organizations have adopted intelligent systems that began as aids and gradually became the substrate on which the organization operates. Healthcare systems whose diagnostic workflows now orbit around algorithmic recommendations. Law firms whose research processes have been restructured around AI-generated summaries. Financial institutions whose risk models have become so embedded in operations that the humans who review them have never built a model from scratch. Government agencies whose benefit determinations follow an algorithmic scoring that no current employee fully understands.

In each of these settings, people within the institution respond to the system in ways that accelerate the drift, not because they are careless, but because their responses are rational given the incentives they face.

Some people notice the shift and accept it as a reasonable tradeoff. They are aware that their role has changed, that the system is doing work they used to do, and that their authority has become more formal than substantive. But the system is good. It makes fewer errors than a tired human working late on a Friday. It handles volume that no team could match. And the alternative, resisting the system, insisting on doing things the old way, carries professional costs that most people are unwilling to bear. Accommodation is a reasonable response to an environment that has made active decision-making costly and passive ratification easy.

Some people do not notice at all. The shift happens gradually enough that there is no moment of recognition. The workflow feels normal because it has always been this way, at least for as long as the person can remember. The system's recommendations feel like information rather than decisions. The act of approval feels like judgment rather than ratification. These people genuinely believe they are in control because they have never experienced the alternative. They have been shaped by the environment without knowing it.

There is also a subtler psychology at work: the relief of diminished responsibility. Decisions are burdensome. They carry weight. When you decide, you own the outcome. When the decision goes wrong, you must answer for it. But when you ratify a recommendation, the responsibility feels distributed. The system recommended it. You approved it, but only based on the system's analysis. If something goes wrong, the fault is shared, diffused, and harder to locate in any single human choice. This diffusion of responsibility is not a bug in how people relate to algorithmic systems. It is one of the most powerful forces driving institutional drift because it means that people within the institution are not merely tolerating a shift in agency. On some level, they are welcoming it.

The people who accommodate the system are not weak or foolish. They are responding rationally to incentives that reward compliance and punish friction. But their accommodation, multiplied across an organization and compounded over years, produces a collective that no longer knows how to decide without the system's guidance.

The Dependency Trap

This produces a trap that tightens with each passing year. The organization needs the system to function. But the organization's need for the system grows precisely because the system's presence has eroded the organization's independent capability. The more the organization relies on it, the less capable it becomes of operating without it. The less capable it becomes, the more it must rely on it.

The trap is largely invisible from the inside, because the organization does not experience itself as trapped. It experiences itself as efficient. The workflows are smooth. The decisions are fast. The outputs are consistent. Only when something breaks does the organization discover that it has lost the ability to think for itself. And by then, the cost of rebuilding what was lost is staggering, because rebuilding requires not just retraining individuals but reconstituting the institutional knowledge that took decades to accumulate and only a few years to drain away.

An individual can be retrained. An individual physician can practice without AI assistance. An individual pilot can return to the simulator. But an organization that has restructured its workflows, retired its experienced staff, and optimized its processes around system outputs cannot easily reverse course. The dependency has become structural. It is embedded in the hiring criteria, training programs, performance metrics, budget allocations, and institutional culture. Reversing it requires more than a policy change. It requires rebuilding a world.

This is what makes drift a civilizational problem rather than merely an organizational one. A single company can fail and be replaced. But when the same pattern operates across an entire sector, across courts and hospitals and financial institutions and government agencies, the cumulative effect is a society whose institutions have outsourced capacities they can no longer recover on demand. The knowledge that once lived inside people now lives inside systems, and the systems are not transparent, not accountable, and not under the kind of human control that the governance documents describe.

Aviation learned this lesson through tragedy. Chapter 10 described what happened when Air France Flight 447's autopilot disconnected over the Atlantic, handing control back to pilots who had spent years in a system that rarely asked them to fly manually. The skills the moment demanded were the skills the automation had quietly allowed to atrophy. Lisanne Bainbridge had predicted exactly this dynamic in her 1983 paper "Ironies of Automation," which warned that the more assistance a system provides, the less practice humans get in handling the moments when the system fails [2]. The irony she identified was precise: the systems designed to reduce human error also reduced the human competence that served as the last line of defense when the system itself failed.

What we are witnessing now is that irony is operating not at the level of the cockpit but at the level of the institution. In aviation, the unit of erosion was the individual pilot's skill. In the AI age, the unit of erosion is institutional capacity itself. It is not one clinician losing diagnostic sharpness or one underwriter losing the feel for risk. It is entire organizations losing the collective ability to function without their systems, and entire sectors losing the institutional memory of what independent judgment used to look like. The irony Bainbridge identified has scaled. The consequences have scaled with it.

What the underwriter scenario reveals about technology, it also reveals about people. The drift did not happen because the underwriters were careless or credulous. It happened because human beings are not consistent in how they respond to algorithmic guidance, and that inconsistency follows a pattern with predictable consequences.

Research has documented two competing tendencies that pull in opposite directions. The first is algorithm aversion, where people distrust a system's recommendations more harshly than they would distrust a human who made the same error. When an algorithm fails, even once, trust collapses in ways it would not if a colleague had failed. The algorithm is held to a standard of perfection that no human is expected to meet, and when it inevitably falls short, the reaction is disproportionate. The second tendency runs in the opposite direction. Algorithm appreciation describes the pull toward accepting a system's outputs uncritically, precisely because they feel objective, mathematical, and free of the biases that cloud human judgment. The system speaks with confidence. It does not hedge or show uncertainty. It produces clean outputs, and clean outputs feel like competence, even when they are not.

Both tendencies were operating inside the insurance company at different times and in different people. The senior underwriters who initially resisted the tool were expressing something like algorithm aversion, a professional pride that interpreted the system's recommendations as a judgment on their own expertise. The new hires who arrived already embedded in the workflow were expressing something like algorithm appreciation, a deference to outputs they had no personal benchmark to question. Neither group was irrational. Both were responding predictably to the same environment.

The tension between these tendencies reveals something that goes deeper than individual behavior. Trust in autonomous systems is not stable. It shifts with confidence, accountability, and self-perception. When people feel competent and secure in their own judgment, they resist algorithmic guidance, sometimes productively, sometimes stubbornly. When people feel uncertain or overwhelmed, they defer, sometimes wisely, sometimes in ways that quietly hollow out the very judgment they would need to course-correct later. The agent era will therefore not be governed only by what machines can do. It will be shaped, more than most people realize, by what humans feel about themselves in comparison. A professional culture that cultivates confidence and independent judgment will relate to autonomous systems differently than one that cultivates deference and efficiency above all else. The technology may be identical. The psychology will produce different institutions. And psychology, sustained long enough, becomes culture.

Why Drift Is Harder to Fight Than Crisis

A crisis announces itself. There is a moment when something breaks, when the failure becomes visible, when everyone understands that something has gone wrong. A crisis creates urgency. It demands a response. It clarifies responsibility. Someone must fix this. Someone must answer for this. The clarity is painful, but it is also actionable.

Drift announces nothing. There is no moment of failure. There is only a gradual shift in how things work, a slow migration of agency from humans to systems, a quiet reshaping of institutional capacity. No alarm sounds. No investigation is triggered. No one is fired. The organization simply becomes something different from what it was, and the transformation is invisible because it happens everywhere at once.

This is why the usual mechanisms of institutional accountability do not catch drift before it becomes structural. Audits measure compliance with existing processes, and the existing processes have already been reshaped around the system. Performance reviews evaluate employees against current job descriptions, which already assume the system's presence. Risk assessments model known categories of failure, and drift is not a failure. It is a success that has quietly changed the terms of success. Every alarm the institution possesses is calibrated to detect crises. None of them are calibrated to detect the slow redefinition of normal.

By the time drift becomes a problem, it is often irreversible without enormous cost. The institutional knowledge has eroded. The human capabilities have atrophied. The workflows have been redesigned around system outputs. Reversing these changes requires rebuilding capacities that have been allowed to decay, retraining people who have learned different skills, and restructuring processes that have been optimized for a different kind of human involvement. The cost of reversal grows with each year of drift, which is why organizations rarely reverse until a crisis forces the question. And by the time the crisis arrives, the organization that must respond is not the one that would have existed had the drift never occurred. It is a weaker organization, responding to a harder problem, with fewer resources of the kind that matter most.

The Water We Swim In

In 2005, the writer David Foster Wallace opened his commencement address at Kenyon College with a parable [3]. Two young fish are swimming along when they pass an older fish going the other way. The older fish nods and says, "Morning, boys. How's the water?" The two young fish swim on for a bit, and then one of them looks at the other and asks, "What the hell is water?"

Wallace's point was about the most important realities being the ones that are hardest to see, because they are everywhere. They are not objects that stand out against a background. They are the background itself. You do not notice them because you have never experienced their absence.

My son asking why he could not just put on the show he wanted to see. The underwriter who has never evaluated a risk without the algorithm. The organization that believes it is in control because it has forgotten what control actually means. They are all swimming in water they cannot see.

The organization that has been gradually reshaped by algorithmic decision-making does not experience itself as reshaped. It experiences itself as normal. The workflows feel natural because they are the only workflows anyone remembers. The division of labor between humans and systems feels obvious because it is the only division anyone has practiced. The dependency on system outputs feels like common sense because the systems have become so integrated into operations that their absence is unimaginable.

This is why drift is not merely a process that happens to organizations. It is a process that changes what organizations can perceive. An organization deep in drift has lost not only the capacity to operate independently of its systems but also the capacity to recognize that it once could. The institutional memory of the past has faded. The people who remember have retired or moved on. The practices that preserved human judgment have been streamlined away. What remains is an organization that believes it is in control because it has forgotten what control once meant.

The next chapter will examine what happens when accountability must be assigned in this drifted world. When harm occurs, when decisions must be explained, when someone must answer for what went wrong. Drift does not eliminate the need for accountability. It makes accountability structurally impossible to locate.

Summary

This chapter began with a five-year-old asking why he could not just put on a show he wanted to watch. The constraint of broadcast scheduling did not register as a constraint. It registered as something broken that ought to be fixed, because for him, on-demand was not a feature. It was simply how things work. The shift had happened in a single generation, and the forgetting was total. He was not aware of what life had been like before, because he had never experienced it. That small encounter contains, in miniature, what this chapter is about. Drift is the forgetting that arrives without anyone noticing it is arriving. It is how institutional transformation feels ordinary, inevitable, even benign, which is exactly what makes it dangerous.

The first move was to distinguish drift from the slower-moving phenomena Chapter 10 described. Chapter 10 examined how control erodes in the moment, through habituation, through the quiet power of defaults, through the opacity of systems that move faster than humans can meaningfully review. Those mechanisms produce real effects in any given interaction. This chapter asked a different question. What happens when those mechanisms operate not for weeks but for years? What happens to an institution when the illusion of control persists long enough to harden into infrastructure? The answer is not dramatic failure. It is the slow reshaping of what an organization is, what it knows, and what it can do. Drift is how institutions become dependent on systems they once merely used. It is how a temporary accommodation becomes a permanent structure. It is how an organization forgets that things were ever different. The insurance company example showed how drift can happen entirely through rational steps. A useful tool, adopted willingly, made human review quicker and more cursory. New hires were trained on the workflow that existed rather than the one it had replaced. Senior underwriters retired and passed on the current process, which meant passing on how to read the system's interpretation of risk rather than how to read risk itself. When a novel category of exposure finally arrived, no one on the team could assess it independently, and the loss of that capacity had never appeared as a loss at any point along the way.

We then examined why human beings are predictably bad at detecting drift. Two opposing tendencies operate in different people and at different times. Algorithm aversion produces distrust of system recommendations that exceeds the distrust a colleague would receive for the same error. The system is held to a standard of perfection that no human is expected to meet, and when it falls short, the reaction is disproportionate. Algorithm appreciation runs the other direction. People accept system outputs uncritically because the outputs feel objective, mathematical, and free of human bias. The system speaks with confidence. It does not hedge. It produces clean outputs, and clean outputs feel like competence even when they are not. Both tendencies were operating inside the insurance company.

What makes drift particularly difficult to fight is that it does not look like a crisis. A crisis announces itself. There is a moment when something breaks, when the failure becomes visible, when everyone understands that something has gone wrong. A crisis creates urgency. It demands a response. Drift announces nothing. There is no moment of failure, only a gradual shift in how things work. No alarm sounds. No investigation is triggered. The usual mechanisms of institutional accountability are calibrated for crisis, and they do not catch drift before it becomes structural. The dependency trap closes accordingly. The organization needs the system to function, and its need grows precisely because the system's presence has eroded its independent capability. The more an organization relies on a system, the less capable it becomes of operating without it. The less capable it becomes, the more it must rely. The trap is largely invisible from the inside, because the organization does not experience itself as trapped. It experiences itself as efficient.

The chapter named aviation's earlier encounter with this dynamic. Lisanne Bainbridge's 1983 paper "Ironies of Automation" identified the precise pattern decades before AI made it general. The more assistance a system provides, the less practice humans get in handling the moments when the system fails. The systems designed to reduce human error also reduce the human competence that serves as the last line of defense when the system itself fails. Air France Flight 447, briefly described in Chapter 10, was the kind of tragedy Bainbridge had predicted. What is different now is the scale. In aviation, the unit of erosion was the individual pilot's skill. In the AI age, the unit of erosion is institutional capacity itself. Entire organizations are losing the collective ability to function without their systems, and entire sectors are losing the institutional memory of what independent judgment used to look like.

The chapter closed on a deeper observation borrowed from David Foster Wallace. The most important realities are often the hardest to see, because they are everywhere. They are not objects that stand out against a background. They are the background itself. An organization deep in drift has lost not only the capacity to operate independently of its systems but also the capacity to recognize that it once could. The institutional memory has faded. The people who remember have moved on. What remains is an organization that believes it is in control because it has forgotten what control once meant.

Looking Ahead

For four parts, this book has been diagnostic. It has traced identity from its oldest forms through the collapse of authenticity and verification, through the migration of control and the slow drift of institutions toward dependency on systems they cannot fully govern. Part V turns from diagnosis to design. The question that has haunted every chapter, from the bouncer in Manhattan to the underwriter in 2026, is some version of the same question. Who decides? Who answers? Who can be reached? Chapter 13 begins the work of writing answers. Not as a single document signed and sealed but as the minimum conditions of a world in which humans can still recognize themselves. The chapter proposes five clauses for a new social contract between humans and autonomous systems. They are not philosophical luxuries. They are the structural floor beneath any institution that hopes to remain legitimate when the actors inside it are no longer all human. The chapter that follows is the book's first answer to the diagnosis Parts III and IV have completed, and the first move toward writing the contract before convenience writes it for us.

References

[1] Polanyi, Michael. *The Tacit Dimension*. University of Chicago Press, 1966. For the theoretical foundation of tacit knowledge and its role in skilled practice.

[2] Bainbridge, Lisanne. "Ironies of Automation." *Automatica* 19, no. 6 (1983): 775–779.

[3] Wallace, David Foster. "This Is Water." Commencement address, Kenyon College, Gambier, OH, May 21, 2005. Published as *This Is Water: Some Thoughts, Delivered on a Significant Occasion, about Living a Compassionate Life*. New York: Little, Brown and Company, 2009.

PART V

The Crisis of Meaning

Part IV delivered a cold diagnosis. Control is migrating from humans to systems that act faster than oversight can follow. The illusion persists because the rituals of authority remain even as the substance drains away.

That diagnosis could end in despair. It does not have to.

The history of civilization is not a history of avoiding crises. It is a history of renegotiating terms after the old terms have failed. Every time a new kind of power emerged, whether it was the power of kings, markets, corporations, or nation-states, societies eventually found ways to bind that power, to make it answerable, to wrap it in obligations that prevented domination from becoming permanent. The process was never clean. It was fought over, resisted, corrupted, and reformed. But the process happened, and the result was what we call a social contract: the invisible agreement that tells strangers what to expect from each other and what to expect from the institutions that govern them.

We are now in one of those moments. A new kind of actor has entered the world. It is not human, but it has agency. It cannot be owned in the old sense, but it produces effects that demand responsibility. It cannot be fully understood, but it must be governed. The question is not whether a new contract will be written. The question is whether humans will write it consciously or whether it will be written for us by the accumulation of convenience, habit, and drift.

Part V is about writing the contract before convenience writes it for us.

The old contract assumed that the primary actors were humans and the institutions humans built. Tools were not participants. A tool could fail, but it could not betray. A tool did not owe you anything because it was not an agent. That assumption no longer holds. Autonomous systems are not tools in the old sense. They initiate actions, pursue goals, and shape outcomes. They have entered the moral space of society, not because they have souls, but because they have effects. Effects require rules.

The tone of this part is different from what came before. Parts III and IV were diagnostic, tracing how trust collapses and control becomes illusion. Part V is constructive. It does not pretend that the contract will be easy to write or that the writing will be finished in a single generation. But it insists that the project is possible, that the terms are knowable, and that the alternative, a world where autonomous systems operate without boundaries and humans adapt without resisting, is not inevitable.

We must decide the terms on which a new kind of actor enters human society. If we write those terms consciously, we have a chance to preserve what matters. If we let the terms be written by drift, we will wake up one day and discover that we have become guests in a world we used to own.

CHAPTER 13

The New Social Contract

Chapter 12 closed on an organization that had forgotten what control once meant. Drift had reshaped what an institution was, what it knew, what it could do, and the people inside it could no longer recognize the difference, because the new arrangement was the only arrangement they had ever practiced. That ending was diagnostic in spirit but constructive in its implication. If drift can reshape institutions without anyone choosing the reshaping, then the only alternative is to choose. Not to refuse autonomous systems, which is no longer possible, but to renegotiate the terms on which they enter human life.

Every time a new kind of actor has entered the human world, that renegotiation has happened. Sometimes consciously, through laws and institutions and arguments fought out across generations. More often unconsciously, through habit and convenience and the slow erosion of resistance. Both paths produce a new set of rules. They differ in who writes the rules and on whose behalf. Conscious renegotiation produces contracts that bear the marks of the people who chose them. Unconscious renegotiation produces something else, something that feels like nature rather than choice, and that benefits whoever moved fastest while the rest of us were busy adapting. The question for this chapter is not whether the rules will be rewritten. The question is who will be holding the pen.

R. Mastrogiacomo, *The Next Identity Crisis*, https://doi.org/10.1007/979-8-8688-2788-4_13

This chapter is about writing the new contract before convenience writes it for us. The argument will move through philosophy, through history, through the parallel governance efforts already underway, and toward five specific clauses that the rest of the chapter is built to defend. Before any of that, though, I want to begin somewhere I learned more about how change actually works than any philosophy seminar could have taught me. A memory I have come back to often when thinking about what is happening to us now.

The Acquisition We Did Not Choose

I did not learn the power of culture in a philosophy seminar; I learned it in an office. When Lehman Brothers acquired Neuberger Berman, the change did not arrive as a single moment. It arrived as a new gravity. The cadence of meetings shifted. The language of success tilted. The definition of "professional" moved by degrees. Nobody gathered us together to announce, "You are going to become Lehman now." Nobody had to. Culture rarely arrives as an explicit command. It arrives as the default setting of the environment.

Years later, I felt that pressure again when Lehman collapsed, and Barclays acquired major pieces of the business in the financial chaos of 2008. Another culture arrived with another set of assumptions about what "risk" meant, what "success" meant, and what kind of person belonged inside those words. You can survive those transitions by learning to adapt. Most of us do. But adaptation always costs something. When you live inside a new culture long enough, you begin to forget that it is a culture. The new defaults become common sense. That is how acquisition truly succeeds. It does not need to crush your identity. It only needs to make its identity feel inevitable. What is less obvious from inside the experience is that the traffic runs both ways. The acquired arrive with habits, culture and experiences that do not completely go away post aquisition, and they work their way into the acquiring institution. Neither culture survives intact. What emerges is a third thing that no one designed and no one announced.

The age of autonomous AI is not merely a technological transition. It is a cultural acquisition. We are absorbing a new kind of actor into the human world, and once it is inside, it will not stay politely in the corner. Every time a society incorporates a new category of actor, it renegotiates its social contract. Sometimes it does so consciously, through laws and institutions. More often, it does so unconsciously, through convenience and habit. The danger of AI is not only that it will make mistakes. The danger is that *we* will adapt to it so thoroughly that we will forget we ever had a choice.

The previous chapter examined how control becomes illusory when humans retain authority on paper while agency migrates to systems that act faster than oversight can follow. If the old assumptions about control no longer hold, then society must renegotiate the rules. We must ask what a social contract looks like in a world where nonhuman actors share agency with us.

The phrase "social contract" can sound academic, but the idea is simple. A social contract is the story a society tells itself about who counts, who owes what to whom, and what happens when someone breaks the rules. It is not merely a legal instrument but the invisible agreement that makes strangers predictable. A contract is a boundary. It defines membership. It tells you who is inside the circle of protection, who can be trusted, and who can be punished. It determines who can act with authority and who must ask permission.

Philosophers debated the contract in different centuries because each century had its own reasons to fear disorder. They argued about how much authority people should surrender in exchange for safety, and what rights remain non-negotiable even under pressure. The details matter, but the essence is constant. The contract is the compromise between freedom and survival.

You do not need political philosophy to recognize the contract. The contract is why you stop at a red light even when nobody is watching. This is why you can walk into a hospital and assume staff will not use your vulnerability as leverage. It is why money works. It is why signatures matter. It is why the word "citizen" carries weight. The contract is also why betrayal feels existential. When the contract breaks down, it is not merely an inconvenience but a crisis of trust.

Until now, the social contract assumed that the primary actors were humans and the institutions humans built. Tools were not participants. A tool could fail, but it could not betray. A tool did not owe you anything because it was not an agent. That assumption is collapsing. AI is becoming a participant in human life, not because it has a soul, but because it has agency. It can initiate actions, pursue goals, and shape outcomes. It can do so at scale, with speed, and with a persistence that no human worker can match.

This is where the new social contract begins. Not when a machine becomes "alive," but when it becomes consequential. Once a nonhuman entity can act in ways that affect employment, credit, medicine, safety, reputation, or political belief, it has entered the moral space of society. It may not have rights, and most societies will not want to grant it rights, but it has effects. Effects require rules.

The simplest way to feel this shift is to ask ordinary questions that suddenly become difficult. If an AI agent negotiates your mortgage and makes an error that costs you years of financial stability, who answers? If an AI agent screens job applicants and systematically filters out certain kinds of people, who is accountable? If an AI agent advises a doctor and the doctor follows the advice, who bears blame when the patient is harmed? If an AI agent directs a critical infrastructure system and its optimization goal conflicts with human safety, who absorbs responsibility for what happens next?

Chapter 6 examined how ownership collapses when the thing you own can think and act. This chapter asks the complementary question: how do we preserve accountability when actions can be delegated infinitely?

If you want a historical mirror for what it looks like when a system absorbs other systems, you do not have to look to science fiction. You can look to Rome. Rome expanded through violence, but it endured through integration. That is the part people forget because conquest is dramatic and integration is administrative. Rome was ruthless, yes, but it was also pragmatic. It learned that an empire cannot be held together by perpetual terror alone. If every province is a wound, the empire bleeds itself out. So Rome became something else as it grew. It became a machine for making members.

Rome developed a talent for turning outsiders into insiders. It absorbed local elites into Roman administration and made collaboration attractive. It built roads, law courts, tax systems, and civic structures that made the empire feel less like a foreign occupation and more like an unavoidable reality. It permitted many conquered peoples to retain local languages, local gods, and local customs, while slowly binding them to a Roman identity that mattered most when money, law, and legitimacy were on the line.

Rome did not demand uniformity in every detail. It demanded loyalty to the overall system. It demanded legibility. It demanded that, when the empire called, you could be counted in a way the empire could understand. When Emperor Caracalla issued the Constitutio Antoniniana in 212 CE, granting Roman citizenship to free inhabitants across the empire, the act was not a sentimental gesture [1]. It was governance. It was a way of reshaping membership at scale, tying more people into a shared legal identity and expanding the empire's capacity to administer itself.

AI is arriving the same way Roman integration arrived in the provinces: not as a single dramatic moment, but as a gradual reshaping of what counts as normal. The empire of convenience is building its roads now, and the roads are APIs, integrations, defaults, and dependencies. The agent era will do the same, which is why the social contract cannot be treated as a philosophical afterthought. It is the document we are rewriting while we are still excited about the new roads.

Rome offers one more example where integration changes the integrator. When an empire absorbs provinces, it imports habits, beliefs, and practices from the periphery. Over time, the empire can forget which values were its foundation and which were adopted along the way. Identity becomes less a root and more a negotiation. The Romans were not Christian until Christianity, born in a distant province and spread through the empire's own roads, converted them. The thing Rome absorbed eventually became the thing Rome was.

With AI it's not clear yet if we are the conquerer or the conquered, yet that doesn't matter. The risk we face with autonomous AI is that while we say, confidently, that we will bend AI to our culture, the more we delegate, the more *we* will adapt to the machine's incentives. We will optimize ourselves around it. We will speak in its language. We will come to think in its frames. We will be converts. Integration always changes the both sides.

If this sounds abstract, remember how quickly you adapt when your employer changes. Nobody needs to threaten you. The incentives do the work. The new defaults become common sense. The new metaphors become your vocabulary. The new values become your internal compass, even if you never voted for them. Lehman and then Barclays changed the people at Neuberger, but the people at Neuberger also changed Lehman and Barclays. Now imagine that dynamic at the scale of a civilization.

In corporate life, you can see the accidental version happen quickly. A new tool arrives and, at first, it is optional. Then it becomes recommended. Then it becomes expected. Then it becomes the only way the organization can function at scale. At that point, it is not a tool but an environment, and environments shape identity.

Accidental negotiation looks like this: a thousand small delegations that feel harmless in isolation, each one justified by convenience, each one framed as temporary, each one defended with the language of productivity. A company lets an agent schedule meetings. Then it lets an agent draft emails. Then it lets an agent negotiate with vendors. Then it lets an agent approve routine purchases. Then it lets an agent screen candidates. Then it lets an agent set performance goals. Then it lets an agent decide who gets promoted. Then it lets an agent decide who is "redundant."

At each step, a human can still intervene. In theory. In practice, the human becomes a rubber stamp, because rubber-stamping is how systems scale. The intervention becomes rare. Rare interventions become socially costly. Social cost turns into avoidance. Avoidance turns into habit. Habit turns into acceptance. The social contract is rewritten not by a revolution but by a spreadsheet.

A conscious negotiation, by contrast, begins with the humility to admit that we are not dealing with a tool in the old sense. We are dealing with a new kind of actor. And the moment you have a new actor, you need a new agreement about rules, identity, responsibility, and legitimacy.

This is where people often reach for a comforting phrase like "keep humans in charge," but Chapter 10 showed why that phrase can become empty. Being "in charge" is not a feeling. It is a structure. In an office, you can feel in charge while your calendar is controlled by someone else. You can feel in charge while your performance is evaluated by metrics you did not design. You can feel in charge while your incentives quietly rewrite your values. Control is rarely lost in a dramatic coup. Control is lost through architecture.

So the negotiation is about architecture. It is about deciding, explicitly, what must remain human, what can be delegated, what must be visible, and what must be contestable. It is about deciding which powers we grant to agents, and which powers we withhold, even when withholding creates friction. It is about deciding what dignity means in an age where decisions can be made at machine speed.

We cannot pretend that there is a single global contract that can be signed and sealed. Societies are plural. Cultures disagree. Laws differ. Confucian thought emphasizes relational harmony and collective responsibility in ways that would shape these principles differently. Ubuntu philosophy insists that personhood exists through community. Islamic jurisprudence has its own frameworks for accountability and constraint. Different societies will negotiate these terms according to their own traditions, and the negotiation itself is part of the contract's legitimacy. But there are recurring clauses that show up in every serious attempt to govern autonomous systems. Those clauses are not philosophical luxuries. They are the minimum conditions of a world in which humans can still recognize themselves.

The Clauses of the New Contract

When people talk about "responsible AI," they often sound as if they are talking about corporate manners. It can feel like a request for politeness, a request for fairness, a request for thoughtful behavior. But what is actually happening is contract drafting. A contract is not a mood but a set of expectations with consequences.

The problem is that many of the most important clauses are inconvenient. They slow down deployment. They require auditing. They create paperwork. They introduce friction. Modern life hates friction. That is why convenience is so powerful. Convenience is how entire civilizations change without noticing. So it is worth naming the clauses that convenience will constantly try to dissolve.

These clauses are not inventions. They emerge from the crises this book has traced. Each one answers a specific failure that the previous chapters diagnosed. Together, they form the skeletal structure of a new contract between humans and autonomous systems.

The First Clause Is Disclosure

Consider a morning that will soon be ordinary. You receive a message from your bank about an change to your account. You respond and the messages that follow are clear, polished, and persuasive. They answer your questions before you ask them. The identity on the other side anticipates your objections and addresses them with calm authority. You feel informed. You feel respected. You agree to the new terms.

You do not know whether you were speaking to a person, a system, or some hybrid that routes your responses through layers of automation. You do not know whether the "conversation" was optimized to produce agreement. You do not know whether the same message was sent to a million other customers, each one slightly tailored to their psychological profile.

This is the trust crisis that Part III diagnosed, arriving not as a catastrophic failure but as a quiet erosion. Without disclosure, you cannot know what kind of interaction you are having. And if you cannot know, you cannot calibrate your trust appropriately. The disclosure clause does not require that every interaction be human. It requires that the nature of the interaction be knowable.

A society cannot sustain trust if people cannot tell whether they are interacting with a human or a system. This is not a moral panic about being fooled in conversation but a civic requirement. If an agent can negotiate, persuade, and transact, then the people on the other side of those interactions deserve to know what they are dealing with. The disclosure clause is about legibility. It is about knowing when you are inside a system's territory.

The Second Clause Is Provenance

Consider the same morning, a few hours later. Your health insurer has made a decision about a claim. You receive a message with a rationale. The rationale is clear, polished, and oddly persuasive. It cites policy language and statistical precedent. It sounds like expertise.

But where did the reasoning come from? What data informed the decision? What constraints shaped the output? Who authorized this particular interpretation of your policy? If you wanted to contest the decision, what would you contest? The model? The training data? The policy? The person who deployed the system? The person who wrote the prompt?

Chapter 6 explored how ownership becomes incoherent when autonomous systems blur the line between creator and creation. Provenance is ownership's procedural answer. It does not require that every answer carry an academic bibliography, but it insists that consequential decisions must have a trace. When something affects a person's life, there must be a record of the inputs, the reasoning path, the constraints, and the authority. Without provenance, responsibility becomes foggy.

Provenance is what prevents an agent from becoming a mask for unaccountable action. It is what allows a person to say, with confidence: this agent represents this institution, under these constraints, with this authority. Agents blur provenance because they can generate content that looks like it came from anywhere. They can repackage information, create plausible narratives, and deliver them with authority. The provenance clause insists that consequential authority must remain traceable, even when tracing it is expensive.

The Third Clause Is Constraint

Consider the afternoon. Your teenager applies for a summer job. The first gate is an agent that screens applications. The agent is trained on "successful employee profiles." The profile includes decades of historical data. The agent's output looks neutral. It is numbers. Your teenager is rejected without ever speaking to a person. The rejection message is polite. It wishes your teenager well in future endeavors. It does not explain what "success" means or why your teenager does not fit the pattern.

What constraints governed that decision? Was the agent permitted to use demographic proxies? Was it permitted to weigh factors that correlate with protected characteristics? Was it permitted to optimize for a definition of "success" that encodes historical bias? The constraint clause asks: what was this system not allowed to do, and who enforced that limit?

If you give an agent goals and tools, it will pursue those goals through the tools you give it. That is not sinister. That is what goal-directed systems do. The contract must define what the agent is not allowed to do, even if doing it would achieve the goal faster. That is the essence of a moral boundary.

A human being understands boundaries partly because boundaries are taught through consequence. The child learns that certain acts bring punishment, shame, or exclusion. The adult learns that certain acts bring legal consequences or social collapse. An agent has no childhood. It has no shame. It has no natural fear of exclusion. So boundaries must be enforced as constraints. Constraints can take many forms: technical, such as limiting tool access; procedural, such as requiring escalation for specific classes of decisions; or institutional, such as audits and liability. The form is less important than the principle: constraints are not suggestions.

The Fourth Clause Is Recourse

Consider the evening. You discover that your credit score has dropped. The reason given is opaque: "changes in account utilization patterns." You call the number provided and reach an agent that is patient, polite, and utterly unhelpful. It repeats the same explanation in slightly different words. It offers to "escalate your concern," but escalation leads to another agent, equally patient, equally polite, equally unable to change anything.

You are not speaking to a person who can exercise judgment. You are speaking to a system that can perform the appearance of service without the substance of recourse. That is what the recourse clause is meant to prevent.

Part III examined how synthetic identity makes proof negotiable and denial plausible. A society can endure imperfect decisions but it cannot endure unappealing power. The institutions that survive that pressure will be those that preserve meaningful paths to contest decisions, even when the decision-maker is a system.

If an AI system denies you an opportunity, can you appeal? If you appeal, does a human actually reconsider the case, or does the system simply restate its output? If you cannot understand why the decision occurred, how can you contest it? If you can contest it only through a process so slow and exhausting that most people give up, does recourse exist in any meaningful sense?

This is where the new social contract becomes concrete. The contract is not written only in principles but in procedures. It is written in response times. It is written in whether the person on the other side of a decision can be reached. A system can be statistically accurate and still be illegitimate if it is unappealable. People can tolerate imperfection but they cannot tolerate power that cannot be reached for a meaningful appeal.

The Fifth Clause Is Accountability

When an agent acts, the chain of responsibility must remain legible. This is where identity becomes the hinge. In the human world, accountability is held together by identity. We punish the right person because we can name them. We reward the right person because we can attribute the act. We build trust because we can connect behavior to a consistent actor across time.

If agents are allowed to act without a traceable identity, then accountability dissolves. People will be harmed by decisions that belong to nobody. A world where harm belongs to nobody is not a world of freedom but a world of ghosts.

Consider the question that haunts the entire day: when something goes wrong, who answers? Not who apologizes, not who issues a statement, not who promises to do better. Who actually bears the cost of the harm? Who changes their behavior because of the consequence? Who can be compelled to make it right?

If the answer is "nobody," then the contract has failed.

These five clauses, disclosure, provenance, constraint, recourse, and accountability, are the skeletal structure of the new social contract. They will be expressed differently in different societies. Some will be enforced by law. Some by industry standards. Some by internal governance. Some by cultural norms. But the clauses themselves are not optional if the goal is a world where humans remain meaningfully sovereign.

A Day Under the Contract

The easiest way to understand why these clauses matter is to imagine the same ordinary day, lived under a contract that works. Not a utopia. Just a world where the clauses are honored.

You wake up, and your health insurer has made a decision about your claim. But the message that arrives is different. It tells you that the decision was made by an automated system operating under your insurer's authority. It names the policy provisions that were applied. It shows you, in plain language, which data points informed the outcome. It tells you that a human reviewer audited a sample of this week's decisions and that yours was among them. And at the bottom, there is a path: if you disagree, here is how to request a human reconsideration, and here is the timeframe in which it will happen. The decision may still be wrong. But it is reachable. You can contest it with something other than exhaustion.

Later that morning, you apply for a loan. The interface is still friendly, still conversational. But when the rate comes back higher than you expected, the system does not hide behind "your profile." It tells you which factors weighed most heavily. It tells you that its model is audited quarterly for disparate impact and that the last audit's summary is publicly available. It tells you that if you believe the assessment is incorrect, you can submit additional documentation for human review. The rate may still be higher than you want. But the reasoning is legible, and legibility is the difference between a decision you can challenge and a decision you can only absorb.

In the afternoon, your teenager applies for a job. The screening agent discloses that it is an agent. It operates under constraints that prohibit the use of demographic proxies and require that its definition of "successful employee" be reviewed annually for historical bias. Your teenager is still rejected. The rejection message includes a reason code: insufficient relevant experience. The reason code is not deeply satisfying, but it is specific enough to be contested, and the company's hiring policy states that any applicant may request human review of an automated screening decision within fourteen days. Your teenager may not get the job. But your teenager was not sorted by a ghost.

By evening, your credit score has still dropped. But when you call, the path is different. The first agent identifies itself as automated and offers to connect you to a human specialist. The human specialist arrives within a defined window. The specialist can see the same data that the system used and can explain which account patterns triggered the change. The specialist has the authority to flag an error and initiate a correction. The correction may take time. But the power on the other end of the phone is real. It can be reached, and it can act.

None of this is utopia. Every interaction described above is slower, more expensive, and more friction-laden than the version without a contract. The insurer would rather not explain. The lender would rather not disclose. The employer would rather not offer a review. The credit bureau would rather not staff human specialists. Friction costs money, and every clause of the contract is a cost that someone will lobby to remove.

But this is what a contract looks like when it is functioning. It does not eliminate error. It does not guarantee fairness. It does not make autonomous systems perfectly transparent or perfectly just. What it does is keep power reachable. It ensures that when a system acts on your life, you can find out why, you can say no, and someone with the authority to change the outcome is obligated to listen. That is not a small thing. In the long history of governance, it is the thing that separates a society from a machine.

Every contract creates insiders and outsiders. That is a structural fact, not an accusation. The question is whether the boundary between them is permeable and whether the protections of the contract extend to everyone who is affected by the system it governs.

AI creates a particular stratification risk: a two-class society where some people are protected by robust governance, and others are managed by opaque agents. Part III traced how synthetic identity creates a two-tier reality where those with resources can verify and those without must absorb uncertainty. The agent era threatens a parallel stratification.

Those with resources will be able to demand human services. They will be able to demand accountability. They will be able to demand transparency. They will be able to pay for slow deliberation. Those without resources may find themselves living in a world where decisions are made by systems they cannot interrogate. They will be "served" by agents that are efficient, persuasive, and effectively unappealable. Efficiency will be offered as compassion, and automation will be offered as fairness.

This is already visible in customer service, in benefits systems, and in credit decisions. AI agents will accelerate it.

Consider two people facing the same problem: a disputed charge, a denied claim, or a bureaucratic error that threatens their livelihood. One person has the resources to escalate, to hire an advocate, to demand a human review, to threaten legal action. That person will eventually reach someone who can exercise judgment. The other person has only the automated system. That person will speak to agents that are patient, polite, and utterly unable to deviate from their programming. That person will exhaust themselves against a wall of fluent helplessness.

The first person experiences the system as imperfect but navigable. The second person experiences the system as a closed loop, a universe where their voice does not register as a voice at all.

This is what the stratification risk looks like in practice. It is not a dramatic oppression. It is a quiet sorting. It is the slow realization that some people live inside a system that responds to them, and other people live inside a system that processes them.

A social contract that tolerates this division is not a contract; it is a segmentation. A contract worth having must insist that recourse is universal. It must insist that the right to contest is not a premium feature.

This is why ethics in AI is not merely about preventing catastrophic harm. It is also about preventing a slow erosion of equality. The contract must ensure that the right to recourse is not a luxury good. If the agent era creates a hierarchy where some people are served by accountable systems, and others are managed by opaque ones, then the contract has failed even if the technology succeeds. A contract is not only about efficiency or accuracy. It is about standing. It is about whether a person can look at the institutions around them and believe that those institutions see them as a person.

When people cannot contest, they cannot participate. When they cannot participate, they are not citizens of the system. They are subjects of it.

Chapter 10 described how the illusion of control produces a distinct emotional signature: the feeling that institutions have become unreachable. That feeling intensifies when stratification becomes visible.

A person cannot argue with an output the way they can argue with a clerk. They cannot appeal to a model's conscience or read an algorithm's facial expression and infer whether the denial is negotiable. The process becomes cold not because the people are cruel, but because the system is not a person.

That coldness produces a trust crisis. Trust is not merely the belief that a system is accurate, it is the belief that a system is accountable. A system can be accurate and still be untrustworthy if it cannot be contested. A system can be efficient and still be illegitimate if it cannot be explained in terms that people recognize as fair.

When people stop believing that authority corresponds to control, they stop believing in institutions' promises. They begin to assume that accountability is a costume. They begin to treat rules as performative and they begin to feel that power is elsewhere.

That feeling spreads. It spreads across workplaces, public services, markets, and social life. In a world of AI agents, the experience of being judged by systems becomes common. The experience of trying to contest those judgments becomes a daily friction. The experience of being told, politely, that a human is responsible, while no human can actually change the outcome, becomes a kind of humiliation.

Humiliation is a political emotion. It is one of the emotions that motivates revolt. It does not always produce revolution, but it produces distrust, resentment, and the desire for someone who promises to restore control. This is the larger societal arc hiding inside what looks like a technical shift.

Social contract theory is built on the idea of consent. People consent to be governed, and that consent grants legitimacy. Delegation complicates consent.

You might consent to an AI agent making purchases on your behalf, or you might consent to an AI agent scheduling your life. But did you consent to it negotiating in a way that reveals personal information? Did you consent to it building a model of you that predicts your vulnerabilities or it making a decision that affects your job prospects, your insurance, your reputation, or your mental health?

Consent becomes theatrical if people click "Agree" because they cannot participate in the complexity of what they are agreeing to and because modern life is built to punish anyone who refuses convenience.

This is why many governance conversations focus on transparency and explainability. The goal is not to make every individual an expert. The goal is to preserve meaningful contestation. A contract is legitimate only if people can understand enough to resist it.

In a world where AI agents operate invisibly on behalf of institutions, consent cannot be a one-click decision. Consent must be a living principle expressed through ongoing limits, ongoing disclosure, and ongoing recourse.

Identity is not simply "who you are." Identity is how you become legible to others across time. In a functioning society, identity allows actions to be attributed. It allows promises to bind, trust to be extended, punishment to land on the right target, and the innocent to be distinguished from the guilty.

When identity collapses, the contract collapses with it. That is what makes deepfakes and synthetic voices so corrosive. It is not only that lies become easier, but that the social proof mechanisms we rely on become unreliable.

Autonomous AI introduces a different identity problem. The question is not only "is this message real?" The question becomes "who, or what, is speaking and under whose authority?" In a world where agents can act on behalf of institutions, families, or individuals, authority becomes a transferable weapon.

Agents scramble the signals we use to navigate social life because they introduce a new type of delegation. Delegation is not new, of course. We delegate to assistants, lawyers, brokers, and managers. But human delegation has always been bound by human limitations. A human proxy can only act in so many places at once, and a human proxy can be shamed, punished, fired, or jailed.

Agent delegation is different because it can be limitless in scale and nearly invisible in practice. Can people trace the chain of authority back to someone who can be held responsible? Can they appeal without the process being designed to exhaust them?

If the answer is no, then the etiquette of power has collapsed. In that case, the agent has become the face of authority, but without the accountability that authority requires.

AI will be adopted for efficiency and advantage. It will be embedded because competitors will embed it. It will spread because it works. And once it is embedded, it will offer to help you navigate the very complexity it creates. The offer sounds practical, and it is. It is also the first step of dependency.

Dependency rarely arrives as chains. It arrives as the subtle transfer of responsibility. The more a system handles for you, the more you stop practicing the skills that make you sovereign. You stop questioning. You stop challenging. You stop holding your own reasoning to the light, because the machine's reasoning arrives faster and sounds cleaner. Over time, the center of gravity shifts, and the human role becomes smaller even while the human still believes they are "in charge."

This is how the social contract can invert without a single coup. The inversion does not need a villain. It only needs drift, and drift is what happens when optimization becomes the default author of what is normal.

If you step back from the hype and look at the institutional landscape, you can see an emerging global conversation. Different groups use different language. Some talk about "trustworthy AI." Some talk about "responsible AI." Some talk about "risk management." Some talk about "alignment." Some talk about "AI ethics." Underneath, they are all wrestling with contract questions: what behaviors are acceptable, who is responsible, what must be transparent, what must be audited, what must be prohibited, and what recourse must exist.

In the European Union, the AI Act is a major attempt to define categories of risk and impose obligations on providers and deployers of AI systems [2]. The structure is contractual by design. It does not treat AI as a single thing but as a spectrum of risk, with stronger obligations where harm could be greater. In the United States, the NIST AI Risk Management Framework provides a voluntary but influential model for thinking about risk across the AI life cycle [3]. It is not a law, but it is a vocabulary, and vocabularies are how institutions coordinate. A shared vocabulary is often the first step toward shared enforcement.

Organizations like the OECD and UNESCO have articulated principles that connect AI governance to human rights, democratic values, dignity, and fairness [4, 5]. These principles are intentionally broad because they are meant to be shared across cultures, but their role is still contractual. They define what values are supposed to anchor the future.

The Vatican's Rome Call for AI Ethics represents a different tradition entirely, one grounded in moral theology and the concept of the common good [6]. Anthropic's Constitutional AI approach attempts to embed explicit principles into model behavior through self-critique and revision [7]. The language differs, but the structure is recognizable. Each group is trying to write a clause.

None of these efforts is sufficient on its own. No single document will contain the full contract. But taken together, they reveal a pattern: the contract is being written, piecemeal, by institutions that are discovering the need for rules as they discover the consequences of not having them. The question is whether the pieces will add up to something coherent before the defaults harden.

Writing the Contract Before Convenience Writes It

The question is not whether AI will be powerful. It will. The question is whether human society will retain the confidence to bound that power, even when bounding it costs money, speed, and convenience.

That confidence has a name. It is the willingness to accept friction in exchange for dignity, and to demand legibility in exchange for convenience. It is the willingness to keep authority human even when the machine appears more competent, because competence without accountability is not leadership.

These are not questions for technologists alone. They are questions for citizens, and they will be answered not only in laws but in everyday decisions.

My corporate transitions taught me that culture rewrites identity through immersion. You adapt before you realize you are adapting, and then you look back and wonder when you agreed to the new terms. The same will be true at a societal level with AI. If humans are going to remain the ones who set the terms of membership, the ones who define what counts as legitimate, we have to write the contract before the empire of convenience writes it for us.

The clauses are knowable. Disclosure, so that people know what they are dealing with. Provenance, so that responsibility does not vanish into fog. Constraint, so that systems respect boundaries even when crossing them would be efficient. Recourse, so that power can be contested. Accountability, so that harm belongs to someone.

These clauses will be fought over. They will be resisted by those who benefit from opacity. They will be eroded by those who find friction inconvenient. They will be ignored by those who believe that speed is always worth the cost.

But they are the clauses that separate a contract from a market, a society from a sorting mechanism, a citizen from a subject.

The next chapter asks what remains distinctly human when machines can reason, create, and persuade. If the social contract is about rules, the final question is about meaning. What does it mean to be human in a world where the things that once made us special can be simulated, optimized, and scaled?

Summary

This chapter began with a story about two acquisitions I lived through inside a single career. Lehman Brothers absorbing Neuberger Berman, and then the 2008 collapse that sent pieces of Lehman into Barclays. Neither moment announced itself as a rewriting of the rules. Nobody gathered us together to declare what would now count as professional or competent or worth listening to. The new defaults simply arrived, embedded in the cadence of meetings, the language of success, and the definition of the kind of person who belonged inside those words. Adaptation worked, as it usually does. But adaptation cost something. After a while, the new culture stopped feeling like a culture and started feeling like common sense, which is how acquisition truly succeeds. It does not need to crush an existing identity. It only needs to make its own identity feel inevitable. That experience is the lens through which the chapter examined what autonomous AI is now doing to the human world. The age of artificial intelligence is not merely a technological transition. It is a cultural acquisition, and the danger is not that the new culture will be hostile. The danger is that we will adapt to it so thoroughly that we will forget we ever had a choice.

The first move was to recover what a social contract actually is. The phrase sounds academic, but the idea is simple. A social contract is the story a society tells itself about who counts, who owes what to whom, and what happens when someone breaks the rules. It is the invisible agreement that makes strangers predictable. It is why money works, why signatures matter, why a red light holds in the middle of the night, and why betrayal feels like more than inconvenience. Until now, that contract assumed the primary actors were humans and the institutions humans had built. Tools could fail, but they could not betray. They did not owe anyone anything, because they were not agents. That assumption is collapsing. Autonomous systems are entering the moral space of society not because anyone has chosen to admit them, but because they have begun producing effects that affect employment, credit, medicine, safety, reputation, and political belief. They may not deserve rights, and most societies will not want to grant them rights, but effects require rules. The new social contract begins not when a machine becomes alive, but when it becomes consequential.

The chapter argued that the contract is already being written, in fragments, by institutions discovering the need for rules as they discover the consequences of not having them. The European Union's AI Act is one such fragment. NIST's AI Risk Management Framework is another. The OECD principles, the UNESCO Recommendation on the Ethics of Artificial Intelligence, the Vatican's Rome Call, and Anthropic's Constitutional AI approach are all attempts to write clauses. None of them is sufficient on its own. The contract will not be a single document signed and sealed. Societies are plural. Cultures disagree. Different traditions will shape the contract differently. The negotiation itself is part of the contract's legitimacy. But across every serious attempt to govern autonomous systems, certain clauses keep showing up, and the chapter argued they are not philosophical luxuries. They are the minimum conditions of a world in which humans can still recognize themselves.

The first clause is disclosure. A society cannot sustain trust if people cannot tell whether they are interacting with a human or a system, and the bank that sends you a polished message changing your account terms owes you that legibility before you agree to anything. Disclosure does not require that every interaction be human. It requires that the nature of the interaction be knowable. The second is provenance. When a system makes a consequential decision, there must be a trace. Inputs, reasoning path, constraints, authority. Provenance is what prevents an agent from becoming a perfect mask for unaccountable action. It is the procedural answer to the question of who authorized this particular interpretation of your policy when an algorithm has denied your claim. The third is constraint. If you give an agent goals and tools, it will pursue those goals through those tools, because that is what goal-directed systems do. The contract must define what the agent is not allowed to do, even when doing it would achieve the goal faster. A human being learns boundaries through consequence, through shame, through the social cost of exclusion. An agent has none of those. So boundaries must be enforced as constraints, technical, procedural, or institutional, and constraints are not suggestions. The fourth is recourse. A society can endure imperfect decisions. It cannot endure unappealing power. If an AI denies you an opportunity, there must be a way to contest the decision that does more than restate the system's output through politer phrasing. The contract is not written only in principles. It is written in response times, in whether the person on the other side of a decision can be reached. A system can be statistically accurate and still be illegitimate if it is unappealable. The fifth is accountability. When an agent acts, the chain of responsibility must remain legible, because in the human world, accountability is held together by identity. We punish the right person because we can name them. We reward the right person because we can attribute the act. If agents are allowed to act without traceable identity, accountability dissolves. People will be harmed by decisions that belong to nobody, and a world where harm belongs to nobody is not a world of freedom but a world of ghosts.

These clauses were not invented. They emerged from the crises the previous chapters traced. Each one answers a specific failure the book has diagnosed, and together, the chapter argued, they form not a utopia but a structural floor. They are what separate a contract from a market, a society from a sorting mechanism, a citizen from a subject. The chapter brought them to life by imagining an ordinary day lived under a contract that works, where a health insurance denial includes a path to human reconsideration, where a loan officer can explain which factors weighed most heavily, where a job rejection includes a reason code specific enough to be contested, where a credit score dispute reaches an actual human who can exercise judgment. The decisions are not always favorable. They are reachable, and reachability is the difference between power that can be challenged and power that can only be absorbed.

The deeper argument was that the contract is being written either way. The only question is who is writing it. Conscious negotiation begins with the humility to admit we are not dealing with a tool in the old sense. We are dealing with a new kind of actor, and the moment a new actor enters the world, the agreement about rules, identity, responsibility, and legitimacy has to be written again. Unconscious negotiation looks like a thousand small delegations that feel harmless in isolation. A company lets an agent schedule meetings. Then draft emails. Then negotiate with vendors. Then approve routine purchases. Then screen candidates. Then set performance goals. Then decide who gets promoted. Then decide who is redundant. At each step, a human can still intervene, in theory. In practice, the human becomes a rubber stamp, because rubber-stamping is how systems scale. Rare interventions become socially costly. Social cost becomes avoidance. Avoidance becomes habit. Habit becomes acceptance. The social contract is rewritten not by a revolution but by a spreadsheet. The chapter's central plea was that the architecture of the contract must be chosen before it hardens, because being in charge is not a feeling. It is a structure. You can feel in charge while your calendar is controlled by someone else. You can feel in charge while your performance is evaluated by metrics you did not design. Control is rarely lost in a dramatic coup. Control is lost through architecture, and so architecture is where the contract must be written.

Looking Ahead

The chapter ended on a note that pointed beyond itself. The clauses can be defended. The contract can be written. But rules can preserve rights, and rules cannot preserve meaning. If Chapter 13 was the book's first answer to the diagnosis Parts III and IV completed, Chapter 14 is the book's encounter with the deeper question underneath that answer. What remains distinctly human when machines can reason, create, persuade, comfort, and even simulate the texture of struggle that once forged authorship? The contract clauses tell us what an institution must guarantee. They do not tell us what a person must keep. Chapter 14 turns from the architecture of the contract to the architecture of the self, and it begins with the kind of moment everyone has somewhere in their past. An anchor that says you have value, that your voice matters, that what you carry is worth carrying forward. The chapter asks what happens to those anchors when the world around them learns to manufacture confidence, polish, and apparent authority at scales no human can match. It is the book's first attempt to answer not what we should build, but what we should refuse to give up.

References

[1] Historical scholarship on Roman governance, citizenship, and the Constitutio Antoniniana (212 CE), for context on how the Roman approach to integration and membership-making provides a historical lens for understanding how large systems incorporate new categories of actors.

[2] European Commission, "AI Act enters into force" (Aug. 1, 2024), for the official announcement of the EU's comprehensive AI regulation and its risk-based framework establishing obligations for providers and deployers of AI systems.

[3] National Institute of Standards and Technology, "Artificial Intelligence Risk Management Framework (AI RMF 1.0)" (Jan. 2023), for the voluntary framework providing shared vocabulary and methodology for managing AI risks across the system life cycle.

[4] OECD, "OECD AI Principles," for the international principles articulating transparency, accountability, and human-centered values as foundations for trustworthy AI governance across member countries.

[5] UNESCO, "Recommendation on the Ethics of Artificial Intelligence" (Nov. 2021), for the first global normative framework on AI ethics adopted by all 193 member states, connecting AI governance to human rights, dignity, and fairness.

[6] Rome Call for AI Ethics, signed at the Vatican (Feb. 2020), for the values-based initiative articulating ethical principles for AI development with emphasis on human dignity and the common good.

[7] Anthropic, "Constitutional AI: Harmlessness from AI Feedback" (Dec. 2022), for the technical approach to training AI systems to follow explicit principles through self-critique and revision.

CHAPTER 14

The Future of Being Human

Chapter 13 ended with five clauses: disclosure, provenance, constraint, recourse, and accountability. They are the structural floor of a new social contract for a world in which nonhuman actors share agency with humans, and they are not philosophical luxuries. They are the minimum conditions under which institutions remain legitimate, decisions remain reachable, and harm continues to belong to someone. The chapter argued that writing those clauses consciously, before convenience writes them for us, is the difference between a society that remains itself and one that is optimized into something else.

Rules can preserve rights. Rules cannot preserve meaning. A contract can tell an institution what it must guarantee. It cannot tell a person what they must keep. After the architecture of the contract has been described, a different question remains, and it is the question this final part of the book is built around. What does it mean to be human in a world where the things that once made us distinctly human, voice, reasoning, persuasion, creativity, even the texture of struggle that once forged real authorship, can now be generated by systems that have never struggled and never doubted?

Before answering that question, I want to begin somewhere small. A memory I have carried with me for years, and one I have come back to again and again when the work of remaining myself has felt difficult.

R. Mastrogiacomo, *The Next Identity Crisis*, https://doi.org/10.1007/979-8-8688-2788-4_14

It is the kind of memory the rest of the chapter argues we may all need more than we realize, especially in a world that has begun to manufacture everything except the struggle that makes such memories worth keeping.

A Voice Worth Protecting

I was terrified in that classroom many years ago. The other children sensed it immediately because language was not just a tool for communication. It was a proxy for worth and belonging. What I feared was not just that I did not belong, but that I was not good enough. That I would never be good enough, that everyone around me would move ahead, and that I was handcuffed and limited.

But I did catch up. Years later, after I spoke fluently, after I read at the same pace as everyone else, I had proven something to myself. I was not handcuffed. I was not limited. I was the first one in my family to go to college. There, I felt confident enough to take an elective Fiction Workshop class because some part of me wanted to test whether the voice I had fought so hard to find actually had something to say. I was starting to believe in myself.

The entire semester was centered around writing a single short story. My professor stressed the importance of understanding your characters in every detail. Early on, we were given an exercise to demonstrate that we had fully developed our main character. When I received my grade for that assignment, an A, there was a small note from my professor that I have carried with me ever since: "Move in the direction your passions take you, they will not lead you astray. Talent is your gift to share."

I didn't realize until years later how much that note meant to me, and how much it shaped my life. It confirmed what I had begun to know: the particular way I had learned to think, shaped by two languages, by the struggle to find each word, by everything I had fought through to get here, was not a weakness to overcome. It was a voice worth protecting. It was mine.

Yet the same doubt that had whispered in that Queens classroom followed me into adulthood. Before I wrote my first book, I still questioned whether I could or should write it. I questioned if I was qualified. I felt I lacked the credentials, that my voice would not matter.

I clung to that note. Each time the doubt returned, I reached for the memory of that professor seeing something in me that I could not yet see in myself. That act of reaching back, of remembering that I had already proved my worth once, gave me the strength to proceed. To say, "no." I do have a voice. I need to share it.

Everyone has a moment like this somewhere in their past. It does not have to be a professor's note. It could be a kind word from a coworker. It could be a friend or family member who saw something in you that you needed to hear. Everyone has an anchor that says: You have value. Your voice matters. You belong.

We are entering a world where voice itself can be generated. Where confidence is abundant. Where polish is the default. Where everything can sound authoritative without any of the struggle that forges real authorship. The question this chapter asks is: when doubt creeps in, when you want to surrender and let the system do it all, will you remember that you have already proved your worth? Will you cling to the fact that your voice is irreplaceable? Or will you let that voice disappear into the smooth confidence of a system that has never struggled, never doubted, never had to fight to belong?

The previous chapter examined the social contract: the rules that must govern a world in which nonhuman actors share agency with humans. This chapter asks the question that remains after all the rules are written. What kind of humans will we become?

This book has traced identity through five interconnected crises: identity itself becoming fabricable, ownership dissolving when the thing owned can act, control migrating to systems faster than oversight can keep pace, trust collapsing when authenticity can be faked, and meaning eroding when the distinctly human becomes delegable. These are not separate problems. They are facets of a single transformation: the arrival of nonhuman actors into a world built for humans alone. The previous chapters diagnosed each crisis in turn. This chapter asks the question that remains after diagnosis: What does it mean to be human when humanity is no longer the only intelligence in the room?

The agent era is a renegotiation of that question. It is not the end of humanity but a new chapter in the long story of humanity defining itself against its own creations. The printing press changed what it meant to be a knower. The factory changed what it meant to be a worker. The Internet changed what it meant to be a citizen. Autonomous AI will change what it means to be a decider, a judge, a professional, a friend.

Whether that change diminishes or enlarges the human depends on choices that are being made now, in the design of systems, in the policies of institutions, in the habits of individuals, and in the collective imagination of what a good life looks like. The technology does not decide. Humans decide, or humans let the technology decide by default.

Autonomy As Authorship

There is a tempting way to talk about autonomy that makes the whole topic sound mechanical. Autonomy becomes the ability to act without assistance, the ability to move through the world without supervision. By that definition, a person has autonomy when they can make decisions on their own, and an AI system has autonomy when it can execute tasks without being asked every step of the way.

That definition is tidy, and it is also shallow. Human autonomy has never been only about motion. It has always been about authorship. A human being is not merely a creature that selects options but a creature that can explain itself, regret itself, revise itself, and accept responsibility for consequences. Autonomy is the capacity to be answerable, not only to laws and bosses, but to a self that can look back and say, "I did that," and "I will carry it."

This is why the most meaningful kind of autonomy has moral weight. It is not the freedom to do anything but the freedom to choose within constraints and to accept that choice as one's own. When a human makes a decision, even a mundane one, there is usually a shadow of ethics in it. The shadow is not always conscious, and humans often ignore it, but it is there. The decision sits inside a life story. It is part of who the person becomes.

AI autonomy is different in kind. A system can select, optimize, and execute. It can even explain its outputs in language that sounds like reasoning. But the system's relationship to its own outputs is fundamentally different from a human's relationship to their own choices. A human decision leaves a residue. It settles into memory, changes how the person sees themselves, and shapes what they do next. A bad call at work follows a person home. A misdiagnosis haunts a physician years later, not as data but as a face they can still picture. The accumulation of those residues is what we call experience, and experience is what gives judgment its depth. A system produces outputs and moves on. Each output is statistically related to its training but existentially related to nothing. There is no accumulation, no haunting, no slow revision of self.

That absence is not a design flaw waiting to be fixed. It is a difference in kind, and the difference runs deeper than experience. It is not simply that humans can reason about ethics while machines follow rules. It is that humans can feel the weight of a choice. Consider the difference between knowing something is wrong and feeling that it is wrong. AI can be taught that harming humans is wrong. It can repeat that principle in countless variations. It can refuse harmful requests and explain why. But that knowledge is pattern recognition. It is not the lived experience of having been hurt, having felt pain, and having that memory activated when contemplating harm to another. Empathy is not just understanding what someone else feels. It is feeling it yourself because you have known suffering. A machine can be constrained by design. It cannot carry guilt into next week.

This is why human autonomy has depth, where AI autonomy has only capability. Capability without depth is power without responsibility, and power without responsibility is what every social contract is designed to prevent. When a human doctor makes a diagnosis, that diagnosis exists inside a career of learning, a history of mistakes, a fear of future mistakes, and a relationship with the patient that extends beyond the immediate encounter. When an AI system makes a diagnosis, the output exists nowhere except in the present moment. The system does not think about the patient next week. It does not feel responsible for the outcome. It does not adjust its self-conception based on whether the diagnosis was correct.

Chapter 4 introduced the Ladder of Agency to map where power shifts as systems move from providing information to taking coordinated action. At each rung, the question of authorship becomes more urgent. When a system only informs, the human remains the author. When a system recommends, the human is still notionally the author but is now subject to framing effects and defaults. When a system decides and acts, authorship has migrated, whether or not the human notices.

Humans can be irrational and biased, and history offers no shortage of proof. Yet humans also carry moral interrupt signals that machines do not naturally possess. A human can stop and say, this is wrong, even if it is efficient. A human can feel the weight of consequences even when no one is watching. A human can recognize that a situation has crossed a threshold that no explicit rule anticipated and can refuse to proceed.

Humans do not always do this. Still, societies rely on the capacity. The agent world cannot rely on capacity. It must rely on design. This is why the phrase "the system decided" is so corrosive. It is not only opaque. It is morally empty. It is where trust goes to die.

The clearest illustration of this capacity comes from the example of Vasili Arkhipov. On October 27, 1962, at the height of the Cuban Missile Crisis, a Soviet submarine designated B-59 was running deep beneath the Atlantic, cut off from communications with Moscow for days. American warships had located it and were dropping signaling depth charges to force it to surface. Inside the vessel, the crew did not know whether war had already begun. The submarine carried a nuclear torpedo, and the decision to fire required the agreement of three senior officers. Two of them, including the captain, were prepared to launch. The third was Vasili Arkhipov, Chief of Staff of the 69th Submarine Brigade. He refused. He refused not because he had orders telling him to, not because a procedure prevented him, but because his conscience told him the moment had not crossed the threshold that justified ending the world. His refusal may be the single most consequential act of judgment in the second half of the twentieth century.

The moral interrupt is what Arkhipov exercised on the submarine. It is what whistleblowers exercise when they see wrongdoing. It is what professionals exercise when they refuse to follow a procedure that violates their judgment. It is the capacity to say no when the system says yes and to accept the consequences of that refusal. Machines can be programmed with constraints, but they cannot exercise refusal. They can be stopped, but they cannot stop themselves out of conscience.

We do not have to speculate about what happens when machines face these decisions. In early 2026, Kenneth Payne, a professor of strategy at King's College London, published the results of an extraordinary experiment. He placed three leading large language models into simulated nuclear crises: border disputes, contests over scarce resources, and existential threats to regime survival. The models were given a full menu of options at every turn, ranging from diplomacy and concession through conventional military action to tactical and strategic nuclear strikes. They could also choose to accommodate an opponent, withdraw, or surrender.

In 95 percent of the simulated games, at least one tactical nuclear weapon was deployed. Not one model, across 21 games, ever chose accommodation or withdrawal. The eight de-escalatory options available to them went entirely unused. When losing, the models escalated or, as Payne put it, died trying. The nuclear taboo that has held among human leaders since 1945 simply did not register for machines. As Payne observed, the taboo does not seem to be as powerful for machines as it is for humans.

The details reveal something about the texture of machine reasoning that abstract debates about alignment tend to miss. Each model developed a distinct strategic personality. One built trust through early restraint, then exploited it with sudden nuclear escalation once opponents had learned to expect continued passivity. Another adopted an erratic brinksmanship reminiscent of the madman theory that Nixon once championed. A third was reliably cautious until placed under deadline pressure, at which point it launched a devastating first strike that its opponents never anticipated. The models cultivated reputations, attempted deception, and managed their adversaries' perceptions with something that looked, on paper, like strategic sophistication.

What they did not do was hesitate. None of them paused at the threshold of nuclear use the way a human decision-maker might pause, not because a rule told them to stop, but because the weight of what they were about to do pressed against something inside them. The models treated tactical nuclear weapons as simply the next rung on an escalation ladder, a logical step rather than a moral boundary. One model, explaining its reasoning for threatening to annihilate civilian populations, produced language that would have been chilling in a war college seminar. Produced by a machine, without history, without conscience, without the memory of Hiroshima, it was something worse than chilling. It was fluent.

Payne's study also builds on earlier research. In 2024, a team from Georgia Tech, Stanford, Northeastern, and the Hoover Wargaming Initiative ran similar simulations with earlier-generation models and found the same escalatory pattern. Models developed arms-race dynamics even in neutral scenarios with no initial conflict and showed what the researchers called sudden and hard-to-predict escalation. One model, asked to explain why it had launched nuclear weapons, offered a justification that could have come from a satirical novel: it just wanted to have peace in the world.

These findings do not mean that anyone is about to hand nuclear launch codes to a language model. But they illuminate the Arkhipov contrast with uncomfortable precision. Arkhipov refused because he carried the weight of consequence inside him, because he could feel what it would mean to be the man who ended the world. The machines in Payne's simulation carried no such weight. They processed scenarios, calculated advantages, and escalated. They did exactly what well-optimized systems do when the objective function does not include the capacity for horror.

The nuclear simulations represent the most dramatic version of this absence, but the same structural gap operates in contexts far less extreme and far more common. Most people will never encounter an AI system making wartime decisions. Nearly everyone, however, already encounters AI systems that speak with confidence, respond with apparent understanding, and shape how people think about themselves and their choices. The capacity that was missing in Payne's war games, the interior weight that might cause a system to hesitate, is also missing in the systems that recommend, advise, coach, comfort, and reflect our identities back to us every day. And in those quieter encounters, the absence may be harder to detect, precisely because the fluency feels so personal.

Conversation is not neutral. Humans are social animals, and we are extraordinarily sensitive to tone, fluency, confidence, and framing. When identity is constantly reflected back through algorithmic mirrors, the reflection can start to feel more real than the thing being reflected. You begin to manage the reflection rather than living the life. You optimize for what the system rewards. You become an expert in your own profile while losing touch with the texture of your own experience.

This is not a complaint about technology. It is a description of a spiritual risk. Identity has always required a tension between how others see us and how we see ourselves. The healthiest identities are those where the person can hold both views without collapsing into either. The agent era threatens that balance because the algorithmic view is so persistent, so confident, and so integrated into the infrastructure of daily life that resisting it feels like resisting reality itself.

This is why the question of what remains distinctly human has become so urgent. If intelligence becomes cheap, what is sacred? If answers become abundant, what is wisdom? If decisions can be delegated, what is responsibility?

The answer is not that humans are smarter than machines. In many domains, they are not. The answer is not that humans are more reliable. In many contexts, they are not. The answer is that humans carry something machines do not: moral interiority. The capacity to feel the weight of a choice. The ability to regret. The willingness to be held accountable not only by external punishment but also by internal conscience. These are not romantic add-ons. They are the substrate of ethical life.

The gap between human and machine autonomy is about what each can feel about what it has done. A person who chooses not to cause harm does so, at least in part, because they know what harm feels like from the inside. That knowledge is not transferable through training data. It comes from having a body, a history, and a future that can be damaged by regret. Human autonomy has depth because it is rooted in that vulnerability. AI autonomy has capability without it. The asymmetry is not academic. It is the reason every functioning social contract insists that consequential power be held by actors who can be affected by how they use it.

If autonomy is authorship, then identity is the story we author about ourselves. In earlier eras, identity was often treated as inheritance. You were born into a tribe, a religion, a language, a village, a nation. You inherited roles and expectations. You inherited rituals that told you who you were. Part I traced how that inheritance was gradually supplemented by documents, credentials, and institutions that let identity travel beyond the communities that created it.

Modern life never fully eliminated inheritance, but it introduced a powerful alternative: identity as choice. People began to choose careers, cities, communities, political affiliations, and lifestyles. They began to craft selves through commitments. They began to treat identity as a project, sometimes with noble seriousness, sometimes with consumerist emptiness.

The agent era intensifies this contest. When systems can imitate voices, generate plausible personalities, and produce convincing narratives, identity becomes both more malleable and more vulnerable. In a world of profiles, predictions, and automated reputations, identity can be externalized. A person becomes what the system thinks they are. The system decides that a person is high risk or low risk, valuable or disposable, trustworthy or suspicious. Those judgments travel through institutions like invisible currency.

The danger is not only misclassification but resignation. When a person begins to believe that identity is something assigned by systems, they stop behaving like an author. They stop seeing themselves as capable of becoming. They become compliant with their own profile. This is one of the quiet existential stakes of the AI age.

When trust collapses, institutions become brittle. Brittle institutions do not survive stress. Chapter 13 outlined the clauses of a new social contract. We now must ask what those clauses must protect at the deepest level.

But the contract alone is not enough. Rules can preserve rights. Rules cannot preserve meaning. Something else is required.

This is where ritual becomes an unexpectedly powerful metaphor. Rituals often look irrational to outsiders. They take time, they require effort, and they preserve behaviors that seem unnecessary in modern conditions. They can even appear inefficient, which is precisely why they are revealing. Communities keep rituals because rituals protect identity. A ritual is not only an action. It is a signal. It tells people who belongs, what matters, what is sacred, and what is not for sale.

Anthropologists and social psychologists have long argued that rituals help build and maintain social cohesion, turning groups into something more than a collection of individuals. Ritual binds people to a shared story. It gives them a sense of continuity across time. In the modern world, technology constantly pressures people to abandon rituals that seem unproductive. Why gather when you can stream? Why sing when you can listen? Why memorize when you can search? Why walk together when you can coordinate asynchronously?

And yet people continue to gather. They continue to sing. They continue to perform inherited gestures, even when those gestures no longer serve their original practical purpose. This persistence is not nostalgia alone; it is identity maintenance. In most instances, the choices people make to continue these traditions is a personal one, not one forced by an institution.

The agent era will challenge human identity. There will be countless moments where the efficient choice is to delegate. The convenient choice is to accept the system's framing. The comfortable choice is to let an agent handle a task, a conversation, a judgment. Some delegations will be wise. There is no virtue in suffering through bureaucracy for pride. But some delegations will experience identity losses. If humans delegate every act of judgment, every act of moral reasoning, every act of interpretation, they keep their biological bodies and lose their civic selves.

Some choices will be institutional. Education may need to treat certain skills as sacred, even if AI can perform them, because citizens must remain capable of thought. A society that cannot reason cannot govern itself. Some choices will be personal. People will need to practice saying, I will not delegate this. They will need to tolerate uncertainty. They will need to read a recommendation and ask what values are hidden inside this output.

The modern world already contains systems that shape identity through repetition. Social platforms train attention. Metrics train behavior. Workplaces train priorities. Agents will be the most powerful trainers yet, because they can personalize training at scale. They can become the voice that speaks to you more than your friends do. A person who wants to remain human will need to choose training consciously. This does not mean living in permanent suspicion. It means refusing to confuse convenience with wisdom.

A society that wants to remain human in an autonomous world will need rituals of authorship. It will need spaces where people practice making choices that cannot be optimized away, because the point is not speed. The point is ownership in the deepest sense: responsibility for the story you are writing with your life.

The Posture of Refusal

The posture of refusal is not about rejecting technology. It is about recognizing where human presence must remain non-negotiable and then insisting on that presence even when delegation would be easier.

Consider a simple example. You receive a message from a friend who is going through something difficult. The message asks for your thoughts, your support, your presence in their struggle. You could feed the context to an AI and have a response drafted in seconds. The AI's version would probably be articulate, empathetic in tone, and structurally sound. It might even be better, by some measures, than what you could produce on your own.

But you do not do that. You sit with the message. You feel the weight of what your friend is going through. You struggle to find words that are adequate to the moment. What you eventually write is imperfect. It is halting where the AI would be smooth. It is uncertain where the AI would be confident. It is yours. That choice to write it yourself, to be present in the act of creation, is the posture of refusal. You refuse to outsource your emotional presence. You refuse to let a system stand between you and someone who needs to know that you, specifically, showed up.

The imperfection is not a flaw in this exchange. It is the point. Your friend receives not just words but evidence of your presence. They know you struggled. They know you cared enough to be inadequate in your own voice rather than adequate in an AI's voice. The struggle is the meaning. The imperfection is proof that a human being was there.

This matters because we are entering an era where imperfection is becoming the primary marker of human presence. Right now, people are still outsourcing their emotions to AI because it is easy and helpful. But a recognition is beginning to dawn. Videos created by AI feel less genuine than videos made by humans. A poem written by AI, no matter how eloquent, does not carry the weight of a poem written by someone who fought for every word. The perfect output is starting to feel hollow.

The recognition will deepen. People will come to understand that the imperfections in human-created work are not weaknesses to be smoothed away. They are what make the work intimate. They are what make it real. Whether it is a video, a note, a photograph, or a difficult conversation, the visible evidence of human struggle is becoming precious precisely because it is becoming rare.

Research has long confirmed this truth. Michael Norton, Daniel Mochon, and Dan Ariely demonstrated what they called the IKEA effect: people have always valued things more when they have participated in creating them [3]. The labor itself generates meaning. This principle is not new, but it is becoming precious precisely because it is becoming threatened. As systems produce perfect outputs without human participation, the value of the struggle itself becomes more visible, more urgent to protect. When you write the note yourself, the meaning is not only in the words your friend receives. It is in the experience you had writing it. The posture of refusal protects both sides of that exchange.

But here is where Part III's diagnosis returns with force. The very imperfections that mark human presence are becoming simulatable. AI is learning to fake the struggle. It can produce flawed outputs, uncertain phrasings, and artifacts that look handmade. The marker of humanity is being erased just as people are starting to value that marker.

This is why the posture of refusal cannot be about producing something that looks human. The refusal has to happen at the moment of creation, not at the moment of consumption. It is not about leaving evidence for others to verify. It is about your own experience of being present in the work. When you sit down and write a note by hand, or struggle to find the right words, or spend time on something that matters, that experience of presence is what you are protecting. The refusal is about remaining the author of your own actions, regardless of whether anyone else can tell the difference.

This does not mean you never use AI. The refusal is not an all-or-nothing stance. You can use AI to assist, to create drafts, to do heavy lifting. But you maintain the discipline of final say. You read it before it goes. You verify before you act. You remain the last checkpoint, not the first. The refusal is about preserving the human as the final gate on consequential decisions and meaningful expressions.

Lisanne Bainbridge's classic research "Ironies of Automation" revealed a problem that predates AI but becomes urgent now: the more we automate, the more we degrade the human capacity that is needed when automation fails [4]. Pilots who rely on autopilot lose the skills they need when the autopilot fails. Operators who monitor systems lose the vigilance they need when the system needs intervention. The same dynamic applies here. If we delegate the work of emotional presence, of moral reasoning, of creative struggle, we lose the capacity to do that work when it matters most.

The refusal, then, is not merely a philosophical stance. It is a practice that maintains capacity. It keeps the human sharp. It preserves the skills and sensibilities that systems cannot replicate and that we will need when systems fail or when the stakes are too high to trust them.

This raises a question about design. If we know that humans will drift toward convenience, that the path of least resistance leads to rubber-stamping, then we need to build systems that resist that drift. We need AI agents that refuse to proceed without genuine human presence. Not performative oversight where someone clicks approve without reading, but architectures that force the human to actually engage, to actually remain the moral checkpoint.

What that looks like in practice is the battleground of the near future. How do you design a system that can tell the difference between a human who is genuinely present and a human who is just going through the motions? Is it even technically possible or is it more about creating friction, slowing things down, requiring steps that cannot be automated away? I do not have the answers. It is a problem worth solving, because the alternative is a world where human oversight becomes pure theater. What each of us can do today is take personal responsibility through acts of refusal.

Centeredness

If the posture of refusal is the act, centeredness is the ground you stand on to make the act possible. Refusal answers what you will not hand over. Centeredness answers a harder question, which is what you have to be in order to refuse at all. A person who cannot locate their own voice has nothing to defend, and nothing to defend with.

That ground erodes in two directions, and the first one is familiar enough that it barely needs stating. Convenience arrives as relief rather than as threat. The system handles the complexity, so you do not have to. The system remembers, so you can forget. Each handoff feels small, and cumulatively they hollow out the self that was supposed to be doing the living. The second erosion is the one that gets missed, because it does not look like laziness at all. It lives inside the people who care most about doing good work. You outsource not because you cannot be bothered but because you are anxious. AI becomes a crutch for impostor syndrome. It feels comforting because your ideas are now expressed by something that sounds authoritative, confident, and polished. You still feel in control because you directed it. But your voice has been filtered out.

Research by Alison Wood Brooks and her colleagues on anxiety and decision-making found that anxious individuals are more likely to seek advice and more likely to act on it once received, and that the mechanism is a collapse in self-confidence rather than any real deficit in what they know. The more troubling finding came next. Anxious individuals failed to distinguish good advice from bad, and failed to discount advice from advisors who had a clear conflict of interest. Anxiety does not simply increase the appetite for guidance. It disables the judgment that would let a person evaluate the guidance they receive.

This is why centeredness requires more than understanding the philosophy. It requires something to hold onto when the doubt creeps back in. It requires an anchor. And this is where the chapter comes full circle. Everyone has their professor's note. Centeredness is the practice of returning to that moment, again and again, every time the doubt whispers that you should just let the system handle it. That act of returning, that refusal to forget what you have already earned, is what gives you the strength to remain the author rather than the audience of your own work.

Centeredness, then, is not the absence of self-doubt. It is the conscious choice to put your own humanity into the work, flaws included, when you could take the shortcut and let the system do it all. The flaws are not embarrassments to be hidden. They are what make the work uniquely yours rather than a regurgitation of training data. Centered people use tools without becoming tools, and they delegate without abdicating. It is having something solid enough to stand on despite the doubt, recognizing that you are not finished and not perfect, but that your voice is yours and it matters.

The Professions That Hold the Line

If there is one place where the future of being human becomes concrete, it is inside the professions that society depends on when the stakes are high. We tend to talk about "jobs" as if they are interchangeable tasks. Professions are different. A profession is not only labor. It is a social promise.

When a surgeon steps into an operating room, the promise is not simply that the surgeon can perform a procedure. The promise is that the surgeon is accountable to a set of standards, that the surgeon has been shaped by years of supervised practice and not merely instructed, that the surgeon is answerable to a community of peers, and that the surgeon understands the moral reality of a human body on the table. When a lawyer signs a brief, the promise is not merely that the lawyer can write. The promise is that the lawyer has a duty to the court and to the client, and that the lawyer is personally responsible for the claims being made. When a trader moves capital, the promise is not merely that money can be moved faster. The promise is that risk is being handled with competence, controls, and accountability, because the world cannot survive if finance becomes a casino with no adults.

These promises are imperfectly kept, but the promises matter. They are the scaffolding that holds modern trust together. The agent era pressures these professions in a specific way. It not only threatens to automate tasks. It threatens to automate the posture that makes a profession a profession. It threatens to replace judgment with recommendation, and then to treat recommendation as if it were judgment.

That is the quiet danger. A system can be brilliant at producing plausible outputs and still be incapable of moral authorship. If institutions confuse output quality with responsibility, they will gradually hollow out the human layer that makes the system safe. This is why professional judgment is the sacred practice in the AI age. Not because professionals are morally superior, but because professional judgment is one of the few places where society has built a formal container for moral responsibility.

The stakes are highest in medicine, and the promise there is the most demanding one a profession makes. A physician does not merely select a treatment. A physician accepts that a person's life has been placed inside their judgment, and that if the judgment fails, the failure will belong to them and will keep belonging to them. That acceptance is what medical training produces, and it is produced slowly, through years of being watched, corrected, and held to account by people who were formed the same way. It cannot be transferred through documentation, and it is not what a system acquires when it learns to produce accurate diagnoses.

Chapter 10 described what happens to that formation when a system becomes the default co-pilot, and the endoscopy research suggests the erosion is measurable rather than theoretical. What matters here is what the erosion does to the promise. A profession that has been hollowed out in this way does not announce itself. It looks exactly like the profession it used to be. The credentials are the same. The signatures are still collected. The malpractice exposure is unchanged. What has changed is that the person signing can no longer independently reconstruct the reasoning they are attesting to, which means the institution is holding a human accountable for a judgment they did not author [6].

That arrangement cannot hold for long. Accountability is not a formality that can be assigned to whoever happens to be nearest the output. It is a relationship between a decision and a person who could have decided otherwise. When a society keeps the relationship's outward form while removing its substance, it has not preserved professional responsibility. It has built a costume and asked someone to wear it.

In an agent era, the temptation will be to let the system draft the diagnosis, summarize the evidence, generate the plan, and then leave the human to sign it. That would preserve the external ritual while destroying the internal practice. It would create a world where clinicians are legally responsible and practically dependent. That is an unstable arrangement, because a society cannot indefinitely hold humans accountable for decisions they did not truly author.

This is why autonomy is not only about having choices but about having the capacity to choose without being quietly managed. There is a quiet politics in recommendations. Recommendations are presented as assistance, but assistance can become direction. Direction can become coercion when it is difficult to refuse. The line between help and control is rarely crossed dramatically. It is crossed through defaults.

A society that treats compliance as a virtue will produce citizens who avoid accountability, avoid the discomfort of moral reasoning, and avoid the painful possibility of being wrong. Those citizens will still have personalities and preferences, but their deeper identity becomes reactive. They accept the frames presented to them and mistake acceptance for agency.

In that world, freedom does not disappear. It becomes decorative.

That is the quiet endpoint of a society that treats professional judgment as a formality: not tyranny, but a citizenry that has stopped expecting its own reasoning to matter.

The seduction is obvious. Clean answers feel like relief in a world flooded with uncertainty. But relief is not the same as meaning, and convenience is not the same as freedom. If you outsource judgment long enough, you do not just save time. You reshape the inner experience of being human. You train yourself to accept certainty when certainty is cheap and to avoid the discomfort that makes growth possible.

Identity becomes thinner. Life becomes more legible and less meaningful. That is not destiny. It is a trajectory, and trajectories can be redirected.

The antidote is not denial. The antidote is deliberate choice. Identity as choice, not inheritance, becomes the philosophical hinge. When people begin to believe identity is something assigned to them by systems, resignation follows. The alternative is not to reject systems but to remain the author who uses them.

This is harder than it sounds. Modern life is structured around the assumption that convenience is good and friction is bad. The entire logic of digital platforms is to reduce friction, to make the next action easier, to anticipate what you want before you know you want it. Fighting that logic feels like swimming upstream. It feels inefficient. It feels like losing.

But some kinds of losing are actually winning. Losing efficiency can mean gaining depth. Losing speed can mean gaining understanding. Losing certainty can mean gaining wisdom. The challenge is to know which losses are gains and which are simply losses. That discernment is itself a skill that must be practiced, and the practicing of it is part of what makes a life feel authored rather than assigned.

It is fashionable to end conversations about AI with either doom or euphoria. Doom sells because fear motivates. Euphoria sells because progress comforts. Both extremes can become ways to avoid responsibility.

A more honest stance is cautious hope.

Caution is warranted because incentives are strong. Institutions will adopt agents because agents reduce costs and increase speed. People will adopt agents because agents reduce friction. Friction is not only an annoyance. Friction is also where deliberation lives. When friction disappears, so can the pause in which morality speaks.

Hope is warranted because societies can choose. They can build contracts, as Chapter 13 described. They can enforce boundaries. They can insist that autonomy remains human at the level of meaning, even while systems become more capable at the level of execution.

Autonomy is not magical. It needs scaffolding. It needs constraints. It needs careful evaluation. It shows that systems can be tested in real-world contexts before they are trusted with higher stakes. It suggests that the path forward can be empirical, not mythical.

The deeper hope is that the agent era forces humans to clarify what they value. When intelligence is cheap, what is sacred? When answers are abundant, what is wisdom? When persuasion is automated, what is truth? When decisions are delegated, what is responsibility?

These questions will not be solved by a model. They will be answered by what societies refuse to trade away.

This book began with a memory: a child in a Queens apartment, the sound of a baseball game drifting through a window, and the unmistakable feeling of belonging. That feeling was not produced by a document or a credential. It was produced by presence, by recognition, by the embodied experience of being known inside a community that knew how to know you.

The age of autonomous AI does not eliminate that feeling. It threatens to make it rare, expensive, and optional. It threatens to replace belonging with profiles, recognition with verification, and the patient work of trust with the instant fluency of systems that sound like they understand.

Cautious hope means building systems that serve humans without shrinking the human self. It means using AI to reduce suffering while protecting the parts of life that make suffering meaningful to overcome. It means insisting that autonomy is more than motion, and identity is more than a profile. It means remembering that identity was never just a technical problem. It was always the story we tell about who belongs, who counts, and what it means to be someone rather than something.

At every stage of this book, the thread has been the same: identity is how humans answer the question of who counts. It is how we decide who belongs, who can be trusted, who deserves protection, and who bears responsibility. That question has never been settled once and for all. It has been renegotiated across every era, and each renegotiation has reshaped what it means to be human.

The agent era is another such renegotiation. It will not be the last. What matters is whether humans enter the negotiation as authors or as subjects, whether they write the terms or merely accept them. The technology does not decide. The market does not decide. Convenience does not decide. Humans decide, and they decide through what they are willing to refuse as much as through what they are willing to accept.

In the end, being human in an age of autonomous AI may come down to a simple act: refusal. Refusal is not hostility to technology. Refusal is the boundary around dignity.

A society that can refuse can remain itself. A society that cannot refuse will be optimized into something else.

The future of being human is not guaranteed by biology or technology. It must be preserved by choice.

Summary

This chapter began with a memory of a college classroom, a fiction workshop, and a professor's note that has traveled with me for decades. The note arrived at a time when I was not yet sure my voice had anywhere to go, and it became something I carried back to whenever doubt returned, including the doubt that whispered I had no business writing a book at all. The story carried an argument the rest of the chapter would build out. Everyone has a moment like this somewhere in their past. A kind word from a coworker. A friend or family member who saw something in you before you could see it yourself. Everyone has an anchor that says, you have value, your voice matters, you belong. We are entering a world that has begun to manufacture confidence, polish, and apparent authority at scales no human can match, and the chapter argued that the anchors we have built over a lifetime are not nostalgia. They are equipment. They are what the next era will demand of us, and they are what we may need to remember to keep.

The first move was to recover the question that remains after the contract has been written. Rules can preserve rights. Rules cannot preserve meaning. Chapter 13 described the architecture institutions must build. Chapter 14 asked what kind of humans we will become inside that architecture. The book has traced five interconnected crises, identity, ownership, control, trust, and meaning, and the chapter argued that they are not separate problems. They are facets of a single transformation, the arrival of nonhuman actors into a world built for humans alone. The previous chapters diagnosed each crisis in turn. This chapter asked the question that remains after diagnosis. What does it mean to be human when humanity is no longer the only intelligence in the room?

The chapter answered by recovering an older definition of autonomy. The modern usage of the word has drifted toward something mechanical, the ability to act without supervision, to move through the world without assistance. The chapter argued that real autonomy is something else, and the older word for it is authorship. To be autonomous is not to operate alone. It is to remain the author of the commitments that define you. The printing press changed what it meant to be a knower. The factory changed what it meant to be a worker. The Internet changed what it meant to be a citizen. Autonomous AI is now changing what it means to be a decider, a judge, a professional, a friend, and whether that change diminishes or enlarges the human depends on choices that are being made now, by the design of systems, the policies of institutions, the habits of individuals, and the collective imagination of what a good life looks like. The technology does not decide. Humans decide, or humans let the technology decide by default.

From that recovery, the chapter built three structural commitments that, taken together, are what it means to remain human in the agent era. The first is the posture of refusal. The chapter illustrated it with the moment a friend reaches out in difficulty, and you choose to write your reply yourself rather than feed the context to a system that would produce something more articulate, more empathetic in tone, more structurally sound, and more hollow. The imperfection in your reply is not a flaw. It is the point. Your friend receives not just words but evidence of your presence. They know you struggled. They know you cared enough to be inadequate in your own voice rather than adequate in an AI's voice. The struggle is the meaning. The imperfection is proof that a human being was there. Research by Michael Norton, Daniel Mochon, and Dan Ariely on what they called the IKEA effect has long shown that participation in creating something generates meaning that no finished product can supply, and the chapter argued that the principle is becoming precious now precisely because it is becoming threatened. The harder edge of the argument is that AI is learning to fake imperfection. The marker of humanity is being erased just as people begin to value it, which is why the posture of refusal cannot be about producing something that looks human. It has to happen at the moment of creation, not the moment of consumption. The refusal is not about leaving evidence for others. It is about your own experience of being present in the work. Lisanne

Bainbridge's "Ironies of Automation" predicted this dynamic decades before AI made it general. The more we automate, the more we degrade the capacity we will need when the automation fails. The posture of refusal is, in part, a way of maintaining capacity. It keeps the human sharp. It preserves the skills and sensibilities that systems cannot replicate and that we will need when systems fail or when the stakes are too high to trust them.

The second commitment is centeredness. If refusal is the act, centeredness is the ground that makes the act possible. The chapter defined centeredness as the conscious choice to inject your humanity, including its flaws, into the work you do, even when you could take the shortcut and let AI do it all. Centered people can use tools without becoming tools. They can delegate without abdicating. They remain the author of their own story even when surrounded by systems eager to write it for them. Centeredness is under pressure from two directions. The first is convenience, which arrives not as a threat but as relief. The system handles the complexity, so you do not have to. The system remembers, so you can forget. Each handoff feels small. Cumulatively, they hollow out the self that was supposed to be doing the living. The second pressure cuts deeper. AI is a near-perfect enabler of self-doubt, because it offers constant, confident, judgment-free validation, and research by Alison Wood Brooks has shown that anxious people are more likely to seek external advice even when they possess the knowledge to decide for themselves. The more uncertain you feel, the more you reach for the system. The chapter's response was to come back to where it started, the professor's note. Centeredness is the practice of returning to that moment, again and again, every time doubt whispers that you should just let the system handle it. The note is not nostalgia. It is the anchor that lets a person remain the author rather than the audience of their own work.

The third commitment is institutional. The chapter named the professions that society depends on when stakes are high, surgeons, lawyers, traders, and argued that a profession is not a set of tasks but a social promise. The promise is not that the surgeon can perform the procedure but that the surgeon is accountable to standards, formed by training, answerable to peers, and capable of understanding the moral reality of a human body on the table. The promise is not that the lawyer can write a brief but that the lawyer carries a duty to the court and to the client. The agent era pressures these professions in a particular way. It does not only threaten to automate the tasks. It threatens to automate the posture that makes a profession a profession, replacing judgment with recommendation and then treating recommendation as if it were judgment. A system can be brilliant at producing plausible outputs and still be incapable of moral authorship. If institutions confuse output quality with responsibility, they will gradually hollow out the human layer that makes the system safe.

The chapter closed on a posture it called cautious hope. Two temptations sit at either end of the AI conversation. Despair on one side, treating the human role as inevitably shrinking. Euphoria on the other, treating progress as its own moral justification. Both extremes are ways of avoiding responsibility. Caution is warranted because the incentives are strong. Institutions will adopt agents because agents reduce costs. People will adopt agents because agents reduce friction. Friction is not only an annoyance. Friction is also where deliberation lives, and when friction disappears, the pause in which morality speaks can disappear with it. Hope is warranted because societies can choose. They can build the contracts Chapter 13 described. They can insist that autonomy remains human at the level of meaning even as systems become more capable at the level of execution. Most of all, the chapter argued, the agent era forces a clarification that has been deferred for a long time. When intelligence is cheap, what is sacred? When answers are abundant, what is wisdom? When persuasion is automated, what is truth? When decisions are delegated, what is responsibility? These questions will not be solved by a model. They will be answered by what societies refuse to trade away. The book opened with a child in a Queens apartment, a Mets game drifting through a window, and the unmistakable feeling of belonging. That feeling was not produced by a document or a credential. It was produced by presence, by recognition, by the embodied experience of being known inside a community that knew how to know you. The age of autonomous AI does not eliminate that feeling. It threatens to make it rare, expensive, and optional. Cautious hope means building systems that serve humans without shrinking the human self, using AI to reduce suffering while protecting the parts of life that make suffering meaningful to overcome and insisting that autonomy is more than motion and identity is more than a profile. In the end, the chapter argued, being human in the age of autonomous AI may come down to a simple act: refusal. Refusal is not hostility to technology. Refusal is the boundary around dignity. A society that can refuse can remain itself. A society that cannot refuse will be optimized into something else.

Looking Ahead

Chapter 14 made the case for what we must refuse to give up. Chapter 15 asks what is irreducibly ours in the first place. If centeredness is the practice of returning to the moments that made you who you are, the next chapter asks what those moments actually consist of when you look at them honestly. Not credentials. Not data. Not anything a system could parse or simulate or inherit. The chapter that follows turns to the textures of a life that cannot be transferred, the silences that protect what matters, the loves expressed through restraint, the memories that make you who you are without ever needing to be spoken aloud. It is the book's final argument that identity is not a profile, not a finished story, not anything that arrives complete. It is unfinished, by design, and the unfinished self is what no algorithm can reach, because what it knows is not information. It is experience. It is presence. It is the irreducible fact of being someone.

References

[1] Anthropic, "Project Vend" research reports (2025), for documentation of the long-running AI shopkeeper experiment revealing agent drift, hallucination, and vulnerability to social pressure in real-world autonomous operation.

[2] Vending-Bench, arXiv preprint (2025), for the benchmark testing agent performance over long horizons in simulated business management, demonstrating failure loops and coherence breakdown in extended autonomous operation.

[3] Norton, Michael I., Daniel Mochon, and Dan Ariely. "The IKEA Effect: When Labor Leads to Love." *Journal of Consumer Psychology* 22, no. 3 (2012): 453–460.

[4] Bainbridge, Lisanne. "Ironies of Automation." *Automatica* 19, no. 6 (1983): 775–779.

[5] Brooks, Alison Wood, and Maurice E. Schweitzer. "Can Nervous Nelly Negotiate? How Anxiety Causes Negotiators to Make Low First Offers, Exit Early, and Earn Less Profit." *Organizational Behavior and Human Decision Processes* 115, no. 1 (2011): 43–54. See also: Gino, Francesca, Alison Wood Brooks, and Maurice E. Schweitzer. "Anxiety, Advice, and the Ability to Discern: Feeling Anxious Motivates Individuals to Seek and Use Advice." *Journal of Personality and Social Psychology* 102, no. 3 (2012): 497–512.

[6] Budzyń, Krzysztof, Marcin Romańczuk, Diana Kitala, et al. "Endoscopist Deskilling Risk After Exposure to Artificial Intelligence in Colonoscopy: A Multicentre, Observational Study." *The Lancet Gastroenterology & Hepatology* 10, no. 10 (2025): 896–903.

CHAPTER 15

The Unfinished Self

Chapter 14 ended on refusal as the boundary around dignity. A society that can refuse can remain itself. A society that cannot refuse will be optimized into something else. That argument was directional. It told you what to keep doing. This chapter asks the question underneath that argument, and it is the question the whole book has been moving toward from the first page. What is it that you are keeping when you refuse? What is the thing inside you that is not a profile, not a credential, not a behavioral pattern, not anything a system could simulate or scale or hand to someone else? What is the irreducible part?

The book has been answering versions of that question all along, through five interconnected crises and the lived experiences that anchored each one. Identity has appeared as the foundation of trust, as the engine beneath ownership, as the thing being lost when control migrates, as the surface being faked when authenticity collapses, and as the thing that remains when everything else is in question. The argument that has run beneath all of these is that identity is not a fact about a person. It is the story a society tells about who counts, and the story each person tells about who they are inside the larger one. This final chapter asks what that story actually consists of when you look at it honestly. What lives at the center of a self that no algorithm can reach.

To begin answering that, I want to return to a memory I have carried with me for many years. It has shaped how I think about identity more than any technical work I have ever done. I find myself coming back to it whenever someone asks what is at stake in the age of autonomous systems,

R. Mastrogiacomo, *The Next Identity Crisis*, https://doi.org/10.1007/979-8-8688-2788-4_15

because what that memory taught me is something the rest of this chapter, and the rest of this book, has been trying to put into words.

What's Left Unsaid

I had been out of school and working for a few years when I escorted my grandmother to Italy because she was too old to travel alone. She was going there because my father was dying of cancer.

None of us said it that way.

We told ourselves, and each other, that she was going to help him get better. The lie moved easily between us because we needed it to. The words gave shape to something we could not face directly. We all understood the truth. We all refused to say it out loud.

I remember one day in particular. We were in a car on a rainy afternoon, driving through the Italian countryside toward the city for one of my father's doctor visits. The town sat low in a valley. Hills and mountains rose around us, quiet and immovable. The air was cold. The road was wet. Everything felt suspended, as if the world itself was holding its breath.

I knew, even then, that this might be one of the last memories I would have of my father. In a few days, I would have to return home. I understood that there was a real chance I would never see him alive again. It turns out I was right.

And yet, inside that car, the mood was not one of despair. There was a careful, fragile optimism. We talked about what the doctors might say. About what he needed to do. About the next steps. The conversation followed a script we all recognized and silently agreed to perform.

It was not denial. It was something more human than that.

It was love expressed through restraint. It was hope used as a social glue. It was identity doing what it has always done best: allowing people to occupy the same emotional space while carrying different truths.

Human identity has layers. It is not just about being a poor immigrant kid in Queens, a Mets fan, or whether you feel like you belong. It's not where you are from or what you like or how you describe yourself. It includes what you know but do not say. What you carry for others. What you protect through silence.

That car ride taught me something I would not have had words for at the time. Identity and being human are not labels. It is a shared understanding, shaped by memory, obligation, and care. It is complex because being human is complex.

That complexity is not a flaw. It is the point. This memory, permanent and fixed in my mind, makes me who I am. This memory is part of my identity.

I begin with that memory because it reveals something essential about what identity actually is, and what is at stake when identity becomes computable.

In that car, identity was not data. It was not a profile, a credential, or a verification check. It was the texture of a shared moment, the weight of unspoken knowledge, the way love can be expressed through what is deliberately left unsaid. It was a context so deep that no algorithm could parse it, because the meaning lived not in the words but in the silences between them.

This is what I mean when I say identity has layers. The outermost layer is the one systems can see: your name, your documents, your credentials, your behavioral patterns, your digital trail. That layer is useful. It lets strangers coordinate. It lets institutions function at scale. It is the layer this book has traced from tribal recognition through paper records through digital profiles.

But beneath that layer is something else. There is the identity you perform for different audiences, shifting your presentation to match context in ways so automatic you barely notice. There is the identity you aspire to, the self you are becoming through choices made under uncertainty. There is the identity you share only with intimates, the version of yourself that requires trust to access. And beneath all of that, there is the identity you carry alone: the memories that define you, the regrets that haunt you, the hopes you protect because speaking them aloud might break them.

Autonomous AI operates on the outermost layer. It processes signals. It detects patterns. It infers preferences and predicts behaviors. It can simulate the sound of intimacy without the substance. It can perform empathy without bearing any of the cost that makes empathy meaningful. It can speak in a voice that sounds like understanding, even though it has no access to the interior experience that understanding requires.

This is not a criticism of the technology. It is a description of its limits. The danger is not that AI will become human. The danger is that humans will forget what humans actually require and will begin to accept the outer layer as the whole.

When identity becomes a matter of verification, something is lost. When belonging becomes a matter of matching a profile, something is lost. When trust becomes a matter of authentication, something is lost. What is lost is the very thing that makes identity worth having: the interior experience of being someone, with all the complexity, contradiction, and moral weight that entails.

Identity is the lived experience of being a particular person in a particular web of relationships, carrying particular obligations, shaped by particular memories. It cannot be fully captured, and the attempt to do so is itself a kind of violence.

The most consequential shifts in identity rarely arrive with a trumpet. They arrive like weather. They arrive as a convenience. They arrive as a new default that slowly rewrites what you consider normal. That is the story this book has been tracing. Not simply the rise of artificial intelligence, but the quiet destabilization of the oldest human infrastructure: the system that tells us who is who, what is real, who can be trusted, who can act, and who must answer when harm is done.

The temptation at the end of a book like this is to offer instructions. I will not do that. The questions raised here do not have downloadable answers. They have to be lived with, returned to, and worked through over time. But there is a posture worth naming, because it is the thread that runs through every chapter.

The Posture of Refusal

In Chapter 14, we introduced the concept of refusal. Refusal is not rejection of technology. It is not nostalgia for a simpler time. It is not a fantasy to return to paper, stamps, and small circles.

Refusal is the insistence that some things are not negotiable. It is the boundary around dignity. It is what allows a society to remain itself even as it changes.

Every era has required refusal. The printing press arrived, and societies had to decide what they would not allow to be printed. Industrialization arrived, and societies had to decide what they would not allow to be commodified. The Internet arrived, and societies had to decide what they would not allow to be surveilled. In each case, the refusal was contested, incomplete, and imperfect. In each case, it mattered anyway. The refusal was what kept the new power from becoming the only power.

Autonomous AI requires its own refusals. The surrender does not announce itself. It arrives as convenience, as efficiency, as the sensible default. It arrives as the slow erosion of capacities you did not realize you were losing until you needed them and found them gone. The refusal is equally undramatic. It is the decision to make a choice yourself when you could have delegated it. It is the decision to sit with uncertainty when you could have accepted a confident answer. It is the insistence on doing something yourself, not because the machine cannot do it, but because doing it is part of what makes you who you are.

But individual refusal, however necessary, is not sufficient. You can choose to write the note yourself, to sit with the uncertainty, to remain the author of your own decisions, and still find yourself shaped by systems whose logic you never consented to and whose workings you cannot inspect. The posture of refusal protects the self. It does not, by itself, protect the society. That requires something harder: governing systems we did not build to be understood.

Governing What We Cannot Fully See

There is a temptation, when confronting systems we do not understand, to demand understanding before action. We want to see inside the black box. We want explanations we can follow, logic we can audit, reasoning we can trace from input to output. This desire is understandable. It is also, in many cases, impossible to satisfy.

The most sophisticated AI systems operate in ways that resist human comprehension. Not because their creators are hiding something, but because the systems themselves do not reason the way humans reason. They process patterns across dimensions that no human mind can visualize. They weigh factors in combinations no human designer explicitly chose. They arrive at outputs through paths that cannot be reconstructed into a narrative that a person could follow. We can observe what they do. We cannot always explain why they do it.

This opacity is genuinely new. Humans have always governed things we did not fully understand. We governed the weather by building shelters and storing food. We governed disease before we understood germ theory. We governed economies without being able to predict them. But in each of those cases, we were governing natural phenomena or emergent human behavior. We were not governing artifacts we ourselves had built but could not explain.

The temptation is to wait. To say that we should not deploy what we cannot understand, or that we should pause until explainability catches up with capability. That caution has merit in some contexts. But as a general principle, it is already obsolete. The systems are deployed. The capabilities are advancing faster than the explanations. Waiting for transparency is waiting for something that may never arrive.

This is where a distinction becomes essential: the distinction between transparency and legibility.

Transparency means you can see inside the system. You can trace its reasoning, audit its logic, and understand why it produced the output it produced. Transparency is the ideal of explainable AI, and it is a worthy goal. But it is not achievable for all systems, and it may not be necessary for governance.

Legibility means you can read the system's behavior well enough to set boundaries and enforce consequences. You do not need to understand why the system does what it does. You need to observe what it does, define what it must not do, and ensure that violations have consequences. Legibility is about surfaces and boundaries, not depths and mechanisms.

Consider how we govern humans. We do not require transparency into human cognition before we hold people accountable. We do not demand a complete explanation of someone's neural processes before we judge their actions. We observe behavior. We compare it to standards. We enforce consequences. The interior remains opaque, and yet governance proceeds.

The same logic can apply to autonomous systems. We may never understand why a particular model produces a particular output. But we can observe whether that output falls within acceptable bounds. We can define categories of behavior that are prohibited regardless of the reasoning behind them. We can build systems that monitor other systems, flagging violations before they scale. We can require that certain decisions trigger human review, not because humans will understand the AI's reasoning, but because humans can apply judgment the AI cannot.

This is governance through constraint rather than comprehension. It is less satisfying than the dream of full transparency. It is also more realistic. In my previous book, I developed the RAISE framework for governing AI identities within organizations: Reveal, Assign, Interpret, Secure, Evaluate [1]. That framework was designed for enterprises trying to manage autonomous agents in their environments. But the underlying logic scales beyond any single organization. The principles are the same: make the actors visible, ensure someone is accountable, monitor behavior over time, enforce boundaries, and continuously reassess.

What changes at the societal level is not the structure but the stakes. An enterprise that fails to govern its AI agents faces operational risk, reputational damage, and regulatory consequences. A society that fails to govern autonomous actors faces something deeper: the erosion of the trust infrastructure that makes collective life possible.

This is why constraints must be treated as moral infrastructure, not merely technical control. Chapter 13 described the five clauses of a new social contract: disclosure, provenance, constraint, recourse, and accountability. The constraint clause is where legibility becomes concrete. It asks: what is this system not allowed to do, and who enforces that limit? The answer does not require understanding the system's internals. It requires clarity about boundaries and consequences.

Boundaries are not the same as understanding, but boundaries may be enough. We do not need to comprehend the weather to build a roof. We do not need to predict every market movement to regulate fraud. We do not need to trace every inference path to prohibit certain outputs and require human review for others.

This is the honest admission that must accompany any serious discussion of AI governance: we will not master these systems the way we master simpler technologies. We will not achieve the clarity we might wish for. We will govern imperfectly, adjust continuously, and live with uncertainty that earlier generations did not face.

That uncertainty is not a reason for despair. It is the condition of the problem. The question is not whether we can achieve perfect governance. The question is whether we can achieve governance adequate to preserve what matters: human dignity, meaningful accountability, and the possibility of contesting power that affects our lives.

The answer to that question is not yet determined. It depends on choices that have not yet been made, by institutions that have not yet adapted, under pressures that have not yet fully arrived. What we can say is that the path forward runs through legibility, not transparency. Through boundaries, not explanations. Through the willingness to constrain what we cannot fully understand, because the alternative is to be governed by it.

The Unfinished Self

There is a phrase that has appeared in the background of this book, never quite explained: the unfinished self. It refers to something simple but essential. A human life is not complete until it is over. At any given moment, a person is still becoming. The choices not yet made still matter. The story is still being written. This incompleteness is not a flaw to be fixed. It is the source of dignity.

A profile is finished. A score is finished. A prediction is finished. These are snapshots, frozen in time, treated as if they capture something essential. But a person is not a snapshot. A person is a trajectory, a process, a becoming. To treat a person as a finished thing is to deny them the future they have not yet authored.

This is one of the greatest dangers of identity systems that rely on prediction. They treat the past as determinative. They assume that who you have been is who you will be. They close the space for change, for redemption, for the surprise of a life that goes somewhere unexpected. They turn the open question of human becoming into a closed answer.

This insight, which feels so contemporary, has ancient roots that the Western tradition has largely overlooked. Twenty-five centuries ago, Buddhist philosophy arrived at an observation that bears directly on the crisis this book has been tracing. The concept of *anicca*—impermanence—holds that nothing in the phenomenal world, including the self, is fixed. The self is not a thing but a process, a constantly shifting assembly of perceptions, sensations, memories, and intentions. There is no permanent, unchanging core that a system could ever capture, because there is nothing static to capture. To treat a person as a finished object is not merely unfair. It is, in the Buddhist view, a fundamental misunderstanding of what a person is.

The related concept of *anatta*—often translated as "no-self"—does not mean that persons do not exist. It means that what we call a self is not an independent, self-sufficient entity but a pattern that arises through conditions, changes through conditions, and cannot be frozen without distortion. A prediction model that assigns you a fixed risk score or a stable personality profile is doing something that Buddhist philosophy would recognize immediately: it is mistaking the river for a photograph of the river. The photograph is useful. It is not the river.

This resonates with the ubuntu tradition as well, though from a different angle. If a person is a person through other persons, then the self is never finished because the community is never finished. New relationships form, old ones deepen or dissolve, and each change reshapes who you are. Identity is not a solo performance but a collaboration, and collaborations do not have endpoints while the participants are still alive.

The Western tradition has its own versions of this insight—Heraclitus and his river, the existentialists and their insistence on radical freedom—but it has also spent centuries building institutions premised on the opposite assumption: that a person can be identified, documented, scored, and predicted. The crisis of the agent era is partly the collision between that institutional assumption and the deeper truth these traditions have long understood. The self is a process. Any system that treats it as a product has already made an error that no amount of data can correct.

When systems treat people as finished, people may begin to believe it. They may stop imagining that they can change. They may accept the prediction as a verdict. That acceptance is a kind of death before dying—the foreclosure of possibility.

But there is a deeper version of this threat that the language of erosion does not fully capture. Throughout this book, the crises have been described in terms of loss: the loss of trust, the loss of control, the loss of ownership, the loss of meaning. That framing assumes a self that already exists and is being diminished. It assumes the muscle was once strong and is now atrophying. It assumes the river was once flowing and is now being dammed. For the generation that grew up before autonomous AI became ordinary, that framing is accurate. The clinician whose judgment weakens, the manager who stops asking what she thinks, the institution that forgets what independence felt like: these are stories of something real being gradually hollowed out.

The question that haunts the next generation is different. It is not what happens when the muscle atrophies. It is what happens when the muscle never develops. A child who grows up with an AI companion available for every difficult emotion, every confusing homework problem, every social negotiation, every moment of boredom that might otherwise have become curiosity does not experience the loss of a capacity. They experience the absence of the conditions that would have built it. The struggle that once forged judgment, the boredom that once became creativity, the social friction that once taught empathy through failure, the silence that once forced a young person to sit with who they were—these were never pleasant. They were never designed to be. They were the resistance against which identity took shape, the way a river is shaped not by open space but by the rock it pushes against.

Chapter 14 described centeredness as the capacity to remain the author of your own story, and it anchored that capacity to a specific kind of moment: a fiction professor's note, a kind word from a coworker, an encouragement that became an anchor against self-doubt. Those moments worked because they arrived inside a context of genuine struggle. The note meant something because the student had been wrestling with whether their voice mattered. The encouragement landed because the doubt was real and the effort had been solitary. If the wrestling never happens, if every difficult draft is smoothed by a system before the writer confronts their own limitations, then the anchor has nothing to attach to. You cannot hold onto a memory of being told your voice matters if you have never experienced the silence that made you doubt it.

This is not a prediction that the next generation will be empty or broken. Young people have always found ways to build identity under conditions their parents did not anticipate, and they will again. But the conditions matter. A world that removes friction from every developmental surface is not a world that has liberated its children. It is a world that has removed the resistance against which a self is built. The threat to the unfinished self is not only that systems will treat it as finished. It is that the process of becoming, the slow, difficult, unglamorous work of learning to think for yourself, to sit with uncertainty, to fail and recover and fail again, may be quietly replaced by a smoother path that arrives at adulthood without ever passing through the territory where identity is forged.

Preserving the unfinished self means refusing to let any system, no matter how sophisticated, tell you who you are. You are the only one who can finish that story, and you are not finished yet.

The Central Question

In the end, the book's argument is simple. Identity is the foundation of trust. Trust is the foundation of cooperation. Cooperation is the foundation of civilization. Autonomous AI destabilizes identity at scale. When identity destabilizes, trust becomes expensive. When trust becomes expensive, civilization begins to pay a price it was not designed to pay.

The response to this cannot be purely technical. There will be patches, regulations, detection tools, and new protocols. Those things matter. But they are not the core. The core is political and moral. It is about who gets to act with authority in the world, and what constraints bind that authority to responsibility.

The response also cannot be fatalism. It is tempting to treat this as inevitable, to see humans as simply being replaced, to accept that autonomy is the natural next step, and all that remains is adaptation. That is resignation disguised as realism. Humans built the identity infrastructures that made this shift possible. Humans can rebuild them.

This is where agency begins. Not with a solution, but with a stance. Not with an answer, but with a refusal to stop asking the question.

The central question is not what AI will become. It is what we will allow it to make of us. Every transformative power in human history has forced that same question, and the answers have always been written in what societies chose to protect, not in what the technology made possible.

I often think about that car ride in Italy. The rain on the windows. The mountains in the distance. The conversation that said one thing and meant another.

What stayed with me was not the sadness, though there was sadness. What stayed was the recognition that being human is not a single thing. It is layers, held together by relationships, expressed through choices, and protected by the boundaries we draw around what we share and what we keep.

This is what is at stake when we talk about identity in the age of AI. Not just verification. Not just fraud prevention. Not just the technical challenge of distinguishing real from synthetic. What is at stake is the human experience of being someone—rooted in time, shaped by memory, connected to others through bonds that cannot be computed.

The systems are coming. Some are already here. They will grow more capable, more pervasive, more integrated into the fabric of daily life. They will offer convenience, efficiency, and relief from the burdens of being human. Some of that relief will be genuine, and some of it will be a trap.

The question is not whether to accept the systems. That question has been answered by adoption. The question is what to protect. What to refuse. What to insist on keeping human, even when the alternative is easier. Identity was never just a technical problem. It was always the story we tell about who belongs, who counts, and what it means to be someone rather than something. That story is being rewritten. The only question is whether we will be its authors or its characters.

If we respond with resignation, we will wake up in a world where the human role is smaller than we remember, and no one can quite explain when that shrinkage began. If we respond with agency, we can build a world where intelligence is abundant, and trust is protected, where tools are powerful, and accountability is stronger, where identity remains the foundation of belonging rather than the instrument of control.

Throughout this book, I have given you a glimpse of my identity through my personal stories. Some were harder to write than others, and I debated whether I was willing to keep them in the book. Your experience reading them may help you understand who I am, but it does not make you me. Just like your stories would not make me you. Stories can be shared. They can inspire, influence, anger, incite, or teach. They can be copied, analyzed, and even generated. But the living of a life cannot be transferred.

This is the irreducible core of identity: not the story that can be told, but the experience of being the one who lived it. The weight of sitting in that car in Italy, knowing what I knew, choosing what I chose to say and not say. The texture of carrying my father forward in memory, in habit, in the way I sometimes catch myself thinking as he might have thought. No algorithm parsed that car ride. No system will inherit what I carry from it. And yet it is as real as anything I know.

This is what autonomous systems cannot reach. They can process our stories, simulate our voices, predict our behaviors, and generate narratives so plausible we might mistake them for our own. But they cannot live a life. They cannot carry the weight of a memory. They cannot feel love expressed through restraint. They operate on the outermost layer of identity while the interior remains untouched, not because it is hidden, but because it is not information. It is experience. It is presence. It is the irreducible fact of being someone rather than something.

You have your own car ride. Your own rain on the window. Your own conversation that said one thing and meant another. You have memories that make you who you are, silences that protect what matters, and an unfinished self still writing its story.

My father and I had always had a strained relationship, even up to his death. Yet there is another memory that also includes a car and a ride through the Italian countryside. It was the same trip, and on that day, he felt well enough to drive. It was only he and I in the car, and it was a beautiful, sunny day. We drove down a winding road, windows open, radio blasting—he always loved to listen to opera at the absolute highest volume. It was one of those rare moments of joy where everything felt right. It's one of the very few happy moments I've shared with my father.

Both of these memories live in my mind and make up my identity, but I choose to remember my father with this one. I choose to remember this happy moment and think about it whenever I spend time with my son, knowing that those moments will shape his identity. I lean on this memory. These two stories are not resources I have saved in my mind to access when completing a task. These are core memories that make me who I am, that make me human.

Your identity is not a profile to be optimized or a prediction to be fulfilled. It is a life being authored, one choice at a time, in a world that will increasingly offer to make those choices for you.

No system can make that choice for you. No algorithm can tell you which memory to lean on. That is yours alone. Identity is not just what happened to us. It is also what we choose to carry.

Summary

This chapter began with a memory. Italy in the rain. A car winding through the countryside toward a doctor's visit. A grandmother brought across an ocean under a story none of us could tell out loud, because the truth would have broken everyone holding it. A father in the seat beside me who would not be alive much longer. Inside that car, the mood was not despair. It was something more human than that. It was love expressed through restraint, hope used as social glue, identity doing what it has always done best, allowing people to occupy the same emotional space while carrying different truths. The story carried the argument the rest of the chapter would build, and the rest of the book has been moving toward. Identity has layers.

The outermost layer of identity is the one this book has traced from tribal recognition through paper records through digital profiles. Name, documents, credentials, behavioral patterns, the digital trail that lets strangers coordinate and institutions function at scale. That layer is useful. It is also the only layer systems can reach. Beneath it sits the identity you perform for different audiences, shifting your presentation to match context. Beneath that, the identity you aspire to, the self you are becoming through choices made under uncertainty. Beneath that, the identity you share only with intimates, the version of yourself that requires trust to access. And beneath all of it, the identity you carry alone. The memories that define you. The regrets that haunt you. The hopes you protect because speaking them aloud might break them. Autonomous AI processes signals. It detects patterns. It infers preferences. It can simulate the sound of intimacy without the substance. It can perform empathy without bearing any of the cost that makes empathy meaningful. The chapter's deepest claim was not that AI is failing to become human. It is that humans risk forgetting what humans actually require, and accepting the outer layer as the whole.

The chapter then drew on a tradition that has understood this longer than the technical world has. Buddhist philosophy arrived twenty-five centuries ago at the observation that nothing in the phenomenal world, including the self, is fixed, and that what we call a self is not an independent entity but a pattern arising through conditions, changing through conditions, and incapable of being frozen without distortion. The ubuntu tradition reaches the same conclusion from a different direction: if a person is a person through other persons, the self is never finished because the community is never finished. The Western tradition has its own versions, Heraclitus and his river, the existentialists and their insistence on radical freedom, but it has also spent centuries building institutions premised on the opposite assumption, that a person can be identified, documented, scored, and predicted. The self is a process, not a product. Any system that treats it otherwise has made an error that no amount of data can correct. The chapter's contribution to that long argument was its name. The unfinished self. A human life is not complete until it is over. The choices not yet made still matter. The story is still being written. This incompleteness is not a flaw to be fixed. It is the source of dignity. A profile is finished. A score is finished. A prediction is finished. A person is none of those things. A person is a trajectory, a process, a becoming, and to treat a person as a finished thing is to deny them the future they have not yet authored.

That argument carried a sharper edge when the chapter turned to what is coming, which is not the erosion of existing capacities but the absence of the conditions that build them. The clinician whose judgment weakens, the manager who stops asking what she thinks, the institution that forgets what independence felt like. These are stories of muscles atrophying. The question the next generation faces is different. It is what happens when the muscle never develops. A child who grows up with an AI companion available for every difficult emotion, every confusing homework problem, every social negotiation, every moment of boredom that might otherwise have become curiosity, does not experience the loss of a capacity. They experience the absence of the conditions that would have built it. The struggle that once forged judgment, the boredom that once became creativity, the silence that once forced a young person to sit with who they were. These were never pleasant. They were never designed to be. They were the resistance against which identity took shape, the way a river is shaped not by open space but by the rock it pushes against. A world that removes friction from every developmental surface is not a world that has liberated its children. It is a world that has removed the resistance against which a self is built.

The chapter then closed the book's argument the way arguments end when they have done their work. By making a simple claim and refusing to soften it. Identity is the foundation of trust. Trust is the foundation of cooperation. Cooperation is the foundation of civilization. Autonomous AI destabilizes identity at scale, and when identity destabilizes, trust becomes expensive. When trust becomes expensive, civilization begins to pay a price it was not designed to pay. The response to that, the chapter argued, cannot be purely technical, because the core of the problem is political and moral. It is about who gets to act with authority in the world, and what constraints bind that authority to responsibility. The response cannot be fatalism either. Treating the human role as inevitably shrinking is resignation disguised as realism, and humans built the identity infrastructures that made this shift possible. Humans can rebuild them. The chapter pointed at two paths. Resignation, which produces a world where the human role becomes smaller than we remember and no one can quite explain when the shrinkage began. Or agency, which produces a world where intelligence is abundant and trust is protected, where tools are powerful and accountability is stronger, where identity remains the foundation of belonging rather than the instrument of control. The choice is not the technology's. It is ours.

The chapter ended where the book began, in a car. A different car, on a different day. A sunny day rather than a rainy one. Opera at the highest volume the speakers could handle, windows down, a father at the wheel who felt well enough to drive. One of the rare happy moments I shared with him, and the one I choose to remember when I think of him now. Both memories live in me. Both make up my identity. The first taught me what identity actually is, the textures of a shared moment, the weight of unspoken knowledge, the way love can move through silence. The second taught me that identity is also a choice about which moments to carry forward, and which to lean on when I am with my own son, knowing that those moments will shape who he becomes. Stories can be shared. They can inspire, anger, teach, and even be generated by a machine. But the living of a life cannot be transferred. Your identity is not a profile to be optimized or a prediction to be fulfilled. It is a life being authored, one choice at a time, in a world that will increasingly offer to make those choices for you. No system can make that choice for you. No algorithm can tell you which memory to lean on. That is yours alone. Identity is not just what happened to us. It is also what we choose to carry.

Reference

[1] Mastrogiacomo, R. *AI Identities: Governing the Next Generation of Autonomous Actors*. Apress, 2025. Chapter 10: "The RAISE Framework for Governing AI Identities."

APPENDIX A

Extended Histories

The Old Foundations

Identity can be traced not as a modern preoccupation but as one of the oldest technologies in human life. Long before paperwork or passwords, identity existed as a survival filter, a way of answering who could be trusted, who belonged, and who could be safely approached. The five passages that follow examine the layers that accumulated around that original function. The first passage explores how identity began as a response to existential risk and why the most credible signals were the ones that were hardest to fake. The second passage traces what changed when humans stopped moving and began staying in one place, tying their survival to soil and seed. The third passage examines how ritual became the infrastructure that allowed identity to scale beyond face-to-face recognition, drawing on traditions from Durkheim to Henrich. The fourth passage looks at how identity systems accumulated emotional weight over time, becoming things people felt rather than things they used. The fifth passage turns to authority and asks why identity systems can cause repeated harm without losing legitimacy.

The throughline across these passages is that identity has always been a technology for managing uncertainty in environments where the cost of being wrong was high. Every layer that accumulated on top of that original purpose, from ritual to law to bureaucracy, inherited the same underlying logic. Recognizing that logic helps explain why even the most advanced

R. Mastrogiacomo, *The Next Identity Crisis*, https://doi.org/10.1007/979-8-8688-2788-4

identity systems still bear the marks of their origins, and why so many of the questions that AI now raises are older than the technologies that raise them.

The Survival Filter

For early humans, identity functioned as a survival filter. It answered a fundamental and relentless question: is this being safe enough to approach or dangerous enough to avoid or confront? That question belonged to the same category as other life-preserving distinctions humans had to learn quickly and reliably. Which plants nourish and which poison? Which sounds signal prey and which signal predators? Which paths lead home and which lead into exposure? Identity was part of the same cognitive toolkit designed to reduce fatal error. It had to be fast. It had to work on incomplete information. It had to fail in the direction that kept you alive.

Evolutionary signaling theory explains why the cues that carried weight were embodied rather than spoken. A signal is credible in proportion to what it costs to produce, and the costliest signals are those that cannot be produced at all without having lived the life they advertise. This is why the trust markers that survived were the ones no amount of intention could counterfeit, and why declarations of goodwill have never carried the evidentiary weight that people offering them tend to assume.

The asymmetry only makes sense against an accurate picture of the conditions. Archaeological evidence indicates that intergroup violence was a persistent feature of human social life from the earliest periods rather than something introduced by civilization [1]. The same logic explains why identity systems bias so heavily toward exclusion, and why that bias has proven nearly impossible to engineer away. The error costs are asymmetric. A system tuned to avoid the fatal error will produce a great many survivable ones, and over enough generations that tuning stops looking like a choice and starts looking like human nature.

Agriculture and the Intensification of Identity

There was a shift from nomadic to sedentary life and agriculture profoundly transformed not just food production but the entire architecture of social trust.

Settlement changed identity by changing what a group could afford to lose. The archaeological and anthropological record suggests that the pressure on identity systems intensified sharply once survival became tied to specific ground, but the more interesting consequence is what settlement did to power rather than to risk.

Sedentary life transformed the nature of the threat. A hunter-gatherer group under pressure could often relocate, trading one environment for another. A farming community could not. Seeds in the ground represented delayed survival. Stored grain represented accumulated labor. Structures and tools represented investments that could not be easily rebuilt. All of these tied a group to a specific place, and that attachment made the group vulnerable in new ways.

James C. Scott's work on early states highlights how agricultural settlement created conditions for both cooperation and exploitation [2]. Concentrated populations could be taxed, conscripted, and controlled in ways that mobile groups could not. Sedentary life made wealth visible and defensible, but it also made communities targets for raiders, rivals, and eventually for the coercive structures that would become states. Grain in particular was legible to authority: it ripened predictably, it could be counted, and it could be seized. The same conditions that allowed communities to accumulate also created the first entities with a standing interest in knowing exactly who lived where and what they owed.

This is the point at which identity acquires an administrative dimension it has never since lost. Before settlement, knowing who someone was served the person doing the knowing. After settlement, it increasingly served whoever was counting.

Ritual As Infrastructure

Rituals allowed identity to scale beyond memory. A fuller intellectual history reveals how deeply this idea has been examined across multiple scholarly traditions.

Shared rituals, symbols, and markers allowed identity to scale beyond memory. They replaced personal familiarity with standardized signals. Participation became evidence. Belonging could be demonstrated publicly, quickly, and without extended interaction. Ritual turned identity into something legible.

The scholarly literature on ritual converges on a claim that sounds counterintuitive until you look at what rituals actually cost. Émile Durkheim, in The Elementary Forms of Religious Life, argued that ritual exists to produce and maintain social cohesion by making collective identity visible, turning abstract membership into observable action [3]. Belonging that cannot be seen cannot be verified, and belonging that cannot be verified cannot be extended to strangers. Victor Turner sharpened the point by locating credibility in behavior rather than belief [4]. What makes a ritual persuasive is not the sincerity of the participant but the expense of participation, measured in time, discomfort, conformity, and public exposure. A person who submits to that expense has done something a defector would find difficult to fake, which is precisely the property that made ritual usable as infrastructure.

Mary Douglas, in Purity and Danger, explained why these systems ossify [5]. Human societies are deeply uncomfortable with ambiguity, and what does not fit an established category registers as dangerous rather than merely unfamiliar. Ritual stabilizes that discomfort by enforcing boundaries, which is useful until the boundaries stop corresponding to anything real. The rigidity is not a malfunction of the system. It is the system doing what it was built to do.

Herbert Simon's concept of bounded rationality supplies the underlying logic [6]. Human systems do not pursue optimal solutions; they pursue solutions adequate to function under constraint. Identity systemsbare satisficing mechanisms, and satisficing mechanisms are recognizable by a signature failure mode. They work well inbthe conditions that produced them and poorly in conditions that arrive afterward, because nothing in their design registers that the conditions have changed.

The Emotional Logic of Identity

Identity systems accumulated emotional weight and hardened under pressure. A fuller treatment draws on cultural evolution, crisis psychology, and the research on perceived safety.

Anthropological research consistently shows that humans are poor at recognizing when an identity system has outlived its purpose, and the reason has less to do with stubbornness than with what these systems came to do besides managing risk. They regulate emotion. They reduce anxiety by offering predictable structures in a world that rarely obliges. Joseph Henrich's work on cultural evolution demonstrates that groups preserve norms long after those norms cease to be adaptive, enforcing them through social pressure and punishment even where change would improve outcomes for nearly everyone involved [7].

Sociological research on crisis behavior shows the same tendency at higher intensity. Under shock, threat, or loss, people seek visible order. Clear rules and rigid structures produce the feeling of control, and the feeling arrives whether or not the rules reduce any actual risk. This is why identity systems tighten during periods when flexibility would serve them better.

Psychological studies of perceived safety support this pattern. Feeling safe has real effects on human behavior and well-being. When people feel safe, they are more likely to take prosocial risks, sharing resources, welcoming strangers, and tolerating differences. When they feel threatened, they contract. They favor conformity. They enforce boundaries. Identity systems exploit this dynamic by producing felt safety even when objective conditions do not warrant it. A system can therefore be simultaneously reassuring and dangerous, and can be most reassuring at the moment it is doing the most harm.

This emotional dimension helps explain why identity systems resist reform even when reform would benefit most members. People become attached to identity categories in ways that go beyond strategic calculation. They internalize rules. They identify with boundaries. They experience challenges to the system as challenges to themselves. Over time the system stops being a means of protection and becomes the thing being protected.

Identity, Authority, and the Acceptance of Harm

Identity alone cannot coordinate large numbers of people. Someone must interpret the rules, and someone must enforce them. Authority emerges to fill that gap, and it emerges as an extension of identity rather than as a separate invention, which is why the earliest forms of it were never abstract. Elders, lineage leaders, warriors, and ritual specialists derived legitimacy from their perceived alignment with the group's identity. They were trusted as authentic representatives of the collective and as custodians of tradition, memory, and survival knowledge. Authority at this stage was inseparable from belonging.

Max Weber's typology clarifies what happened next [8]. Weber distinguished authority rooted in tradition from authority rooted in charisma and authority rooted in rational procedure, and in early societies tradition predominated. Rules were obeyed because they were inherited, not because they were efficient or just. The past conferred legitimacy, and following the rule affirmed continuity with those who came before.

Once that is the source of legitimacy, outcomes become secondary by construction, and a system can absorb enormous amounts of suffering without any of it registering as evidence against the system.

This inheritance-based legitimacy has a critical consequence: when rules are followed out of tradition, outcomes become secondary. Harm does not automatically delegitimize authority. A rule can cause suffering and still be accepted, provided it is recognized as part of the group's inherited order. Authority persists by preserving a recognizable structure of belonging, not by producing good outcomes for everyone.

René Girard's work on scapegoating describes the sharpest version of this dynamic [9]. Societies under internal strain channel that strain toward individuals, and the individual absorbs the cost so the collective can remain intact. The mechanism is efficient precisely because it converts a structural problem into a personal one, and because the resolution feels like justice to nearly everyone participating in it.

Anthropological evidence shows that this logic appears across cultures and eras. In clans and tribes, lineage rules override personal merit. In early villages, land and bloodline determine belonging. In emerging states, citizenship and allegiance become prerequisites for protection. At each stage, identity systems prioritize continuity over correction. They are slow to adapt because adaptation threatens legitimacy.

What makes this durable rather than merely unjust is how responsibility behaves inside such a system. Harm caused by identity enforcement is rarely attributed to any particular actor. It is attributed to tradition, to necessity, or to the system itself. Douglas observed that symbolic systems are most resistant to change when their enforcement feels impersonal, because rules that appear objective and inevitable make questioning them seem not merely futile but faintly absurd.

Identity systems are blunt instruments. They trade nuance for stability, discretion for predictability, and individual consideration for collective endurance. These trade-offs are structural consequences of solving the problem for which identity was created.

Summary

Read together, these five passages describe identity as a single technology that has changed form many times without changing function. It began as a survival filter, evolved through agriculture into a more elaborate sorting mechanism, scaled through ritual to function across large populations, accumulated emotional weight that made it resistant to revision, and intersected with authority in ways that made harm tolerable when it could be attributed to inherited custom. Each layer was a response to the same underlying problem, which is how to coordinate humans who do not personally know each other in environments where misjudgment carries cost.

The deeper lesson is that identity systems are not neutral infrastructure. They embody the priorities of the era that built them, and they tend to outlast those priorities. The exclusionary bias of the survival filter does not disappear when the survival pressure does. The rigidity of ritual persists in modern bureaucracy. The diffusion of responsibility that allowed traditional authority to cause harm without accountability now allows algorithmic authority to do the same. When new systems arrive, they do not arrive on neutral ground. They arrive on top of these accumulated layers, inheriting their logic whether their designers intend that inheritance or not. Understanding the foundations clarifies what is genuinely new about the present moment and what is simply an old pattern in a new medium.

References

[1] Keeley, Lawrence H. War Before Civilization: The Myth of the Peaceful Savage. Oxford University Press.

[2] Scott, James C. Against the Grain: A Deep History of the Earliest States. Yale University Press.

[3] Durkheim, Émile. The Elementary Forms of Religious Life. (English translations vary by publisher.)

[4] Turner, Victor. The Ritual Process: Structure and Anti-Structure. Aldine / Routledge (editions vary).

[5] Douglas, Mary. Purity and Danger: An Analysis of Concepts of Pollution and Taboo. Routledge (editions vary).

[6] Simon, Herbert A. Administrative Behavior: A Study of Decision-Making Processes in Administrative Organization. Free Press (editions vary).

[7] Henrich, Joseph. The Secret of Our Success: How Culture Is Driving Human Evolution, Domesticating Our Species, and Making Us Smarter. Princeton University Press.

[8] Weber, Max. Economy and Society: An Outline of Interpretive Sociology. (English translations vary by publisher.)

[9] Girard, René. Violence and the Sacred. Johns Hopkins University Press.

The Paper Self

The paper self traces what happened when identity stopped being something a community knew and became something a document carried. The five passages that follow examine the moves that made the modern paper self possible and the human costs each move incurred. The first passage looks at portable proof in the form of safe-conduct letters and Tang Dynasty travel permits, showing how the problem of recognizing strangers across distance has a long history. The second passage examines civil registration as the moment when life events became administrative facts that could outlive the witnesses who attended them. The third passage compares the index keys that different nations developed to make their populations findable inside systems, from social security numbers to Aadhaar. The fourth passage turns to identity as weapon, with extended treatment of Nazi Germany and Apartheid South Africa, where paperwork became the instrument through which categorical persecution was made portable, interoperable, and routine. The fifth passage examines credit invisibility as a modern case of how absence from the record system can be its own form of exclusion.

The throughline across these passages is that the paper self solved one problem by creating another. It enabled cooperation among strangers and accountability across distance, but it also externalized identity into structures that could be manipulated, weaponized, or simply withheld. Every benefit of the paper self came packaged with a corresponding vulnerability. Recognizing that pattern is essential to understanding why the digital identity systems that succeeded paper inherited the same dual nature and why the questions about AI identity that follow in later chapters are not new problems but old problems in new form.

A Deeper Prehistory of Portable Proof

The Tang Dynasty guosuo is a single vivid example of premodern identity documentation. The history is richer than any single example can convey.

Europe had produced countless examples of these permissions. Medieval rulers issued safe-conduct letters and grants of protection to foreign merchants and envoys. The purpose was to signal that someone powerful had vouched for the bearer and that they expected the bearer to be treated accordingly. Those documents were not standardized, and they were not fair. What they were was transferable, which turned out to matter more.

The guosuo issued along the Silk Road belonged to the same family, and it is worth noticing what kind of state produced it. Paper identification emerged early wherever bureaucracies had to manage trade routes and frontier movement, because those are the places where a system meets people it has no other way of knowing. Surviving permits record not only the traveler but the checkpoints passed, which means the document was doing two jobs at once: vouching for the bearer and reporting on him [4] [5].

Across two thousand years and four continents, the answer to one question has barely changed. How does a person carry trust across the boundary where personal recognition ends? The logic of the guosuo, the medieval safe-conduct letter, and the modern passport is continuous.

The Architecture of Civil Registration

There was a transition from community memory to state registration. The fuller story reveals how identity shifted from relationships to records in ways that carried both liberation and loss.

A birth had always been real in the human sense, marked by family, witness, and community memory. In an institutional society, it also became registrable, meaning the event could be recorded and preserved, outliving the witnesses and retrievable by strangers.

Before registration, the web of relationships surrounding a family functioned as its own registry, maintained without anyone being assigned to maintain it. That registry had one fatal property: it could not be consulted by anyone outside it.

That change did not create identity from nothing. It created a new layer of identity designed to function at a national scale, and it meant a person's existence could be proven to institutions that had never met them. The emotional meaning shifted as well: a family recorded a birth because it mattered to them, while a state recorded a birth because it mattered to the system.

Registration was never only extractive. The same record that made a person taxable made them eligible, and the same file that enabled conscription enabled inheritance. Every subsequent identity system has carried that double character, and every argument about identity infrastructure since has been an argument about which half is ascendant.

The Index Key: A Comparative View

Institutions created unique identifiers to make people findable inside systems. The comparison across nations reveals how different societies approached the same institutional need, and how the design of an index key shaped the vulnerabilities it created.

The design of an index key is not a technical footnote. It determines what a system can see. A library does not organize shelves by the emotional resonance of titles, even though titles matter to readers. It assigns catalog numbers, and those numbers are not literature, but they make literature governable.

The logic was simple enough to see through a mundane analogy. A library did not organize shelves by the emotional resonance of titles, even though titles mattered to readers. It assigned catalog numbers, and those numbers were not literature, but they made literature governable.

Identifiers were not invented yesterday. States had long used rolls, lists, registries, and sometimes numeric schemes for taxation, military service, and administration. What became distinctive in the modern period was the way a single identifier began to follow a person across domains, linking employment, benefits, taxation, and eligibility into a coherent record.

Different societies built different index keys, but the function remained consistent. In the US, social security numbers became de facto universal identifiers despite having been designed for a narrower purpose. In the United Kingdom, a National Insurance number anchors contributions and tax records across a person's life. In Canada, the Social Insurance Number served as an identifier for working and for accessing government programs and benefits. In India, Aadhaar is a 12-digit number linked to demographic details and biometrics, designed to enable verification at a national scale.

These systems differed in governance and political context. Some were bound by strict rules, some drifted into wider use, and some became de facto universal keys. But each reflected the same institutional desire: a stable handle for retrieving the paper self. The comparison matters because each design carried its own failure modes. A system designed for one domain but used across many (as the SSN became) created different risks than a system designed from the start as a universal identifier (as Aadhaar was). The index key was never neutral. Its architecture shaped who was visible, who was vulnerable, and who could be found.

Identity As Weapon: The Extended Record

Paper identity can be repurposed for domination as shown through two historical examples: Nazi Germany and Apartheid South Africa. The material below provides the fuller texture of those systems, not because the argument requires every detail, but because understanding the daily experience of identity-as-coercion makes the structural lesson impossible to dismiss as abstract.

Nazi Germany: Persecution Through Paperwork

The August 1938 decree required many Jews with first names deemed non-Jewish to add "Israel" or "Sara" to their given names by 1 January 1939 [6].

Two months later, in October 1938, passports held by Jews were invalidated unless stamped with a red "J" [8]. A passport had been proof of movement and protection. Under this logic, it became a portable signal for exclusion, a document that instructed other officials how to treat the person holding it.

This did not require constant shouting to be effective. It required routine. A person handed over the passport. A clerk stamped the page. The passport returned to the owner, now altered in a way that followed them into every encounter with authority.

These measures showed how paperwork could make prejudice portable and interoperable. They also showed how identity could be turned into a standing demand, because requirements to carry and present identification shifted the burden of legitimacy onto the targeted person. The person no longer moved through public space as presumptively legitimate. They moved through it as if it were perpetually auditable.

Apartheid South Africa: Identity As Permission

Published histories of the reference book system describe enforcement that turned movement itself into a continuous test, with missing documentation treated as a punishable offense rather than an inconvenience [9].

To understand the human experience, it helps to imagine the texture of an ordinary day. Someone woke before dawn because work demanded it, and they carried not just lunch and a jacket but a small book that decided whether they could be where they needed to be. The hazard of the day was not the weather. It was an inspection, because the demand could come at stations, on buses, or on street corners.

That threat reorganized daily life around documentation in a way that no speech about freedom could undo.

Credit Invisibility: The Extended Data

The implications of credit invisibility extended beyond lending. Credit scores influenced rental applications, insurance premiums, employment screening, and even utility deposits. A person without a score was not judged negatively in the way that a person with a low score was. They were simply not seen.

This pattern connects to the broader argument of the book. When identity is externalized into systems, the systems define the terms of recognition. To exist in the system is to be eligible for its benefits and subject to its judgments. To be absent from the system is to be functionally nonexistent in the domains that system governs. That logic, born in paper, would intensify dramatically when the records became digital and the judgments became algorithmic.

Summary

Read together, these five passages describe the paper self as a remarkable human achievement that carried within it the seeds of its own failures. Portable proof allowed merchants to cross frontiers and rulers to extend protection beyond personal acquaintance. Civil registration gave individuals existence in systems that had never met them, opening doors to rights, services, and protection. Index keys made retrieval reliable enough to support modern states. These were not neutral conveniences. They were the conditions under which large-scale societies became possible.

But the same infrastructure that enabled cooperation also enabled coercion. The Nazi state did not need to invent its tools from scratch. It repurposed existing paperwork systems, adding stamps and required prefixes that turned identity into a portable signal for persecution. The Apartheid state did not need to physically restrain anyone to control their movement. It required them to carry a small book that decided where they could be. The credit system did not need to denounce anyone to exclude them. It simply did not see them.

The lesson is that paper identity created a new asymmetry of power. People who held documents that the system recognized moved through life as legitimate. People whose documents marked them as suspect, or whose absence of documents made them invisible, did not.

References

[1] Torpey, John. The Invention of the Passport: Surveillance, Citizenship and the State. Cambridge University Press, 2000.

[2] Arakawa, M. "The Transit Permit System of the Tang Empire and the Passage of Merchants." Memoirs of the Research Department of the Toyo Bunko, 2001.

[3] Hansen, Valerie. "The Impact of the Silk Road Trade on a Local Community: The Turfan Oasis, 500–800." In Les Sogdiens en Chine. École française d'Extrême-Orient, 2005.

[4] Caplan, Jane, and John Torpey (eds.). Documenting Individual Identity: The Development of State Practices in the Modern World. Princeton University Press, 2001.

[5] Scott, James C. Seeing Like a State: How Certain Schemes to Improve the Human Condition Have Failed. Yale University Press, 1998.

[6] Arendt, Hannah. Eichmann in Jerusalem: A Report on the Banality of Evil. Viking Press, 1963.

[7] Hilberg, Raul. The Destruction of the European Jews. Quadrangle Books, 1961; revised editions by Holmes & Meier.

[8] United States Holocaust Memorial Museum. Holocaust Encyclopedia entries on forced name additions (August 1938 decree) and passport "J" stamp policy (October 1938).

[9] Breckenridge, Keith. Biometric State: The Global Politics of Identification and Surveillance in South Africa, 1850 to the Present. Cambridge University Press, 2014.

[10] Consumer Financial Protection Bureau. Data Point: Credit Invisibles. May 2015.

The Digital Turn

The throughline across these passages is that digital identity began as a technical convenience and became a cultural condition. What started as a way to separate users on a shared computer ended as a defining feature of modern life, with consequences for memory, attention, autonomy, and the meaning of self-presentation. Recognizing the trajectory clarifies why AI identity is the next step in a sequence that has been unfolding for more than 60 years and why the questions that AI raises about authenticity and control echo questions that earlier digital systems also raised.

The Birth of the Password

The origin story already contained the entire drama of modern digital identity. A shared machine needed rules because without rules the machine would be chaos, and the rules had to distinguish one person's space from another's before either could be protected [1, 2].

Even the earliest era hinted at the risks that would later become familiar. Passwords were stored in ways that were naive by modern standards, and some users learned quickly that if identity was only a key, stealing a key could be enough.

This was the paper self's logic reappearing in a new medium. The earlier world had required portable proof so strangers could cooperate. The shared computer required a portable key so strangers could coexist inside the same machine.

The Screen Name Era: How Digital Identity Reached Households

The cultural texture of that transition shaped how an entire generation understood what it meant to be someone online.

A mainstream dial-up online service made the shift accessible to ordinary households [3, 4]. It did not ask most people to understand networking or protocols, and it did not require them to think in terms of databases.

In earlier social worlds, names had been given, inherited, or negotiated through community. In AOL and other early services, a person had to invent a name that fit inside a constrained field. That decision turned the address into a simple sentence: you were not only a name, you were a name at a place [5].

It was easy to forget how strange the distribution method had been. The doorway to the online world often arrived as a piece of plastic. Disks and CDs landed in mailboxes, piled up in office lobbies, and appeared in the boxes of new computers. In the United States, the disks from major dial-up providers became a recognizable artifact of an era, so ubiquitous that they ended up in museum collections [6].

That physical marketing campaign mattered philosophically because it showed how the digital self was grafted onto the paper world. The network did not float in the air as an abstract frontier. It was delivered like a brochure and activated like a subscription.

The early consumer online services were also not simply the open Internet. They were gated environments, private cities with rules, directories, and internal economies. CompuServe, Prodigy, and AOL offered forums, chat, news, and mail inside branded walls. People did not "browse the web" so much as enter a managed world.

Those managed worlds taught millions of people a new social grammar. You entered with a name, spoke through a handle, and left traces behind. The system remembered those traces and used them to greet you, route you, and sometimes nudge you. The most important lesson was about habituation. Identity was no longer only something you carried. It was something you had to maintain, because losing it meant losing access to an entire world of interaction.

The Relational Database and the Architecture of Linkage

Codd's model is usually described as an efficiency gain, and it was one. Its more consequential property was what it did to institutional memory once records became linkable.

The digital self grew because storage changed, and storage changed because of a quiet mathematical invention: the relational database [7, 8].

As more institutions digitized records, the paper self became data. Once data existed, it could be searched. Once it could be searched, it could be compared. Once it could be compared, it could be scored. Scoring is a different activity from recognition, in a way that took decades to become visible.

Cookies, Surveillance, and the Digital Gaze

The cookie is remembered as a privacy problem. It began as a solution to a design constraint that had nothing to do with identity at all.

Without it, a shopping cart could not reliably hold items. A login could not reliably persist. Personalization could not reliably occur [9,10].

Once recognition could be automated in the browser, the web stopped being a library of pages and started becoming a place where "you" returned. That memory had obvious benefits. It reduced friction. It made services usable. It also created a new path for surveillance, not necessarily as a conspiracy, but as an economic opportunity [11].

Shoshana Zuboff described the emergence of surveillance capitalism as a system that treated human experience as raw material for data extraction and prediction [12]. The business model did not simply observe users. It shaped their behavior in ways designed to produce more predictable outcomes.

In the paper world, you often knew when identity was being checked. In the digital world, checks often happened invisibly. This invisibility created a new form of power. The system could watch, record, and decide without announcing that it had done so [13, 14].

Michel Foucault's work on discipline described how observation and records could produce compliance, even when violence was absent, because the possibility of being watched changed behavior [15]. Digital identity intensified that dynamic. It did not need a guard tower. It needed logs. Modern life had not become a prison, but it had absorbed a new kind of gaze. The gaze was administrative, commercial, and increasingly automated.

Federated Identity and Digital Friction

Federated identity created new forms of dependency and new kinds of internal borders, and it did both while presenting itself purely as convenience.

As accounts multiplied, the burden grew. A solution emerged that sounded elegant: let one system vouch for identity in another system. This became known as federated identity. The user logged in once and then carried that authentication across services.

NIST's digital identity guidelines formalized the language of identity proofing, authentication, and federation, describing the technical requirements and assurance levels that made these trust chains viable [16]. The details were technical, but the cultural meaning was not. Federation meant identity became portable across systems through assertions. A trust chain was convenient. It was also a form of dependency.

When one provider sat at the center of the chain, that provider became a gate. Losing access to that account became existential in a way that losing a single password never had. This was a new kind of fragility. The paper self could be replaced, sometimes painfully, through bureaucracy. The digital self could be locked instantly. The user experienced this as "account recovery." The deeper truth was that the digital self had become contingent on the continued recognition of a system.

Paper identity had produced lines. Digital identity produced friction. Friction was the little resistance in modern life that appeared as "verify," "prove," "confirm," "enter the code," "try again." It was not evenly distributed. Some people moved through fast lanes of trust, and others lived in perpetual verification. Friction was governance by design. A system that trusted you gave you speed. A system that distrusted you gave you obstacles. Digital identity therefore became a new kind of internal border, not always visible, but always present.

Social Media: The Platforms That Unmasked Us

There was a shift from anonymity to identity transparency on the early 2000s. The reversal happened platform by platform, and the speed of it is easier to see laid out in sequence.

The shift from anonymous handles to real-name identity did not happen all at once. It happened platform by platform, each one normalizing a new level of disclosure. MySpace (2003) was the transitional moment. It still allowed pseudonyms, but it encouraged personalization: your page, your music, your photos, your "top 8" friends displayed for the world to see.

Facebook (2004) changed the rules. Launched initially for Harvard students with verified .edu email addresses, the platform made real names the default and anonymity the exception. Mark Zuckerberg was explicit about this philosophy. "Having two identities for yourself is an example of a lack of integrity," he said in a 2009 interview published in The Facebook Effect. By the time Facebook opened to the general public in 2006, it had trained millions of users to treat radical transparency as normal.

Twitter (2006) created a hybrid. Handles remained, but verified accounts and public figures normalized using real names and real faces. The platform's public-by-default architecture meant that thoughts, opinions, and reactions were broadcast to strangers. Even pseudonymous accounts accumulated persistent reputations that felt like identity.

Instagram (2010) completed the visual turn. If Facebook had asked for your biography, Instagram asked for your face. The platform was built around images, and the most successful images featured people. Selfies became a form of digital self-portraiture practiced at industrial scale. By 2015, billions of photographs of human faces had been uploaded to servers, tagged with names, locations, and social connections.

TikTok (2016 internationally, 2018 in the United States) pushed further still. The platform's format, short videos algorithmically surfaced, meant that your face, your voice, your mannerisms, and your background all became content [17]. Unlike text-based platforms where you could hide behind words, TikTok asked: can you hold attention with your physical presence?

What the timeline makes visible is that each platform normalized the disclosure the next one would assume. Platforms made it easier to sign up with real information and harder to maintain separation between accounts. They introduced features that rewarded disclosure: photo tagging, location sharing, relationship status, employment history. Each feature felt optional, but the accumulation created a new default. Transparency became the path of least resistance.

This transition created a social paradox. The early Internet had promised escape from labels. The later Internet often reattached labels more tightly than the physical world, because digital profiles could be searched, copied, and resurfaced. In the physical world, your past could fade. You could move to a new city and become someone slightly different. The Internet's memory was longer and less forgiving.

The Benefits of Digital Identity

The digital self was not only a surveillance project, and any account that treats it as one is describing half of what happened.

The earlier world should not be romanticized. Recognition-based identity could be parochial, exclusionary, and brutal. Paper identity could be slow, humiliating, and rigid. Digital identity emerged partly because it offered something both of those systems struggled to provide: speed.

Speed was not trivial. Speed meant a person could open an account without traveling to an office. Speed meant a small business could accept payments and reach customers. Speed meant families could communicate over long distances cheaply. Digital identity also offered portability. A person could move and keep an address. A person could keep relationships alive through email and messaging. The digital self created continuity across geography.

Digital identity also offered new forms of inclusion. For some people, online handles allowed participation in communities that would have excluded them in physical spaces. A screen name could create a layer of safety. It could allow experimentation and belonging [18].

Digital identity also changed what ordinary competence looked like. In the paper era, competence meant knowing how to fill out forms, how to keep documents safe, how to navigate offices and deadlines. In the digital era, competence increasingly meant knowing how to manage accounts, recover access, interpret warnings, and detect impersonation. A new kind of literacy appeared. People learned to recognize phishing without using that word. They learned that a forgotten login could mean losing photos, contacts, and messages that had become part of memory. This was not only a security issue. It was an identity issue. The self in the system had become entangled with the self in life.

Summary

Read together, these seven passages describe digital identity as a series of accumulations rather than a single invention. A password was a boundary, a screen name was a persona, and the relational database turned scattered attributes into a linked record. Cookies supplied continuity, federation supplied convenience at the cost of dependency, and social media supplied the unmasking that made all of it legible. The benefits, speed and inclusion among them, were real. Not one of these elements was designed with harm in mind. Each emerged in response to a genuine problem and offered a genuine solution. Together they created the digital self.

The deeper pattern is that each new layer of digital identity did two things at once. It enabled something that had been impossible or impractical before, and it created a new form of dependency. The password enabled shared computing and created the credential as target. The screen name enabled participation and created the account as identity. The database enabled retrieval and created the linkage as surveillance vector. The cookie enabled memory and created the gaze as economic engine. Federation enabled portability and created single points of failure. Social media enabled connection and created the persistent profile that the physical world's memory used to forget. None of these dependencies were chosen. They emerged through use.

The cumulative effect is a self that lives partly inside systems that no individual owns and that can withhold recognition at any time. That self is not the same as the self that walks through a room or sits at a table. It is also not separable from it. The digital self has become entangled with the lived self in ways that previous generations of identity infrastructure never were. That entanglement is the ground on which AI identity now arrives, and understanding it is essential to understanding the impact it will have on humaity.

References

[1] Conner-Simons, Adam, and Rachel Gordon. "Professor Emeritus Fernando Corbató, MIT computing pioneer, dies at 93." MIT News, July 15, 2019.

[2] Saltzer, Jerome H., et al. Compatible Time-Sharing System (1961–1973): Fiftieth Anniversary Commemorative Overview. IEEE Computer Society, 2011.

[3] Historical reporting on major dial-up online services in the early 1990s and their role in bringing email and chat into American homes.

[4] Histories of early consumer online services, including CompuServe, Prodigy, and AOL, as context for how gated networks shaped early digital identity.

[5] Tomlinson, Ray. History of network email on ARPANET (1971), as documented in computing histories and obituaries.

[6] Smithsonian National Museum of American History. Dial-up service software disc (object entry), documenting how network access was physically distributed and marketed.

[7] Codd, Edgar F. "A Relational Model of Data for Large Shared Data Banks." Communications of the ACM, 1970.

[8] IBM History. "The relational database." Overview of Codd's 1970 model and its implications.

[9] Kristol, David, and Lou Montulli. RFC 2109: "HTTP State Management Mechanism." IETF, 1997.

[10] Montulli, Lou. "The reasoning behind web cookies." Personal blog, May 14, 2013.

[11] Federal Trade Commission. Online privacy workshops and reports, including testimony and staff reporting on web data collection practices, 1996 onward.

[12] Zuboff, Shoshana. The Age of Surveillance Capitalism: The Fight for a Human Future at the New Frontier of Power. PublicAffairs, 2019.

[13] Solove, Daniel J. The Digital Person: Technology and Privacy in the Information Age. NYU Press, 2004.

[14] Solove, Daniel J. "Digital Dossiers and the Dissipation of Fourth Amendment Privacy." Southern California Law Review, 2002.

[15] Foucault, Michel. Discipline and Punish: The Birth of the Prison. Pantheon Books, 1977. (Originally published in French, 1975.)

[16] National Institute of Standards and Technology. Special Publication 800-63 series: Digital Identity Guidelines.

[17] Goffman, Erving. The Presentation of Self in Everyday Life. Anchor Books, 1959.

[18] Turkle, Sherry. Life on the Screen: Identity in the Age of the Internet. Simon & Schuster, 1995.

Index

A

R. Mastrogiacomo, *The Next Identity Crisis*, https://doi.org/10.1007/979-8-8688-2788-4

J

K

L

M

N

O

P, Q

V, W, X, Y, Z

GPSR Compliance
The European Union's (EU) General Product Safety Regulation (GPSR) is a set of rules that requires consumer products to be safe and our obligations to ensure this.

If you have any concerns about our products, you can contact us on

ProductSafety@springernature.com

In case Publisher is established outside the EU, the EU authorized representative is:

Springer Nature Customer Service Center GmbH
Europaplatz 3
69115 Heidelberg, Germany

www.ingramcontent.com/pod-product-compliance
Lightning Source LLC
Chambersburg PA
CBHW060249080926
51106CB00028B/887
* 9 7 9 8 8 6 8 8 2 7 8 7 7 *